The Sense of Beauty

Being the outline of aesthetic theory

by George Santayana

Dover Publications, Inc., New York

This Dover edition, first published in 1955, is an unabridged and unaltered republication of the work first published by Charles Scribner's Sons in 1896.

Library of Congress Catalog Card Number: 55-14673

Manufactured in the United States of America

Dover Publications, Inc.
180 Varick Street
New York 14, N. Y.

PREFACE

THIS little work contains the chief ideas gathered together for a course of lectures on the theory and history of æsthetics given at Harvard College from 1892 to 1895. The only originality I can claim is that which may result from the attempt to put together the scattered commonplaces of criticism into a system, under the inspiration of a naturalistic psychology. I have studied sincerity rather than novelty, and if any subject, as for instance the excellence of tragedy, is presented in a new light, the change consists only in the stricter application to a complex subject of the principles acknowledged to obtain in our simple judgments. My effort throughout has been to recall those fundamental æsthetic feelings the orderly extension of which yields sanity of judgment and distinction of taste.

The influences under which the book has been written are rather too general and pervasive to admit of specification; yet the student of philosophy will not fail to perceive how much I owe to writers, both living and dead, to whom no honour could be added by my acknowledgments. I have usually omitted any reference to them in foot-notes or in the text, in order that the air of controversy might be avoided, and the reader might be enabled to compare what is said more directly with the reality of his own experience.

G. S.

SEPTEMBER, 1896.

CONTENTS

vii

The Sense of Beauty

INTRODUCTION

THE sense of beauty has a more important place in life than æsthetic theory has ever taken in philosophy. The plastic arts, with poetry and music, are the most conspicuous monuments of this human interest, because they appeal only to contemplation, and yet have attracted to their service, in all civilized ages, an amount of effort, genius, and honour, little inferior to that given to industry, war, or religion. The fine arts, however, where æsthetic feeling appears almost pure, are by no means the only sphere in which men show their susceptibility to beauty. In all products of human industry we notice the keenness with which the eye is attracted to the mere appearance of things: great sacrifices of time and labour are made to it in the most vulgar manufactures; nor does man select his dwelling, his clothes, or his companions without reference to their effect on his æsthetic senses. Of late we have even learned that the forms of many animals are due to the survival by sexual selection of the colours and forms most attractive to the eye. There must therefore be in our nature a very radical and wide-spread tendency to observe beauty, and to value it. No account of the principles of the mind can be at all adequate that passes over so conspicuous a faculty.

That æsthetic theory has received so little attention from the world is not due to the unimportance of the subject of which it treats, but rather to lack of an adequate motive for speculating upon it, and to the small success of the occasional efforts to deal with it. Absolute curiosity, and love of comprehension for its own sake, are not passions we have much leisure to indulge: they require not only freedom from affairs but, what is more rare, freedom from prepossessions and from the hatred of all ideas that do not make for the habitual goal of our thought.

Now, what has chiefly maintained such speculation as the world has seen has been either theological passion or practical use. All we find, for example, written about beauty may be

3

divided into two groups: that group of writings in which philosophers have interpreted æsthetic facts in the light of their metaphysical principles, and made of their theory of taste a corollary or footnote to their systems; and that group in which artists and critics have ventured into philosophic ground, by generalizing somewhat the maxims of the craft or the comments of the sensitive observer. A treatment of the subject at once direct and theoretic has been very rare: the problems of nature and morals have attracted the reasoners, and the description and creation of beauty have absorbed the artists; between the two reflection upon æsthetic experience has remained abortive or incoherent.

A circumstance that has also contributed to the absence or to the failure of æsthetic speculation is the subjectivity of the phenomenon with which it deals. Man has a prejudice against himself: anything which is a product of his mind seems to him to be unreal or comparatively insignificant. We are satisfied only when we fancy ourselves surrounded by objects and laws independent of our nature. The ancients long speculated about the constitution of the universe before they became aware of that mind which is the instrument of all speculation. The moderns, also, even within the field of psychology, have studied first the function of perception and the theory of knowledge, by which we seem to be informed about external things; they have in comparison neglected the exclusively subjective and human department of imagination and emotion. We have still to recognize in practice the truth that from these despised feelings of ours the great world of perception derives all its value, if not also its existence. Things are interesting because we care about them, and important because we need them. Had our perceptions no connexion with our pleasures, we should soon close our eyes on this world; if our intelligence were of no service to our passions, we should come to doubt, in the lazy freedom of reverie, whether two and two make four.

Yet so strong is the popular sense of the unworthiness and insignificance of things purely emotional, that those who have taken moral problems to heart and felt their dignity have often been led into attempts to discover some external right and beauty of which our moral and æsthetic feelings should be perceptions or discoveries, just as our intellectual activity is, in men's opinion, a perception or discovery of external fact. These philosophers seem to feel that unless moral and æsthetic judgments are expressions of objective truth, and not merely expressions of human nature, they stand condemned of hopeless triviality. A judgment is not trivial, however, because it rests on human feelings; on the contrary, triviality consists in abstraction from human interests; only those judgments and opinions are truly insignificant which wander beyond the reach of verification, and have no function in the ordering and enriching of life.

Both ethics and æsthetics have suffered much from the prejudice against the subjective. They have not suffered more because both have a subject-matter which is partly objective. Ethics deals with conduct as much as with emotion, and therefore considers the causes of events and their consequences as well as our judgments of their value. Æsthetics also is apt to include the history and philosophy of art, and to add much descriptive and critical matter to the theory of our susceptibility to beauty. A certain confusion is thereby introduced into these inquiries, but at the same time the discussion is enlivened by excursions into neighbouring provinces, perhaps more interesting to the general reader.

We may, however, distinguish three distinct elements of ethics and æsthetics, and three different ways of approaching the subject. The first is the exercise of the moral or æsthetic faculty itself, the actual pronouncing of judgment and giving of praise, blame, and precept. This is not a matter of science but of character, enthusiasm, niceness of perception, and fineness of emotion. It is æsthetic or moral activity, while ethics and æsthetics, as sciences, are intellectual activities, having that æsthetic or moral activity for their subject-matter.

The second method consists in the historical explanation of conduct or of art as a part of anthropology, and seeks to discover the conditions of various types of character, forms of polity, conceptions of justice, and schools of criticism and of art. Of this nature is a great deal of what has been written on æsthetics. The philosophy of art has often proved a more tempting subject than the psychology of taste, especially to minds which were not so much fascinated by beauty itself as by the curious problem of the artistic instinct in man and of the diversity of its manifestations in history.

The third method in ethics and æsthetics is psychological, as the other two are respectively didactic and historical. It deals with moral and æsthetic judgments as phenomena of mind and products of mental evolution. The problem here is to understand the origin and conditions of these feelings and their relation to the rest of our economy. Such an inquiry, if pursued successfully, would yield an understanding of the reason why we think anything right or beautiful, wrong or ugly; it would thus reveal the roots of conscience and taste in human nature and enable us to distinguish transitory preferences and ideals, which rest on peculiar conditions, from those which, springing from those elements of mind which all men share, are comparatively permanent and universal.

To this inquiry, as far as it concerns æsthetics, the following pages are devoted. No attempt will be made either to impose particular appreciations or to trace the history of art and criticism. The discussion will be limited to the nature and elements of our æsthetic judgments. It is a theoretical inquiry and has no directly hortatory quality. Yet insight into the basis of our preferences, if it could be gained, would not fail to have a good and purifying influence upon them. It would show us the futility of a dogmatism that would impose upon another man judgments and emotions for which the needed soil is lacking in his constitution and experience; and at the same time it would relieve us of any undue diffidence or excessive tolerance towards aberrations of taste, when we know what are the broader grounds of preference and the habits that make for greater and more diversified æsthetic enjoyment.

Therefore, although nothing has commonly been less attractive than treatises on beauty or less a guide to taste than disquisitions upon it, we may yet hope for some not merely theoretical gain from these studies. They have remained so often without practical influence because they have been pursued under unfavourable conditions. The writers have generally been audacious metaphysicians and somewhat incompetent critics; they have represented general and obscure principles, suggested by other parts of their philosophy, as the conditions of artistic excellence and the essence of beauty. But if the inquiry is kept close to the facts of feeling, we may hope that the resulting theory may have a clarifying effect on the experience on which it is based. That is, after all, the use of theory. If when a theory is bad it narrows our capacity for observation and makes all appreciation vicarious and formal, when it is good it reacts favourably upon our powers, guides the attention to what is really capable of affording entertainment, and increases, by force of new analogies, the range of our interests. Speculation is an evil if it imposes a foreign organization on our mental life; it is a good if it only brings to light, and makes more perfect by training, the organization already inherent in it.

We shall therefore study human sensibility itself and our actual feelings about beauty, and we shall look for no deeper, unconscious causes of our æsthetic consciousness. Such value as belongs to metaphysical derivations of the nature of the beautiful, comes to them not because they explain our primary feelings, which they cannot do, but because they express, and in fact constitute, some of our later appreciations. There is no explanation, for instance, in calling beauty an adumbration of divine attributes. Such a relation, if it were actual, would not help us at all to understand why the symbols of divinity pleased. But in certain moments of contemplation, when much emotional experience lies behind us, and we have reached very general ideas both of nature and of life, our delight in any particular object may consist in nothing but the thought that this object is a manifestation of universal principles. The blue sky may come to please chiefly because it seems the image of a serene conscience, or of the eternal youth and purity of nature after a thousand partial corruptions. But this expressiveness of the sky is due to certain qualities of the sensation, which bind it to all things happy and pure, and, in a mind in which the essence of purity and happiness is embodied in an idea of God, bind it also to that idea.

So it may happen that the most arbitrary and unreal theories, which must be rejected as general explanations of æsthetic life, may be reinstated as particular moments of it. Those intuitions which we call Platonic are seldom scientific, they seldom explain the phenomena or hit upon the actual law of things, but they are often the highest expression of that activity which they fail to make comprehensible. The adoring lover cannot understand the natural history of love; for he is all in all at the last and supreme stage of its development. Hence the world has always been puzzled in its judgment of the Platonists; their theories are so extravagant, yet their wisdom seems so great. Platonism is a very refined and beautiful expression of our natural instincts, it embodies conscience and utters our inmost hopes. Platonic philosophers have therefore a natural authority, as standing on heights to which the vulgar cannot attain, but to which they naturally and half-consciously aspire.

When a man tells you that beauty is the manifestation of God to the senses, you wish you might understand him, you grope for a deep truth in his obscurity, you honour him for his elevation of mind, and your respect may even induce you to assent to what he says as to an intelligible proposition. Your thought may in consequence be dominated ever after by a verbal dogma, around which all your sympathies and antipathies will quickly gather, and the less you have penetrated the original sense of your creed, the more absolutely will you believe it. You will have followed Mephistopheles' advice:—

> Im ganzen haltet euch am Worte,
> So geht euch durch die sichere Pforte
> Zum Tempel der Gewissheit ein.

Yet reflection might have shown you that the word of the master held no objective account of the nature and origin of beauty, but was the vague expression of his highly complex emotions.

It is one of the attributes of God, one of the perfections which we contemplate in our idea of him, that there is no duality or opposition between his will and his vision, between the impulses of his nature and the events of his life. This is what we commonly designate as omnipotence and creation. Now, in the contemplation of beauty, our faculties of perception have the same perfection: it is indeed from the experience of beauty and happiness, from the occasional harmony between our nature and our environment, that we draw our conception of the divine life. There is, then, a real propriety in calling beauty a manifestation of God to the senses, since, in the region of sense, the perception of beauty exemplifies the adequacy and perfection which in general we objectify in an idea of God.

But the minds that dwell in the atmosphere of these analogies are hardly those that will care to ask what are the conditions and the varieties of this perfection of function, in other words, how it comes about that we perceive beauty at all, or have any inkling of divinity. Only the other philosophers, those that wallow in Epicurus' sty, know anything about the latter question. But it is easier to be impressed than to be instructed, and the public is very ready to believe that where there is noble language not without obscurity there must be profound knowledge. We should distinguish, however, the two distinct demands in the case. One is for comprehension; we look for the theory of a human function which must cover all possible cases of its exercise, whether noble or base. This the Platonists utterly fail to give us. The other demand is for inspiration; we wish to be nourished by the maxims and confessions of an exalted mind, in whom the æsthetic function is pre-eminent. By responding to this demand the same thinkers may win our admiration.

To feel beauty is a better thing than to understand how we

come to feel it. To have imagination and taste, to love the best, to be carried by the contemplation of nature to a vivid faith in the ideal, all this is more, a great deal more, than any science can hope to be. The poets and philosophers who express this æsthetic experience and stimulate the same function in us by their example, do a greater service to mankind and deserve higher honour than the discoverers of historical truth. Reflection is indeed a part of life, but the last part. Its specific value consists in the satisfaction of curiosity, in the smoothing out and explanation of things: but the greatest pleasure which we actually get from reflection is borrowed from the experience on which we reflect. We do not often indulge in retrospect for the sake of a scientific knowledge of human life, but rather to revive the memories of what once was dear. And I should have little hope of interesting the reader in the present analyses, did I not rely on the attractions of a subject associated with so many of his pleasures.

But the recognition of the superiority of æsthetics in experience to æsthetics in theory ought not to make us accept as an explanation of æsthetic feeling what is in truth only an expression of it. When Plato tells us of the eternal ideas in conformity to which all excellence consists, he is making himself the spokesman of the moral consciousness. Our conscience and taste establish these ideals; to make a judgment is virtually to establish an ideal, and all ideals are absolute and eternal for the judgment that involves them, because in finding and declaring a thing good or beautiful, our sentence is categorical, and the standard evoked by our judgment is for that case intrinsic and ultimate. But at the next moment, when the mind is on another footing, a new ideal is evoked, no less absolute for the present judgment than the old ideal was for the previous one. If we are then expressing our feeling and confessing what happens to us when we judge, we shall be quite right in saying that we have always an absolute ideal before us, and that value lies in conformity with that ideal. So, also, if we try to define that ideal, we shall hardly be able to say of it anything less noble and more definite than that it is the embodiment of an infinite good. For it is that incommunicable and illusive excellence that haunts every beautiful thing, and

> like a star
> Beacons from the abode where the eternal are.

For the expression of this experience we should go to the poets, to the more inspired critics, and best of all to the immortal parables of Plato. But if what we desire is to increase our knowledge rather than to cultivate our sensibility, we should do well to close all those delightful books; for we shall not find any instruction there upon the questions which most press upon us; namely, how an ideal is formed in the mind, how a given object is compared with it, what is the common element in all beautiful things, and what the substance of the absolute ideal in which all ideals tend to be lost; and, finally, how we come to be sensitive to beauty at all, or to value it. These questions must be capable of answers, if any science of human nature is really possible.—So far, then, are we from ignoring the insight of the Platonists, that we hope to explain it, and in a sense to justify it, by showing that it is the natural and sometimes the supreme expression of the common principles of our nature.

PART I

THE NATURE OF BEAUTY

§ 1. THE PHILOSOPHY OF BEAUTY IS A THEORY OF VALUES. It would be easy to find a definition of beauty that should give in a few words a telling paraphrase of the word. We know on excellent authority that beauty is truth, that it is the expression of the ideal, the symbol of divine perfection, and the sensible manifestation of the good. A litany of these titles of honour might easily be compiled, and repeated in praise of our divinity. Such phrases stimulate thought and give us a momentary pleasure, but they hardly bring any permanent enlightenment. A definition that should really define must be nothing less than the exposition of the origin, place, and elements of beauty as an object of human experience. We must learn from it, as far as possible, why, when, and how beauty appears, what conditions an object must fulfil to be beautiful, what elements of our nature make us sensible of beauty, and what the relation is between the constitution of the object and the excitement of our susceptibility. Nothing less will really define beauty or make us understand what aesthetic appreciation is. The definition of beauty in this sense will be the task of this whole book, a task that can be only very imperfectly accomplished within its limits.

The historical titles of our subject may give us a hint towards the beginning of such a definition. Many writers of the last century called the philosophy of beauty *Criticism,* and the word is still retained as the title for the reasoned appreciation of works of art. We could hardly speak, however, of delight in nature as criticism. A sunset is not criticised; it is felt and enjoyed. The word "criticism," used on such an occasion, would emphasize too much the element of deliberate judgment and of comparison with standards. Beauty, although often so described, is seldom so perceived, and all the greatest excellences of nature and art are so far from being approved of by a rule that they themselves furnish the standard and ideal by which critics measure inferior effects.

This age of science and of nomenclature has accordingly adopted a more learned word, *Æsthetics,* that is, the theory of perception or of susceptibility. If criticism is too narrow a word, pointing exclusively to our more artificial judgments, æsthetics seems to be too broad and to include within its sphere all pleasures and pains, if not all perceptions whatsoever. Kant used it, as we know, for his theory of time and space as forms of all perception; and it has at times been narrowed into an equivalent for the philosophy of art.

If we combine, however, the etymological meaning of criticism with that of æsthetics, we shall unite two essential qualities of the theory of beauty. Criticism implies judgment, and æsthetics perception. To get the common ground, that of perceptions which are critical, or judgments which are perceptions, we must widen our notion of deliberate criticism so as to include those judgments of value which are instinctive and immediate, that is, to include pleasures and pains; and at the same time we must narrow our notion of æsthetics so as to exclude all perceptions which are not appreciations, which do not find a value in their objects. We thus reach the sphere of critical or appreciative perception, which is, roughly speaking, what we mean to deal with. And retaining the word "æsthetics," which is not current, we may therefore say that æsthetics is concerned with the perception of values. The meaning and conditions of value is, then, what we must first consider.

Since the days of Descartes it has been a conception familiar to philosophers that every visible event in nature might be explained by previous visible events, and that all the motions, for instance, of the tongue in speech, or of the hand in painting, might have merely physical causes. If consciousness is thus accessory to life and not essential to it, the race of man might have existed upon the earth and acquired all the arts necessary for its subsistence without possessing a single sensation, idea, or emotion. Natural selection might have secured the survival of those automata which made useful reactions upon their environment. An instinct of self-preservation would have been developed, dangers would have been shunned without being feared, and injuries revenged without being felt.

In such a world there might have come to be the most perfect organization. There would have been what we should call the expression of the deepest interests and the apparent pursuit of conceived goods. For there would have been spontaneous and ingrained tendencies to avoid certain contingencies and to produce others; all the dumb show and evidence of thinking would have been patent to the observer. Yet there would surely have been no thinking, no expectation, and no conscious achievement in the whole process.

The onlooker might have feigned ends and objects of forethought, as we do in the case of the water that seeks its own level, or in that of the vacuum which nature abhors. But the particles of matter would have remained unconscious of their collocation, and all nature would have been insensible of their changing arrangement. We only, the possible spectators of that process, by virtue of our own interests and habits, could see any progress or culmination in it. We should see culmination where the result attained satisfied our practical or æsthetic demands, and progress wherever such a satisfaction was approached. But apart from ourselves, and our human bias, we can see in such a mechanical world no element of value whatever. In removing consciousness, we have removed the possibility of worth.

But it is not only in the absence of all consciousness that value would be removed from the world; by a less violent abstraction from the totality of human experience, we might conceive beings of a purely intellectual cast, minds in which the transformations of nature were mirrored without any emotion. Every event would then be noted, its relations would be observed, its recurrence might even be expected; but all this would happen without a shadow of desire, of pleasure, or of regret. No event would be repulsive, no situation terrible. We might, in a word, have a world of idea without a world of will. In this case, as completely as if consciousness were absent altogether, all value and excellence would be gone. So that for the existence of good in any form it is not merely consciousness but emotional consciousness that is needed. Observation will not do, appreciation is required.

§ 2. PREFERENCE IS ULTIMATELY IRRATIONAL. We may therefore at once assert this axiom, important for all moral philosophy and fatal to certain stubborn incoherences of thought, that there is no value apart from some appreciation of it, and no good apart from some preference of it before its absence or its opposite. In appreciation, in preference, lies the root and essence of all excellence. Or, as Spinoza clearly expresses it, we desire nothing because it is good, but it is good only because we desire it.

It is true that in the absence of an instinctive reaction we can still apply these epithets by an appeal to usage. We may agree that an action is bad, or a building good, because we recognize in them a character which we have learned to designate by that adjective; but unless there is in us some trace of passionate reprobation or of sensible delight, there is no moral or æsthetic judgment. It is all a question of propriety of speech, and of the empty titles of things. The verbal and mechanical proposition, that passes for judgment of worth, is the great cloak of ineptitude in these matters. Insensibility is very quick in the conventional use of words. If we appealed more often to actual feeling, our judgments would be more diverse, but they would be more legitimate and instructive. Verbal judgments are often useful instruments of thought, but it is not by them that worth can ultimately be determined.

Values spring from the immediate and inexplicable reaction of vital impulse, and from the irrational part of our nature. The rational part is by its essence relative; it leads us from data to conclusions, or from parts to wholes; it never furnishes the data with which it works. If any preference or precept were declared to be ultimate and primitive, it would thereby be declared to be irrational, since mediation, inference, and synthesis are the essence of rationality. The ideal of rationality is itself as arbitrary, as much dependent on the needs of a finite organization, as any other ideal. Only as ultimately securing tranquillity of mind, which the philosopher instinctively pursues, has it for him any necessity. In spite of the verbal propriety of saying that reason demands rationality, what really demands rationality, what makes it a good and indispensable thing and gives it all its authority, is not its own nature, but our need of it both in safe and economical action and in the pleasures of comprehension.

It is evident that beauty is a species of value, and what we have said of value in general applies to this particular kind. A first approach to a definition of beauty has therefore been made by the exclusion of all intellectual judgments, all judgments of matter of fact or of relation. To substitute judgments of fact for judgments of value, is a sign of a pedantic and borrowed criticism. If we approach a work of art or nature scientifically, for the sake of its historical connexions or proper classification, we do not approach it æsthetically. The discovery of its date or of its author may be otherwise interesting; it only remotely affects our æsthetic appreciation by adding to the direct effect certain associations. If the direct effect were absent, and the object in itself uninteresting, the circumstances would be immaterial.

Molière's *Misanthrope* says to the court poet who commends his sonnet as written in a quarter of an hour,

Voyons, monsieur, le temps ne fait rien à l'affaire,

and so we might say to the critic that sinks into the archæologist, show us the work, and let the date alone.

In an opposite direction the same substitution of facts for values makes its appearance, whenever the reproduction of fact is made the sole standard of artistic excellence. Many half-trained observers condemn the work of some naïve or fanciful masters with a sneer, because, as they truly say, it is out of drawing. The implication is that to be correctly copied from a model is the prerequisite of all beauty. Correctness is, indeed, an element of effect and one which, in respect to familiar objects, is almost indispensable, because its absence would cause a disappointment and dissatisfaction incompatible with enjoyment. We learn to value truth more and more as our love and knowledge of nature increase. But fidelity is a merit only because it is in this way a factor in our pleasure. It stands on a level with all other ingredients of effect. When a man raises it to a solitary pre-eminence and becomes incapable of appreciating anything else, he betrays the decay of æsthetic capacity. The scientific habit in him inhibits the artistic.

That facts have a value of their own, at once complicates and explains this question. We are naturally pleased by every perception, and recognition and surprise are particularly acute sensations. When we see a striking truth in any imitation, we are therefore delighted, and this kind of pleasure is very legitimate, and enters into the best effects of all the representative arts. Truth and realism are therefore æsthetically good, but they are not all-sufficient, since the representation of everything is not equally pleasing and effective. The fact that resemblance is a source of satisfaction, justifies the critic in demanding it, while the æsthetic insufficiency of such veracity shows the different value of truth in science and in art. Science is the response to the demand for information, and in it we ask for the whole truth and nothing but the truth. Art is the response to the demand for entertainment, for the stimulation of our senses and imagination, and truth enters into it only as it subserves these ends.

Even the scientific value of truth is not, however, ultimate or absolute. It rests partly on practical, partly on æsthetic interests. As our ideas are gradually brought into conformity with the facts by the painful process of selection,—for intuition runs equally into truth and into error, and can settle nothing if not controlled by experience,—we gain vastly in our command over our environment. This is the fundamental value of natural science, and the fruit it is yielding in our day. We have no better vision of nature and life than some of our predecessors, but we have greater material resources. To know the truth about the composition and history of things is good for this reason. It is also good because of the enlarged horizon it gives us, because the spectacle of nature is a marvellous and fascinating one, full of a serious sadness and large peace, which gives us back our birthright as children of the planet and naturalizes us upon the earth. This is the poetic value of the scientific *Weltanschauung*. From these two benefits, the practical and the imaginative, all the value of truth is derived.

Æsthetic and moral judgments are accordingly to be classed together in contrast to judgments intellectual; they are both judgments of value, while intellectual judgments are judgments of fact. If the latter have any value, it is only derivative, and our whole intellectual life has its only justification in its connexion with our pleasures and pains.

§ 3. CONTRAST BETWEEN MORAL AND ÆSTHETIC VALUES. The relation between æsthetic and moral judgments, between the spheres of the beautiful and the good, is close, but the distinction between them is important. One factor of this distinction is that while æsthetic judgments are mainly positive, that is, perceptions of good, moral judgments are mainly and fundamentally negative, or perceptions of evil. Another factor of the distinction is that whereas, in the perception of beauty, our judgment is necessarily intrinsic and based on the character of the immediate experience, and never consciously on the idea of an eventual utility in the object, judgments about moral worth, on the contrary, are always based, when they are positive, upon the consciousness of benefits probably involved. Both these distinctions need some elucidation.

Hedonistic ethics have always had to struggle against the moral sense of mankind. Earnest minds, that feel the weight and dignity of life, rebel against the assertion that the aim of right conduct is enjoyment. Pleasure usually appears to them as a temptation, and they sometimes go so far as to make avoidance of it a virtue. The truth is that morality is not mainly concerned with the attainment of pleasure; it is rather concerned, in all its deeper and more authoritative maxims, with the prevention of suffering. There is something artificial in the deliberate pursuit of pleasure; there is something absurd in the obligation to enjoy oneself. We feel no duty in that direction; we take to enjoyment naturally enough after the work of life is done, and the freedom and spontaneity of our pleasures is what is most essential to them.

The sad business of life is rather to escape certain dreadful evils to which our nature exposes us,—death, hunger, disease, weariness, isolation, and contempt. By the awful authority of these things, which stand like spectres behind every moral injunction, conscience in reality speaks, and a mind which they have duly impressed cannot but feel, by contrast, the hopeless triviality of the search for pleasure. It cannot but feel that a life abandoned to amusement and to changing impulses must run unawares into fatal dangers. The moment, however, that society emerges from the early pressure of the environment and is tolerably secure against primary evils, morality grows lax. The forms that life will farther assume are not to be imposed by moral authority, but are determined by the genius of the race, the opportunities of the moment, and the tastes and resources of individual minds. The reign of duty gives place to the reign of freedom, and the law and the covenant to the dispensation of grace.

The appreciation of beauty and its embodiment in the arts are activities which belong to our holiday life, when we are redeemed for the moment from the shadow of evil and the slavery to fear, and are following the bent of our nature where it chooses to lead us. The values, then, with which we here deal are positive; they were negative in the sphere of morality. The ugly is hardly an exception, because it is not the cause of any real pain. In itself it is rather a source of amusement. If its suggestions are vitally repulsive, its presence becomes a real evil towards which we assume a practical and moral attitude. And, correspondingly, the pleasant is never, as we have seen, the object of a truly moral injunction.

§ 4. Work and play. We have here, then, an important element of the distinction between æsthetic and moral values. It is the same that has been pointed to in the famous contrast between work and play. These terms may be used in different senses and their importance in moral classification differs with the meaning attached to them. We may call everything play which is useless activity, exercise that springs from the physiological impulse to discharge the energy which the exigencies of life have not called out. Work will then be all action that is necessary or useful for life. Evidently if work and play are thus objectively distinguished as useful and useless action, work is a eulogistic term and play a disparaging one. It would be better for us that all our energy should be turned to account, that none of it should be wasted in aimless motion. Play, in this sense, is a sign of imperfect adaptation. It is proper to childhood, when the body and mind are not yet fit to cope with the environment, but it is unseemly in manhood and pitiable in old age, because it marks an atrophy of human nature, and a failure to take hold of the opportunities of life.

Play is thus essentially frivolous. Some persons, understanding the term in this sense, have felt an aversion, which every liberal mind will share, to classing social pleasures, art, and religion under the head of play, and by that epithet condemning them, as a certain school seems to do, to gradual extinction as the race approaches maturity. But if all the useless ornaments of our life are to be cut off in the process of adaptation, evolution would impoverish instead of enriching our nature. Perhaps that is the tendency of evolution, and our barbarous ancestors amid their toils and wars, with their flaming passions and mythologies, lived better lives than are reserved to our well-adapted descendants.

We may be allowed to hope, however, that some imagination may survive parasitically even in the most serviceable brain. Whatever course history may take,—and we are not here concerned with prophecy,—the question of what is desirable is not affected. To condemn spontaneous and delightful occupations because they are useless for self-preservation shows an uncritical prizing of life irrespective of its content. For such a system the worthiest function of the universe should be to establish perpetual motion. Uselessness is a fatal accusation to bring against any act which is done for its presumed utility, but those which are done for their own sake are their own justification.

At the same time there is an undeniable propriety in calling all the liberal and imaginative activities of man play, because they are spontaneous, and not carried on under pressure of external necessity or danger. Their utility for self-preservation may be very indirect and accidental, but they are not worthless for that reason. On the contrary, we may measure the degree of happiness and civilization which any race has attained by the proportion of its energy which is devoted to free and generous pursuits, to the adornment of life and the culture of the imagination. For it is in the spontaneous play of his faculties that man finds himself and his happiness. Slavery is the most degrading condition of which he is capable, and he is as often a slave to the niggardness of the earth and the inclemency of heaven, as to a master or an institution. He is a slave when all his energy is spent in avoiding suffering and death, when all his action is imposed from without, and no breath or strength is left him for free enjoyment.

Work and play here take on a different meaning, and become equivalent to servitude and freedom. The change consists in the subjective point of view from which the distinction is now made. We no longer mean by work all that is done usefully, but only what is done unwillingly and by the spur of necessity. By play we are designating, no longer what is done fruitlessly, but whatever is done spontaneously and for its own sake, whether it have or not an ulterior utility. Play, in this sense, may be our most useful occupation. So far would a gradual adaptation to the environment be from making this play obsolete, that it would tend to abolish work, and to make play universal. For with the elimination of all the conflicts and errors of instinct, the race would do spontaneously whatever conduced to its welfare and we should live safely and prosperously without external stimulus or restraint.

§ 5. ALL VALUES ARE IN ONE SENSE ÆSTHETIC. In this second and subjective sense, then, work is the disparaging term and play the eulogistic one. All who feel the dignity and importance of the things of the imagination, need not hesitate to adopt the classification which designates them as play. We point out thereby, not that they have no value, but that their value is intrinsic, that in them is one of the sources of all worth. Evidently all values must be ultimately intrinsic. The useful is good because of the excellence of its consequences; but these must somewhere cease to be merely useful in their turn, or only excellent as means; somewhere we must reach the good that is good in itself and for its own sake, else the whole process is futile, and the utility of our first object illusory. We here reach the second factor in our distinction, between æsthetic and moral values, which regards their immediacy.

If we attempt to remove from life all its evils, as the popular imagination has done at times, we shall find little but æsthetic pleasures remaining to constitute unalloyed happiness. The satisfaction of the passions and the appetites, in which we chiefly place earthly happiness, themselves take on an æsthetic tinge when we remove ideally the possibility of loss or variation. What could the Olympians honour in one another or the seraphim worship in God except the embodiment of eternal attributes, of essences which, like beauty, make us happy only in contemplation? The glory of heaven could not be otherwise symbolized than by light and music. Even the knowledge of truth, which the most sober theologians made the essence of the beatific vision, is an æsthetic delight; for when the truth has no further practical utility, it becomes a landscape. The delight of it is imaginative and the value of it æsthetic.

This reduction of all values to immediate appreciations, to sensuous or vital activities, is so inevitable that it has struck even the minds most courageously rationalistic. Only for them, instead of leading to the liberation of æsthetic goods from practical entanglements and their establishment as the only pure and positive values in life, this analysis has led rather to the denial of all pure and positive goods altogether. Such thinkers naturally assume that moral values are intrinsic and supreme; and since these moral values would not arise but for the existence or imminence of physical evils, they embrace the paradox that without evil no good whatever is conceivable.

The harsh requirements of apologetics have no doubt helped them to this position, from which one breath of spring or the sight of one well-begotten creature should be enough to dislodge them. Their ethical temper and the fetters of their imagination forbid them to reconsider their original assumption and to conceive that morality is a means and not an end; that it is the price of human non-adaptation, and the consequence of the original sin of unfitness. It is the compression of human conduct within the narrow limits of the safe and possible. Remove danger, remove pain, remove the occasion of pity, and the need of morality is gone. To say "thou shalt not" would then be an impertinence.

But this elimination of precept would not be a cessation of life. The senses would still be open, the instincts would still operate, and lead all creatures to the haunts and occupations that befitted them. The variety of nature and the infinity of art, with the companionship of our fellows, would fill the leisure of that ideal existence. These are the elements of our positive happiness, the things which, amid a thousand vexations and vanities, make the clear profit of living.

§ 6. ÆSTHETIC CONSECRATION OF GENERAL PRINCIPLES. Not only are the various satisfactions which morals are meant to secure æsthetic in the last analysis, but when the conscience is formed, and right principles acquire an immediate authority, our attitude to these principles becomes æsthetic also. Honour, truthfulness, and cleanliness are obvious examples. When the absence of these virtues causes an instinctive disgust, as it does in well-bred people, the reaction is essentially æsthetic, because it is not based on reflection and benevolence, but on constitutional sensitiveness. This æsthetic sensitiveness is, however, properly enough called moral, because it is the effect of conscientious training and is more powerful for good in society than laborious virtue, because it is much more constant and catching. It is καλοκἀγαθία, the æsthetic demand for the morally good, and perhaps the finest flower of human nature.

But this tendency of representative principles to become independent powers and acquire intrinsic value is sometimes mischievous. It is the foundation of the conflicts between sentiment and justice, between intuitive and utilitarian morals. Every human reform is the reassertion of the primary interests of man against the authority of general principles which have ceased to represent those interests fairly, but which still obtain the idolatrous veneration of mankind. Nor are chivalry and religion alone liable to fall into this moral superstition. It arises wherever an abstract good is substituted for its concrete equivalent. The miser's fallacy is the typical case, and something very like it is the ethical principle of half our respectable population. To the exercise of certain useful habits men come to sacrifice the advantage which was the original basis and justification of those habits. Minute knowledge is pursued at the expense of largeness of mind, and riches at the expense of comfort and freedom.

This error is all the more specious when the derived aim has in itself some æsthetic charm, such as belongs to the Stoic idea of playing one's part in a vast drama of things, irrespective of any advantage thereby accruing to any one; somewhat as the miser's passion is rendered a little normal when his eye is fascinated not merely by the figures of a bank account, but by the glitter of the yellow gold. And the vanity of playing a tragic part and the glory of conscious self-sacrifice have the same immediate fascination. Many irrational maxims thus acquire a kind of nobility. An object is chosen as the highest good which has not only a certain representative value, but also an intrinsic one,—which is not merely a method for the realization of other values, but a value in its own realization.

Obedience to God is for the Christian, as conformity to the laws of nature or reason is for the Stoic, an attitude which has a certain emotional and passionate worth, apart from its original justification by maxims of utility. This emotional and passionate force is the essence of fanaticism, it makes imperatives categorical, and gives them absolute sway over the conscience in spite of their one-sidedness and their injustice to the manifold demands of human nature.

Obedience to God or reason can originally recommend itself to a man only as the surest and ultimately least painful way of balancing his aims and synthesizing his desires. So necessary is this sanction even to the most impetuous natures, that no martyr would go to the stake if he did not believe that the powers of nature, in the day of judgment, would be on his side. But the human mind is a turbulent commonwealth, and the laws that make for the greatest good cannot be established in it without some partial sacrifice, without the suppression of many particular impulses. Hence the voice of reason or the command of God, which makes for the maximum ultimate satisfaction, finds itself opposed by sundry scattered and refractory forces, which are henceforth denominated bad. The unreflective conscience, forgetting the vicarious source of its own excellence, then assumes a solemn and incomprehensible immediacy, as if its decrees were absolute and intrinsically authoritative, not of to-day or yesterday, and no one could tell whence they had arisen. Instinct can all the more easily produce this mystification when it calls forth an imaginative activity full of interest and eager passion. This effect is conspicuous in the absolutist conscience, both devotional and rationalistic, as also in the passion of love. For in all these a certain individuality, definiteness, and exclusiveness is given to the pursued object which is very favourable to zeal, and the heat of passion melts together the various processes of volition into the consciousness of one adorable influence.

However deceptive these complications may prove to men of action and eloquence, they ought not to impose on the critic of human nature. Evidently what value general goods do not derive from the particular satisfactions they stand for, they possess in themselves as ideas pleasing and powerful over the imagination. This intrinsic advantage of certain principles and methods is none the less real for being in a sense æsthetic. Only a sordid utilitarianism that subtracts the imagination from human nature, or at least slurs over its immense contribution to our happiness, could fail to give these principles the preference over others practically as good.

If it could be shown, for instance, that monarchy was as apt, in a given case, to secure the public well-being as some other form of government, monarchy should be preferred, and would undoubtedly be established, on account of its imaginative and dramatic superiority. But if, blinded by this somewhat ethereal advantage, a party sacrificed to it important public interests, the injustice would be manifest. In a doubtful case, a nation decides, not without painful conflicts, how much it will sacrifice to its sentimental needs. The important point is to remember that the representative or practical value of a principle is one thing, and its intrinsic or æsthetic value is another, and that the latter can be justly counted only as an item in its favour to be weighed against possible external disadvantages. Whenever this comparison and balancing of ultimate benefits of every kind is angrily dismissed in favour of some absolute principle, laid down in contempt of human misery and happiness, we have a personal and fantastic system of ethics, without practical sanctions. It is an evidence that the superstitious imagination has invaded the sober and practical domain of morals.

§ 7. ÆSTHETIC AND PHYSICAL PLEASURE. We have now separated with some care intellectual and moral judgments from the sphere of our subject, and found that we are to deal only with perceptions of value, and with these only when they are positive and immediate. But even with these distinctions the most remarkable characteristic of the sense of beauty remains undefined. All pleasures are intrinsic and positive values, but all pleasures are not perceptions of beauty. Pleasure is indeed the essence of that perception, but there is evidently in this particular pleasure a complication which is not present in others and which is the basis of the distinction made by consciousness and language between it and the rest. It will be instructive to notice the degrees of this difference.

The bodily pleasures are those least resembling perceptions of beauty. By bodily pleasures we mean, of course, more than pleasures with a bodily seat; for that class would include them all, as well as all forms and elements of consciousness. Æsthetic pleasures have physical conditions, they depend on the activity of the eye and the ear, of the memory and the other ideational functions of the brain. But we do not connect those pleasures with their seats except in physiological studies; the ideas with which æsthetic pleasures are associated are not the ideas of their bodily causes. The pleasures we call physical, and regard as low, on the contrary, are those which call our attention to some part of our own body, and which make no object so conspicuous to us as the organ in which they arise.

There is here, then, a very marked distinction between physical and æsthetic pleasure; the organs of the latter must be transparent, they must not intercept our attention, but carry it directly to some external object. The greater dignity and range of æsthetic pleasure is thus made very intelligible. The soul is glad, as it were, to forget its connexion with the body and to fancy that it can travel over the world with the liberty with which it changes the objects of its thought. The mind passes from China to Peru without any conscious change in the local tensions of the body. This illusion of disembodiment is very exhilarating, while immersion in the flesh and confinement to some organ gives a tone of grossness and selfishness to our consciousness. The generally meaner associations of physical pleasures also help to explain their comparative crudity.

§ 8. THE DIFFERENTIA OF ÆSTHETIC PLEASURE NOT ITS DISINTERESTEDNESS. The distinction between pleasure and the sense of beauty has sometimes been said to consist in the unselfishness of æsthetic satisfaction. In other pleasures, it is said, we gratify our senses and passions; in the contemplation of beauty we are raised above ourselves, the passions are silenced and we are happy in the recognition of a good that we do not seek to possess. The painter does not look at a spring of water with the eyes of a thirsty man, nor at a beautiful woman with those of a satyr. The difference lies, it is urged, in the impersonality of the enjoyment. But this distinction is one of intensity and delicacy, not of nature, and it seems satisfactory only to the least æsthetic minds.[1]

1 Schopenhauer, indeed, who makes much of it, was a good critic, but his psychology suffered much from the pessimistic generalities of his system. It concerned him to show that the will was bad, and, as he felt beauty to be a good if not a holy thing, he hastened to convince himself that it came from the suppression of the will. But even in his system this suppression is only relative. The desire of individual objects, indeed, is absent in the perception of beauty, but there is still present that initial love of the general type and principles of things which is the first illusion of the absolute,

In the second place, the supposed disinterestedness of æsthetic delights is not very fundamental. Appreciation of a picture is not identical with the desire to buy it, but it is, or ought to be, closely related and preliminary to that desire. The beauties of nature and of the plastic arts are not consumed by being enjoyed; they retain all the efficacy to impress a second beholder. But this circumstance is accidental, and those æsthetic objects which depend upon change and are exhausted in time, as are all performances, are things the enjoyment of which is an object of rivalry and is coveted as much as any other pleasure. And even plastic beauties can often not be enjoyed except by a few, on account of the necessity of travel or other difficulties of access, and then this æsthetic enjoyment is as selfishly pursued as the rest.

The truth which the theory is trying to state seems rather to be that when we seek æsthetic pleasures we have no further pleasure in mind; that we do not mix up the satisfactions of vanity and proprietorship with the delight of contemplation. This is true, but it is true at bottom of all pursuits and enjoyments. Every real pleasure is in one sense disinterested. It is not sought with ulterior motives, and what fills the mind is no calculation, but the image of an object or event, suffused with emotion. A sophisticated consciousness may often take the idea of self as the touchstone of its inclinations; but this self, for the gratification and aggrandizement of which a man may live, is itself only a complex of aims and memories, which once had their direct objects, in which he had taken a spontaneous and unselfish interest. The gratifications which, merged together, make the selfishness are each of them ingenuous, and no more selfish than the most altruistic, impersonal emotion. The content of selfishness is a mass of unselfishness. There is no reference to the nominal essence called oneself either in one's appetites or in one's natural affections; yet a man absorbed in his meat and drink, in his houses and lands, in his children and dogs, is called selfish because these interests, although natural and instinctive in him, are not shared by others. The unselfish man is he whose nature has a more universal direction, whose interests are more widely diffused.

and drives it on to the fatal experiment of creation. So that, apart from Schopenhauer's mythology, we have even in him the recognition that beauty gives satisfaction to some dim and underlying demand of our nature, just as particular objects give more special and momentary pleasures to our individualized wills. His psychology was, however, far too vague and general to undertake an analysis of those mysterious feelings.

But as impersonal thoughts are such only in their object, not in their subject or agent, since all thoughts are the thoughts of somebody: so also unselfish interests have to be somebody's interests. If we were not interested in beauty, if it were of no concern to our happiness whether things were beautiful or ugly, we should manifest not the maximum, but the total absence of æsthetic faculty. The disinterestedness of this pleasure is, therefore, that of all primitive and intuitive satisfactions, which are in no way conditioned by a reference to an artificial general concept, like that of the self, all the potency of which must itself be derived from the independent energy of its component elements. I care about myself because "myself" is a name for the things I have at heart. To set up the verbal figment of personality and make it an object of concern apart from the interests which were its content and substance, turns the moralist into a pedant, and ethics into a superstition. The self which is the object of *amour propre* is an idol of the tribe, and needs to be disintegrated into the primitive objective interests that underlie it before the cultus of it can be justified by reason.

§ 9. THE DIFFERENTIA OF ÆSTHETIC PLEASURE NOT ITS UNIVERSALITY. The supposed disinterestedness of our love of beauty passes into another characteristic of it often regarded as essential, —its universality. The pleasures of the senses have, it is said, no dogmatism in them; that anything gives me pleasure involves no assertion about its capacity to give pleasure to another. But when I judge a thing to be beautiful, my judgment means that the thing is beautiful in itself, or (what is the same thing more critically expressed) that it should seem so to everybody. The claim to universality is, according to this doctrine, the essence of the æsthetic; what makes the perception of beauty a judgment rather than a sensation. All æsthetic precepts would be impossible, and all criticism arbitrary and subjective, unless we admit a paradoxical universality in our judgment, the philosophical implications of which we may then go on to develope. But we are fortunately not required to enter the labyrinth into which this method leads; there is a much simpler and clearer way of studying such questions, which is to challenge and analyze the assertion before us and seek its basis in human nature. Before this is done, we should run the risk of expanding a natural misconception or inaccuracy of thought into an inveterate and pernicious prejudice by making it the centre of an elaborate construction.

That the claim of universality is such a natural inaccuracy will not be hard to show. There is notoriously no great agreement upon æsthetic matters; and such agreement as there is, is based upon similarity of origin, nature, and circumstance among men, a similarity which, where it exists, tends to bring about identity in all judgments and feelings. It is unmeaning to say that what is beautiful to one man *ought* to be beautiful to another. If their senses are the same, their associations and dispositions similar, then the same thing will certainly be beautiful to both. If their natures are different, the form which to one will be entrancing will be to another even invisible, because his classifications and discriminations in perception will be different, and he may see a hideous detached fragment or a shapeless aggregate of things, in what to another is a perfect whole—so entirely are the unities of objects unities of function and use. It is absurd to say that what is invisible to a given being *ought* to seem beautiful to him. Evidently this obligation of recognizing the same qualities is conditioned by the possession of the same faculties. But no two men have exactly the same faculties, nor can things have for any two exactly the same values.

What is loosely expressed by saying that any one ought to see this or that beauty is that he would see it if his disposition, training, or attention were what our ideal demands for him; and our ideal of what any one should be has complex but discoverable sources. We take, for instance, a certain pleasure in having our own judgments supported by those of others; we are intolerant, if not of the existence of a nature different from our own, at least of its expression in words and judgments. We are confirmed or made happy in our doubtful opinions by seeing them accepted universally. We are unable to find the basis of our taste in our own experience and therefore refuse to look for it there. If we were sure of our ground, we should be willing to acquiesce in the naturally different feelings and ways of others, as a man who is conscious of speaking his language with the accent of the capital confesses its arbitrariness with gayety, and is pleased and interested in the variations of it he observes in provincials; but the provincial is always zealous to show that he has reason and ancient authority to justify his oddities. So people who have no sensations, and do not know why they judge, are always trying to show that they judge by universal reason.

Thus the frailty and superficiality of our own judgments cannot brook contradiction. We abhor another man's doubt when we cannot tell him why we ourselves believe. Our ideal of other men tends therefore to include the agreement of their judgments with our own; and although we might acknowledge the fatuity of this demand in regard to natures very different from the human, we may be unreasonable enough to require that all races should admire the same style of architecture, and all ages the same poets.

The great actual unity of human taste within the range of conventional history helps the pretension. But in principle it is untenable. Nothing has less to do with the real merit of a work of imagination than the capacity of all men to appreciate it; the true test is the degree and kind of satisfaction it can give to him who appreciates it most. The symphony would lose nothing if half mankind had always been deaf, as nine-tenths of them actually are to the intricacies of its harmonies; but it would have lost much if no Beethoven had existed. And more: incapacity to appreciate certain types of beauty may be the condition *sine qua non* for the appreciation of another kind; the greatest capacity both for enjoyment and creation is highly specialized and exclusive, and hence the greatest ages of art have often been strangely intolerant.

The invectives of one school against another, perverse as they are philosophically, are artistically often signs of health, because they indicate a vital appreciation of certain kinds of beauty, a love of them that has grown into a jealous passion. The architects that have pieced out the imperfections of ancient buildings with their own thoughts, like Charles V. when he raised his massive palace beside the Alhambra, may be condemned from a certain point of view. They marred much by their interference; but they showed a splendid confidence in their own intuitions, a proud assertion of their own taste, which is the greatest evidence of æsthetic sincerity. On the contrary, our own gropings, eclecticism, and archæology are the symptoms of impotence. If we were less learned and less just, we might be more efficient. If our appreciation were less general, it might be more real, and if we trained our imagination into exclusiveness, it might attain to character.

§ 10. THE DIFFERENTIA OF ÆSTHETIC PLEASURE: ITS OBJECTIFICATION. There is, however, something more in the claim to universality in æsthetic judgments than the desire to generalize our own opinions. There is the expression of a curious but well-known psychological phenomenon, viz., the transformation of an element of sensation into the quality of a thing. If we say that other men should see the beauties we see, it is because we think those beauties *are in the object,* like its colour, proportion, or size. Our judgment appears to us merely the perception and discovery of an external existence, of the real excellence that is without. But this notion is radically absurd and contradictory. Beauty, as we have seen, is a value; it cannot be conceived as an independent existence which affects our senses and which we consequently perceive. It exists in perception, and cannot exist otherwise. A beauty not perceived is a pleasure not felt, and a contradiction. But modern philosophy has taught us to say the same thing of every element of the perceived world; all are sensations; and their grouping into objects imagined to be permanent and external is the work of certain habits of our intelligence. We should be incapable of surveying or retaining the diffused experiences of life, unless we organized and classified them, and out of the chaos of impressions framed the world of conventional and recognizable objects.

How this is done is explained by the current theories of perception. External objects usually affect various senses at once, the impressions of which are thereby associated. Repeated experiences of one object are also associated on account of their similarity; hence a double tendency to merge and unify into a single percept, to which a name is attached, the group of those memories and reactions which in fact had one external thing for their cause. But this percept, once formed, is clearly different from those particular experiences out of which it grew. It is permanent, they are variable. They are but partial views and glimpses of it. The constituted notion therefore comes to be the reality, and the materials of it merely the appearance. The distinction between substance and quality, reality and appearance, matter and mind, has no other origin.

The objects thus conceived and distinguished from our ideas of them, are at first compacted of all the impressions, feelings, and memories, which offer themselves for association and fall within the vortex of the amalgamating imagination. Every sensation we get from a thing is originally treated as one of its qualities. Experiment, however, and the practical need of a simpler conception of the structure of objects lead us gradually to reduce the qualities of the object to a minimum, and to regard most perceptions as an effect of those few qualities upon us. These few primary qualities, like extension which we persist in treating as independently real and as the quality of a substance, are those which suffice to explain the order of our experiences. All the rest, like colour, are relegated to the subjective sphere, as merely effects upon our minds, and apparent or secondary qualities of the object.

But this distinction has only a practical justification. Convenience and economy of thought alone determine what combination of our sensations we shall continue to objectify and treat as the cause of the rest. The right and tendency to be objective is equal in all, since they are all prior to the artifice of thought by which we separate the concept from its materials, the thing from our experiences.

The qualities which we now conceive to belong to real objects are for the most part images of sight and touch. One of the first classes of effects to be treated as secondary were naturally pleasures and pains, since it could commonly conduce very little to intelligent and successful action to conceive our pleasures and pains as resident in objects. But emotions are essentially capable of objectification, as well as impressions of sense; and one may well believe that a primitive and inexperienced consciousness would rather people the world with ghosts of its own terrors and passions than with projections of those luminous and mathematical concepts which as yet it could hardly have formed.

This animistic and mythological habit of thought still holds its own at the confines of knowledge, where mechanical explanations are not found. In ourselves, where nearness makes observation difficult, in the intricate chaos of animal and human life, we still appeal to the efficacy of will and ideas, as also in the remote night of cosmic and religious problems. But in all the intermediate realm of vulgar day, where mechanical science has made progress, the inclusion of emotional or passionate elements in the concept of the reality would be now an extravagance. Here our idea of things is composed exclusively of perceptual elements, of the ideas of form and of motion.

The beauty of objects, however, forms an exception to this rule. Beauty is an emotional element, a pleasure of ours, which nevertheless we regard as a quality of things. But we are now prepared to understand the nature of this exception. It is the survival of a tendency originally universal to make every effect of a thing upon us a constituent of its conceived nature. The scientific idea of a thing is a great abstraction from the mass of perceptions and reactions which that thing produces; the æsthetic idea is less abstract, since it retains the emotional reaction, the pleasure of the perception, as an integral part of the conceived thing.

Nor is it hard to find the ground of this survival in the sense of beauty of an objectification of feeling elsewhere extinct. Most of the pleasures which objects cause are easily distinguished and separated from the perception of the object: the object has to be applied to a particular organ, like the palate, or swallowed like wine, or used and operated upon in some way before the pleasure arises. The cohesion is therefore slight between the pleasure and the other associated elements of sense; the pleasure is separated in time from the perception, or it is localized in a different organ, and consequently is at once recognized as an effect and not as a quality of the object. But when the process of perception itself is pleasant, as it may easily be, when the intellectual operation, by which the elements of sense are associated and projected, and the concept of the form and substance of the thing produced, is naturally delightful, then we have a pleasure intimately bound up in the thing, inseparable from its character and constitution, the seat of which in us is the same as the seat of the perception. We naturally fail, under these circumstances, to separate the pleasure from the other objectified feelings. It becomes, like them, a quality of the object, which we distinguish from pleasures not so incorporated in the perception of things, by giving it the name of beauty.

§ 11. THE DEFINITION OF BEAUTY. We have now reached our definition of beauty, which, in the terms of our successive analysis and narrowing of the conception, is value positive, intrinsic, and objectified. Or, in less technical language, Beauty is pleasure regarded as the quality of a thing.

This definition is intended to sum up a variety of distinctions and identifications which should perhaps be here more explicitly set down. Beauty is a value, that is, it is not a perception of a matter of fact or of a relation: it is an emotion, an affection of our volitional and appreciative nature. An object cannot be beautiful if it can give pleasure to nobody: a beauty to which all men were forever indifferent is a contradiction in terms.

In the second place, this value is positive, it is the sense of the presence of something good, or (in the case of ugliness) of its absence. It is never the perception of a positive evil, it is never a negative value. That we are endowed with the sense of beauty is a pure gain which brings no evil with it. When the ugly ceases to be amusing or merely uninteresting and becomes disgusting, it becomes indeed a positive evil: but a moral and practical, not an æsthetic one. In æsthetics that saying is true—often so disingenuous in ethics—that evil is nothing but the absence of good: for even the tedium and vulgarity of an existence without beauty is not itself ugly so much as lamentable and degrading. The absence of æsthetic goods is a moral evil: the æsthetic evil is merely relative, and means less of æsthetic good than was expected at the place and time. No form in itself gives pain, although some forms give pain by causing a shock of surprise even when they are really beautiful: as if a mother found a fine bull pup in her child's cradle, when her pain would not be æsthetic in its nature.

Further, this pleasure must not be in the consequence of the utility of the object or event, but in its immediate perception; in other words, beauty is an ultimate good, something that gives satisfaction to a natural function, to some fundamental need or capacity of our minds. Beauty is therefore a positive value that is intrinsic; it is a pleasure. These two circumstances sufficiently separate the sphere of æsthetics from that of ethics. Moral values are generally negative, and always remote. Morality has to do with the avoidance of evil and the pursuit of good: æsthetics only with enjoyment.

Finally, the pleasures of sense are distinguished from the perception of beauty, as sensation in general is distinguished from perception; by the objectification of the elements and their appearance as qualities rather of things than of consciousness. The passage from sensation to perception is gradual, and the path may be sometimes retraced: so it is with beauty and the pleasures of sensation. There is no sharp line between them, but it depends upon the degree of objectivity my feeling has attained at the moment whether I say "It pleases me," or "It is beautiful." If I am self-conscious and critical, I shall probably use one phrase; if I am impulsive and susceptible, the other. The more remote, interwoven, and inextricable the pleasure is, the more objective it will appear; and the union of two pleasures often makes one beauty. In Shakespeare's LIVth sonnet are these words:

> O how much more doth beauty beauteous seem
> By that sweet ornament which truth doth give!
> The rose looks fair, but fairer we it deem
> For that sweet odour which doth in it live.
> The canker-blooms have full as deep a dye
> As the perfumèd tincture of the roses,
> Hang on such thorns, and play as wantonly

When summer's breath their maskèd buds discloses.
But, for their beauty only is their show,
They live unwooed and unrespected fade;
Die to themselves. Sweet roses do not so:
Of their sweet deaths are sweetest odours made.

One added ornament, we see, turns the deep dye, which was but show and mere sensation before, into an element of beauty and reality; and as truth is here the co-operation of perceptions, so beauty is the co-operation of pleasures. If colour, form, and motion are hardly beautiful without the sweetness of the odour, how much more necessary would they be for the sweetness itself to become a beauty! If we had the perfume in a flask, no one would think of calling it beautiful: it would give us too detached and controllable a sensation. There would be no object in which it could be easily incorporated. But let it float from the garden, and it will add another sensuous charm to objects simultaneously recognized, and help to make them beautiful. Thus beauty is constituted by the objectification of pleasure. It is pleasure objectified.

PART II

THE MATERIALS OF BEAUTY

§ 12. ALL HUMAN FUNCTIONS MAY CONTRIBUTE TO THE SENSE OF BEAUTY. Our task will now be to pass in review the various elements of our consciousness, and see what each contributes to the beauty of the world. We shall find that they do so whenever they are inextricably associated with the objectifying activity of the understanding. Whenever the golden thread of pleasure enters that web of things which our intelligence is always busily spinning, it lends to the visible world that mysterious and subtle charm which we call beauty.

There is no function of our nature which cannot contribute something to this effect, but one function differs very much from another in the amount and directness of its contribution. The pleasures of the eye and ear, of the imagination and memory, are the most easily objectified and merged in ideas; but it would betray inexcusable haste and slight appreciation of the principle involved, if we called them the only materials of beauty. Our effort will rather be to discover its other sources, which have been more generally ignored, and point out their importance. For the five senses and the three powers of the soul, which play so large a part in traditional psychology, are by no means the only sources or factors of consciousness; they are more or less external divisions of its content, and not even exhaustive of that. The nature and changes of our life have deeper roots, and are controlled by less obvious processes.

The human body is a machine that holds together by virtue of certain vital functions, on the cessation of which it is dissolved. Some of these, like the circulation of the blood, the growth and decay of the tissues, are at first sight unconscious. Yet any important disturbance of these fundamental processes at once produces great and painful changes in consciousness. Slight alterations are not without their conscious echo: and the whole temper and tone of our mind, the strength of our passions, the grip and concatenation of our habits, our power of attention, and the liveliness of our fancy and affections are due to the influence of these vital forces. They do not, perhaps, constitute the whole basis of any one idea or emotion: but they are the conditions of the existence and character of all.

Particularly important are they for the *value* of our experience. They constitute health, without which no pleasure can be pure. They determine our impulses in leisure, and furnish that surplus energy which we spend in play, in art, and in speculation. The attraction of these pursuits, and the very existence of an æsthetic sphere, is due to the efficiency and perfection of our vital processes. The pleasures which they involve are not exclusively bound to any particular object, and therefore do not account for the relative beauty of things. They are loose and unlocalized, having no special organ, or one which is internal and hidden within the body. They therefore remain undiscriminated in consciousness, and can serve to add interest to any object, or to cast a general glamour over the world, very favourable to its interest and beauty.

The æsthetic value of vital functions differs according to their physiological concomitants: those that are favourable to ideation are of course more apt to extend something of their intimate warmth to the pleasures of contemplation, and thus to intensify the sense of beauty and the interest of thought. Those, on the other hand, that for physiological reasons tend to inhibit ideation, and to drown the attention in dumb and unrepresentable feelings, are less favourable to æsthetic activity. The double effect of drowsiness and reverie will illustrate this difference. The heaviness of sleep seems to fall first on the outer senses, and of course makes them incapable of acute impressions; but if it goes no further, it leaves the imagination all the freer, and by heightening the colours of the fancy, often suggests and reveals beautiful images. There is a kind of poetry and invention that comes only in such moments. In them many lovely melodies must first have been heard, and centaurs and angels originally imagined.

If, however, the lethargy is more complete, or if the cause of it is such that the imagination is retarded while the senses remain awake,—as is the case with an over-fed or over-exercised body,—we have a state of æsthetic insensibility. The exhilaration which comes with pure and refreshing air has a marked influence on our appreciations. To it is largely due the beauty of the morning, and the entirely different charm it has from the evening. The opposite state of all the functions here adds an opposite emotion to externally similar scenes, making both infinitely but differently beautiful.

It would be curious and probably surprising to discover how much the pleasure of breathing has to do with our highest and most transcendental ideals. It is not merely a metaphor that makes us couple airiness with exquisiteness and breathlessness with awe; it is the actual recurrence of a sensation in the throat and lungs that gives those impressions an immediate power, prior to all reflection upon their significance. It is, therefore, to this vital sensation of deep or arrested respiration that the impressiveness of those objects is immediately due.

§ 13. THE INFLUENCE OF THE PASSION OF LOVE. Half-way between vital and social functions, lies the sexual instinct. If nature had solved the problem of reproduction without the differentiation of sex, our emotional life would have been radically different. So profound and, especially in woman, so pervasive an influence does this function exert, that we should betray an entirely unreal view of human nature if we did not inquire into the relations of sex with our æsthetic susceptibility. We must not expect, however, any great difference between man and woman in the scope or objects of æsthetic interest: what is important in emotional life is not which sex an animal has, but that it has sex at all. For if we consider the difficult problem which nature had to solve in sexual reproduction, and the nice adjustment of instinct which it demands, we shall see that the reactions and susceptibilities which must be implanted in the individual are for the most part identical in both sexes, as the sexual organization is itself fundamentally similar in both. Indeed, individuals of various species and the whole animal kingdom have the same sexual disposition, although, of course, the particular object destined to call forth the complete sexual reaction, differs with every species, and with each sex.

If we were dealing with the philosophy of love, and not with that of beauty, our problem would be to find out by what machinery this fundamental susceptibility, common to all animals of both sexes, is gradually directed to more and more definite objects: first, to one species and one sex, and ultimately to one individual. It is not enough that sexual organs should be differentiated: the connexion must be established between them and the outer senses, so that the animal may recognize and pursue the proper object.

The case of lifelong fidelity to one mate—perhaps even to an unsatisfied and hopeless love—is the maximum of differentiation, which even overleaps the utility which gave it a foothold in nature, and defeats its own object. For the differentiation of the instinct in respect to sex, age, and species is obviously necessary to its success as a device for reproduction. While this differentiation is not complete,—and it often is not,—there is a great deal of groping and waste; and the force and constancy of the instinct must make up for its lack of precision. A great deal of vital energy is thus absorbed by this ill-adjusted function. The most economical arrangement which can be conceived, would be one by which only the one female best fitted to bear offspring to a male should arouse his desire, and only so many times as it was well she should grow pregnant, thus leaving his energy and attention free at all other times to exercise the other faculties of his nature.

If this ideal had been reached, the instinct, like all those perfectly adjusted, would tend to become unconscious; and we should miss those secondary effects with which we are exclusively concerned in æsthetics. For it is precisely from the waste, from the radiation of the sexual passion, that beauty borrows warmth. As a harp, made to vibrate to the fingers, gives some music to every wind, so the nature of man, necessarily susceptible to woman, becomes simultaneously sensitive to other influences, and capable of tenderness toward every object. The capacity to love gives our contemplation that glow without which it might often fail to manifest beauty; and the whole sentimental side of our æsthetic sensibility—without which it would be perceptive and mathematical rather than æsthetic—is due to our sexual organization remotely stirred.

The attraction of sex could not become efficient unless the senses were first attracted. The eye must be fascinated and the ear charmed by the object which nature intends should be pursued. Both sexes for this reason develope secondary sexual characteristics; and the sexual emotions are simultaneously extended to various secondary objects. The colour, the grace, the form, which become the stimuli of sexual passion, and the guides of sexual selection, acquire, before they can fulfil that office, a certain intrinsic charm. This charm is not only present for reasons which, in an admissible sense, we may call teleological, on account, that is, of its past utility in reproduction, but its intensity and power are due to the simultaneous stirring of profound sexual impulses. Not, of course, that any specifically sexual ideas are connected with these feelings: such ideas are absent in a modest and inexperienced mind even in the obviously sexual passions of love and jealousy.

These secondary objects of interest, which are some of the most conspicuous elements of beauty, are to be called sexual for these two reasons: because the contingencies of the sexual function have helped to establish them in our race, and because they owe their fascination in a great measure to the participation of our sexual life in the reaction which they cause.

If any one were desirous to produce a being with a great susceptibility to beauty, he could not invent an instrument better designed for that object than sex. Individuals that need not unite for the birth and rearing of each generation, might retain a savage independence. For them it would not be necessary that any vision should fascinate, or that any languor should soften, the prying cruelty of the eye. But sex endows the individual with a dumb and powerful instinct, which carries his body and soul continually towards another; makes it one of the dearest employments of his life to select and pursue a companion, and joins to possession the keenest pleasure, to rivalry the fiercest rage, and to solitude an eternal melancholy.

What more could be needed to suffuse the world with the deepest meaning and beauty? The attention is fixed upon a well-defined object, and all the effects it produces in the mind are easily regarded as powers or qualities of that object. But these effects are here powerful and profound. The soul is stirred to its depths. Its hidden treasures are brought to the surface of consciousness. The imagination and the heart awake for the first time. All these new values crystallize about the objects then offered to the mind. If the fancy is occupied by the image of a single person, whose qualities have had the power of precipitating this revolution, all the values gather about that one image. The object becomes perfect, and we are said to be in love.[1] If the stimulus does not appear as a definite image, the values evoked are dispersed over the world, and we are said to have become lovers of nature, and to have discovered the beauty and meaning of things.

To a certain extent this kind of interest will centre in the proper object of sexual passion, and in the special characteristics of the opposite sex; and we find accordingly that woman is the most lovely object to man, and man, if female modesty would confess it, the most interesting to woman. But the effects

[1] Cf. Stendhal, *De l'Amour, passim.*

of so fundamental and primitive a reaction are much more general. Sex is not the only object of sexual passion. When love lacks its specific object, when it does not yet understand itself, or has been sacrificed to some other interest, we see the stifled fire bursting out in various directions. One is religious devotion, another is zealous philanthropy, a third is the fondling of pet animals, but not the least fortunate is the love of nature, and of art; for nature also is often a second mistress that consoles us for the loss of a first. Passion then overflows and visibly floods those neighbouring regions which it had always secretly watered. For the same nervous organization which sex involves, with its necessarily wide branchings and associations in the brain, must be partially stimulated by other objects than its specific or ultimate one; especially in man, who, unlike some of the lower animals, has not his instincts clearly distinct and intermittent, but always partially active, and never active in isolation. We may say, then, that for man all nature is a secondary object of sexual passion, and that to this fact the beauty of nature is largely due.

§ 14. SOCIAL INSTINCTS AND THEIR ÆSTHETIC INFLUENCE. The function of reproduction carries with it not only direct modifications of the body and mind, but a whole set of social institutions, for the existence of which social instincts and habits are necessary in man. These social feelings, the parental, the patriotic, or the merely gregarious, are not of much direct value for æsthetics, although, as is seen in the case of fashions, they are important in determining the duration and prevalence of a taste once formed. Indirectly they are of vast importance and play a great rôle in arts like poetry, where the effect depends on what is signified more than on what is offered to sense. Any appeal to a human interest rebounds in favour of a work of art in which it is successfully made. That interest, unæsthetic in itself, helps to fix the attention and to furnish subject-matter and momentum to arts and modes of appreciation which are æsthetic. Thus comprehension of the passion of love is necessary to the appreciation of numberless songs, plays, and novels, and not a few works of musical and plastic art.

The treatment of these matters must be postponed until we are prepared to deal with expression—the most complex element of effect. It will suffice here to point out why social and gregarious impulses, in the satisfaction of which happiness mainly resides, are those in which beauty finds least support. This may help us to understand better the relations between æsthetics and *hedonics*, and the nature of that objectification in which we have placed the difference between beauty and pleasure.

So long as happiness is conceived as a poet might conceive it, namely, in its immediately sensuous and emotional factors, so long as we live in the moment and make our happiness consist in the simplest things,—in breathing, seeing, hearing, loving, and sleeping,—our happiness has the same substance, the same elements, as our æsthetic delight, for it is æsthetic delight that makes our happiness. Yet poets and artists, with their immediate and æsthetic joys, are not thought to be happy men; they themselves are apt to be loud in their lamentations, and to regard themselves as eminently and tragically unhappy. This arises from the intensity and inconstancy of their emotions, from their improvidence, and from the eccentricity of their social habits. While among them the sensuous and vital functions have the upper hand, the gregarious and social instincts are subordinated and often deranged; and their unhappiness consists in the sense of their unfitness to live in the world into which they are born.

But man is pre-eminently a political animal, and social needs are almost as fundamental in him as vital functions, and often more conscious. Friendship, wealth, reputation, power, and influence, when added to family life, constitute surely the main elements of happiness. Now these are only very partially composed of definite images of objects. The desire for them, the consciousness of their absence or possession, comes upon us only when we reflect, when we are planning, considering the future, gathering the words of others, rehearsing their scorn or admiration for ourselves, conceiving possible situations in which our virtue, our fame or power would become conspicuous, comparing our lot with that of others, and going through other discursive processes of thought. Apprehension, doubt, isolation, are things which come upon us keenly when we reflect upon our lives; they cannot easily become qualities of any object. If by chance they can, they acquire a great æsthetic value. For instance, "home," which in its social sense is a concept of happiness, when it becomes materialized in a cottage and a garden becomes an æsthetic concept, becomes a beautiful thing. The happiness is objectified, and the object beautified.

Social objects, however, are seldom thus æsthetic, because they are not thus definitely imaginable. They are diffuse and abstract, and verbal rather than sensuous in their materials. Therefore the great emotions that go with them are not immediately transmutable into beauty. If artists and poets are unhappy, it is after all because happiness does not interest them. They cannot seriously pursue it, because its components are not components of beauty, and being in love with beauty, they neglect and despise those unæsthetic social virtues in the operation of which happiness is found. On the other hand those who pursue happiness conceived merely in the abstract and conventional terms, as money, success, or respectability, often miss that real and fundamental part of happiness which flows from the senses and imagination. This element is what æsthetics supplies to life; for beauty also can be a cause and a factor of happiness. Yet the happiness of loving beauty is either too sensuous to be stable, or else too ultimate, too sacramental, to be accounted happiness by the worldly mind.

§ 15. THE LOWER SENSES. The senses of touch, taste, and smell, although capable no doubt of a great development, have not served in man for the purposes of intelligence so much as those of sight and hearing. It is natural that as they remain normally in the background of consciousness, and furnish the least part of our objectified ideas, the pleasures connected with them should remain also detached, and unused for the purpose of appreciation of nature. They have been called the unæsthetic, as well as the lower, senses; but the propriety of these epithets, which is undeniable, is due not to any intrinsic sensuality or baseness of these senses, but to the function which they happen to have in our experience. Smell and taste, like hearing, have the great disadvantage of not being intrinsically spatial: they are therefore not fitted to serve for the representation of nature, which allows herself to be accurately conceived only in spatial terms.[1] They have not reached, moreover, the same organization as sounds, and therefore cannot furnish any play of subjective sensation comparable to music in interest.

The objectification of musical forms is due to their fixity and complexity: like words, they are thought of as existing in a social medium, and can be beautiful without being spatial. But tastes have never been so accurately or universally classified and distinguished; the instrument of sensation does not allow such

[1] This is not the place to enter into a discussion of the metaphysical value of the idea of space. Suffice it to point out that in human experience serviceable knowledge of our environment is to be had only in spatial symbols, and, for whatever reason or accident, this is the language which the mind must speak if it is to advance in clearness and efficiency.

nice and stable discriminations as does the ear. The art of combining dishes and wines, although one which everybody practises with more or less skill and attention, deals with a material far too unrepresentable to be called beautiful. The art remains in the sphere of the pleasant, and is consequently regarded as servile, rather than fine.

Artists in life, if that expression may be used for those who have beautified social and domestic existence, have appealed continually to these lower senses. A fragrant garden, and savoury meats, incense, and perfumes, soft stuffs, and delicious colours, form our ideal of oriental luxuries, an ideal which appeals too much to human nature ever to lose its charm. Yet our northern poets have seldom attempted to arouse these images in their sensuous intensity, without relieving them by some imaginative touch. In Keats, for example, we find the following lines:—

> And still she slept in azure-lidded sleep,
> In blanched linen, smooth and lavendered,
> While he from forth the closet brought a heap
> Of candied apple, quince, and plum, and gourd,
> With jellies soother than the creamy curd,
> And lucent syrops tinct with cinnamon;
> Manna and dates in argosy transferred
> From Fez; and spiced dainties, every one
> From silken Samarcand to cedared Lebanon.

Even the most sensuous of English poets, in whom the love of beauty is supreme, cannot keep long to the primal elements of beauty; the higher flight is inevitable for him. And how much does not the appeal to things in argosy transferred from Fez, reinforced with the reference to Samarcand and especially to the authorized beauties of the cedars of Lebanon, which even the Puritan may sing without a blush, add to our wavering satisfaction and reconcile our conscience to this unchristian indulgence of sense!

But the time may be near when such scruples will be less common, and our poetry, with our other arts, will dwell nearer to the fountain-head of all inspiration. For if nothing not once in sense is to be found in the intellect, much less is such a thing to be found in the imagination. If the cedars of Lebanon did not spread a grateful shade, or the winds rustle through the maze of their branches, if Lebanon had never been beautiful to sense, it would not now be a fit or poetic subject of allusion. And the word "Fez" would be without imaginative value if no traveller had ever felt the intoxication of the torrid sun, the languors of oriental luxury, or, like the British soldier, cried amid the dreary moralities of his native land:—

> Take me somewhere east of Suez
> Where the best is like the worst,
> Where there ain't no ten commandments
> And a man may raise a thirst.

Nor would Samarcand be anything but for the mystery of the desert and the picturesqueness of caravans, nor would an argosy be poetic if the sea had no voices and no foam, the winds and oars no resistance, and the rudder and taut sheets no pull. From these real sensations imagination draws its life, and suggestion its power. The sweep of the fancy is itself also agreeable; but the superiority of the distant over the present is only due to the mass and variety of the pleasures that can be suggested, compared with the poverty of those that can at any time be felt.

§ 16. SOUND. Sound shares with the lower senses the disadvantage of having no intrinsic spatial character; it, therefore, forms no part of the properly abstracted external world, and the pleasures of the ear cannot become, in the literal sense, qualities of *things.* But there is in sounds such an exquisite and continuous gradation in pitch, and such a measurable relation in length, that an object almost as complex and describable as the visible one can be built out of them. What gives spatial forms their value in description of the environment is the ease with which discriminations and comparisons can be made in spatial objects: they are measurable, while unspatial sensations commonly are not. But sounds are also measurable in their own category: they have comparable pitches and durations, and definite and recognizable combinations of those sensuous elements are as truly *objects* as chairs and tables. Not that a musical composition exists in any mystical way, as a portion of the music of the spheres, which no one is hearing; but that, for a critical philosophy, visible objects are also nothing but possibilities of sensation. The real world is merely the shadow of that assurance of eventual experience which accompanies sanity. This objectivity can accrue to any mental figment that has enough cohesion, content, and individuality to be describable and recognizable, and these qualities belong no less to audible than to spatial ideas.

There is, accordingly, some justification in Schopenhauer's speculative assertion that music repeats the entire world of sense, and is a parallel method of expression of the underlying substance, or will. The world of sound is certainly capable of in-

finite variety and, were our sense developed, of infinite extensions; and it has as much as the world of matter the power to
interest us and to stir our emotions. It was therefore potentially
as full of meaning. But it has proved the less serviceable and
constant apparition; and, therefore, music, which builds with its
materials, while the purest and most impressive of the arts, is
the least human and instructive of them.

The pleasantness of sounds has a simple physical basis. All
sensations are pleasant only between certain limits of intensity;
but the ear can discriminate easily between noises, that in themselves are uninteresting, if not annoying, and notes, which have
an unmistakable charm. A sound is a note if the pulsations of the
air by which it is produced recur at regular intervals. If there
is no regular recurrence of waves, it is a noise. The rapidity of
these regular beats determines the pitch of tones. That quality
or *timbre* by which one sound is distinguished from another
of the same pitch and intensity is due to the different complications of waves in the air; the ability to discriminate the various
waves in the vibrating air is, therefore, the condition of our
finding music in it; for every wave has its period, and what we
call a noise is a complication of notes too complex for our organs
or our attention to decipher.

We find here, at the very threshold of our subject, a clear instance of a conflict of principles which appears everywhere in
æsthetics, and is the source and explanation of many conflicts of
taste. Since a note is heard when a set of regular vibrations can
be discriminated in the chaos of sound, it appears that the perception and value of this artistic element depends on abstraction,
on the omission from the field of attention, of all the elements
which do not conform to a simple law. This may be called the
principle of purity. But if it were the only principle at work,
there would be no music more beautiful than the tone of a
tuning-fork. Such sounds, although delightful perhaps to a child,
are soon tedious. The principle of purity must make some compromise with another principle, which we may call that of interest. The object must have enough variety and expression to
hold our attention for a while, and to stir our nature widely.

As we are more acutely sensitive to results or to processes, we
find the most agreeable effect nearer to one or to the other of
these extremes of a tedious beauty or of an unbeautiful expressiveness. But these principles, as is clear, are not co-ordinate. The
child who enjoys his rattle or his trumpet has æsthetic enjoyment, of however rude a kind; but the master of technique who

should give a performance wholly without sensuous charm would be a gymnast and not a musician, and the author whose novels and poems should be merely expressive, and interesting only by their meaning and moral, would be a writer of history or philosophy, but not an artist. The principle of purity is therefore essential to æsthetic effect, but the principle of interest is subsidiary, and if appealed to alone would fail to produce beauty.

The distinction, however, is not absolute: for the simple sensation is itself interesting, and the complication, if it is appreciable by sense and does not require discursive thought to grasp it, is itself beautiful. There may be a work of art in which the sensuous materials are not pleasing, as a discourse without euphony, if the structure and expression give delight; and there may be an interesting object without perceived structure, like musical notes, or the blue sky. Perfection would, of course, lie in the union of elements all intrinsically beautiful, in forms also intrinsically so; but where this is impossible, different natures prefer to sacrifice one or the other advantage.

§ 17. Colour. In the eye we have an organ so differentiated that it is sensitive to a much more subtle influence than even that of air waves. There seems to be, in the interstellar spaces, some pervasive fluid, for the light of the remotest star is rapidly conveyed to us, and we can hardly understand how this radiation of light, which takes place beyond our atmosphere, could be realized without some medium. This hypothetical medium we call the ether. It is capable of very rapid vibrations, which are propagated in all directions, like the waves of sound, only much more quickly. Many common observations, such as the apparent interval between lightning and thunder, make us aware of the quicker motion of light. Now, since nature was filled with this responsive fluid, which propagated to all distances vibrations originating at any point, and moreover as these vibrations, when intercepted by a solid body, were reflected wholly or in part, it obviously became very advantageous to every animal to develope an organ sensitive to these vibrations—sensitive, that is, to light. For this would give the mind instantaneous impressions dependent upon the presence and nature of distant objects.

To this circumstance we must attribute the primacy of sight in our perception, a primacy that makes light the natural symbol of knowledge. When the time came for our intelligence to take the great metaphysical leap, and conceive its content as permanent and independent, or, in other words, to imagine *things,* the idea of these *things* had to be constructed out of the materials already present to the mind. But the fittest material for such construction was that furnished by the eye, since it is the eye that brings us into widest relations with our actual environment, and gives us the quickest warning of approaching impressions. Sight has a prophetic function. We are less interested in it for itself than for the suggestion it brings of what may follow after. Sight is a method of presenting psychically what is practically absent; and as the essence of the *thing* is its existence in our absence, the *thing* is spontaneously conceived in terms of sight.

Sight is, therefore, perception *par excellence,* since we become most easily aware of objects through visual agency and in visual terms. Now, as the values of perception are those we call æsthetic, and there could be no beauty if there was no conception of independent objects, we may expect to find beauty derived mainly from the pleasures of sight. And, in fact, form, which is almost a synonym of beauty, is for us usually something visible: it is a synthesis of the seen. But prior to the effect of form, which arises in the constructive imagination, comes the effect of colour; this is purely sensuous, and no better intrinsically than the effects of any other sense: but being more involved in the perception of objects than are the rest, it becomes more readily an element of beauty.

The values of colours differ appreciably and have analogy to the differing values of other sensations. As sweet or pungent smells, as high and low notes, or major and minor chords, differ from each other by virtue of their different stimulation of the senses, so also red differs from green, and green from violet. There is a nervous process for each, and consequently a specific value. This emotional quality has affinity to the emotional quality of other sensations; we need not be surprised that the high rate of vibration which yields a sharp note to the ear should involve somewhat the same feeling that is produced by the high rate of vibration which, to the eye, yields a violet colour. These affinities escape many minds; but it is conceivable that the sense of them should be improved by accident or training. There are certain effects of colour which give all men pleasure, and others which jar, almost like a musical discord. A more general development of this sensibility would make possible a new abstract art, an art that should deal with colours as music does with sound.

We have not studied these effects, however, with enough attention, we have not allowed them to penetrate enough into the soul, to think them very significant. The stimulation of fire-works, or of kaleidoscopic effects, seems to us trivial. But every-thing which has a varied content has a potentiality of form and also of meaning. The form will be enjoyed as soon as attention accustoms us to discriminate and recognize its variations; and meaning will accrue to it, when the various emotional values of these forms ally the new object to all other experiences which involve similar emotions, and thus give it a sympathetic environ-ment in the mind. The colours of the sunset have a brilliancy that attracts attention, and a softness and illusiveness that en-chant the eye; while the many associations of the evening and of heaven gather about this kindred charm and deepen it. Thus the most sensuous of beauties can be full of sentimental suggestion. In stained glass, also, we have an example of masses of colour made to exert their powerful direct influence, to intensify an emotion eventually to be attached to very ideal objects; what is in itself a gorgeous and unmeaning ornament, by its absolute impressiveness becomes a vivid symbol of those other ultimates which have a similar power over the soul.

§ 18. Materials surveyed. We have now gone over those organs of perception that give us the materials out of which we construct objects, and mentioned the most conspicuous pleasures which, as they arise from those organs, are easily merged in the ideas furnished by the same. We have also noticed that these ideas, conspicuous as they are in our developed and operating consciousness, are not so much factors in our thought, independ-ent contributors to it, as they are discriminations and excisions in its content, which, after they are all made, leave still a back-ground of vital feeling. For the outer senses are but a portion of our sensorium, and the ideas of each, or of all together, but a portion of our consciousness.

The pleasures which accompany ideation we have also found to be unitary and vital; only just as for practical purposes it is necessary to abstract and discriminate the contribution of one sense from that of another, and thus to become aware of par-ticular and definable impressions, so it is natural that the dif-fused emotional tone of the body should also be divided, and a certain modicum of pleasure or pain should be attributed to each idea. Our pleasures are thus described as the pleasures of touch, taste, smell, hearing, and sight, and may become elements of beauty at the same time as the ideas to which they are at-tached become elements of objects. There is, however, a remainder of emotion as there is a remainder of sensation; and the importance of this remainder—of the continuum in which lie all particular pleasures and pains—was insisted upon in the beginning.

The beauty of the world, indeed, cannot be attributed wholly or mainly to pleasures thus attached to abstracted sensations. It is only the beauty of the materials of things which is drawn from the pleasures of sensation. By far the most important effects are not attributable to these materials, but to their arrangement and their ideal relations. We have yet to study those processes of our mind by which this arrangement and these relations are conceived; and the pleasures which we can attach to these processes may then be added to the pleasures attached to sense as further and more subtle elements of beauty.

But before passing to the consideration of this more intricate subject, we may note that however subordinate the beauty may be which a garment, a building, or a poem derives from its sensuous material, yet the presence of this sensuous material is indispensable. Form cannot be the form of nothing. If, then, in finding or creating beauty, we ignore the materials of things, and attend only to their form, we miss an ever-present opportunity to heighten our effects. For whatever delight the form may bring, the material might have given delight already, and so much would have been gained towards the value of the total result.

Sensuous beauty is not the greatest or most important element of effect, but it is the most primitive and fundamental, and the most universal. There is no effect of form which an effect of material could not enhance, and this effect of material, underlying that of form, raises the latter to a higher power and gives the beauty of the object a certain poignancy, thoroughness, and infinity which it otherwise would have lacked. The Parthenon not in marble, the king's crown not of gold, and the stars not of fire, would be feeble and prosaic things. The greater hold which material beauty has upon the senses, stimulates us here, where the form is also sublime, and lifts and intensifies our emotions. We need this stimulus if our perceptions are to reach the highest pitch of strength and acuteness. Nothing can be ravishing that is not beautiful pervasively.

And another point. The wider diffusion of sensuous beauty makes it as it were the poor man's good. Fewer factors are needed to produce it and less training to appreciate it. The senses are indispensable instruments of labour, developed by the necessities of life; but their perfect development produces a harmony between the inward structure and instinct of the organ and the outward opportunities for its use; and this harmony is the source of continual pleasures. In the sphere of sense, therefore, a certain cultivation is inevitable in man; often greater, indeed, among rude peoples, perhaps among animals, than among those whose attention takes a wider sweep and whose ideas are more abstract. Without requiring, therefore, that a man should rise above his station, or develope capacities which his opportunities will seldom employ, we may yet endow his life with æsthetic interest, if we allow him the enjoyment of sensuous beauty. This enriches him without adding to his labour, and flatters him without alienating him from his world.

Taste, when it is spontaneous, always begins with the senses. Children and savages, as we are so often told, delight in bright and variegated colours; the simplest people appreciate the neatness of muslin curtains, shining varnish, and burnished pots. A rustic garden is a shallow patchwork of the liveliest flowers, without that reserve and repose which is given by spaces and masses. Noise and vivacity is all that childish music contains, and primitive songs add little more of form than what is required to compose a few monotonous cadences. These limitations are not to be regretted; they are a proof of sincerity. Such simplicity is not the absence of taste, but the beginning of it.

A people with genuine æsthetic perceptions creates traditional forms and expresses the simple pathos of its life, in unchanging but significant themes, repeated by generation after generation. When sincerity is lost, and a snobbish ambition is substituted, bad taste comes in. The essence of it is a substitution of non-æsthetic for æsthetic values. To love glass beads because they are beautiful is barbarous, perhaps, but not vulgar; to love jewels only because they are dear is vulgar, and to betray the motive by placing them ineffectively is an offence against taste. The test is always the same: Does the thing itself actually please? If it does, your taste is real; it may be different from that of others, but is equally justified and grounded in human nature. If it does not, your whole judgment is spurious, and you are guilty, not of heresy, which in æsthetics is orthodoxy itself, but of hypocrisy, which is a self-excommunication from its sphere.

Now, a great sign of this hypocrisy is insensibility to sensuous beauty. When people show themselves indifferent to primary and fundamental effects, when they are incapable of finding pictures except in frames or beauties except in the great masters, we may justly suspect that they are parrots, and that their verbal and historical knowledge covers a natural lack of æsthetic sense. Where, on the contrary, insensibility to higher forms of beauty does not exclude a natural love of the lower, we have every reason to be encouraged; there is a true and healthy taste, which only needs experience to refine it. If a man demands light, sound, and splendour, he proves that he has the æsthetic equilibrium; that appearances as such interest him, and that he can pause in perception to enjoy. We have but to vary his observation, to enlarge his thought, to multiply his discriminations—all of which education can do—and the same æsthetic habit will reveal to him every shade of the fit and fair. Or if it should not, and the man, although sensuously gifted, proved to be imaginatively dull, at least he would not have failed to catch an intimate and widespread element of effect. The beauty of material is thus the groundwork of all higher beauty, both in the object, whose form and meaning have to be lodged in something sensible, and in the mind, where sensuous ideas, being the first to emerge, are the first that can arouse delight.

PART III

FORM

§ 19. THERE IS A BEAUTY OF FORM. The most remarkable and characteristic problem of æsthetics is that of beauty of form. Where there is a sensuous delight, like that of colour, and the impression of the object is in its elements agreeable, we have to look no farther for an explanation of the charm we feel. Where there is expression, and an object indifferent to the senses is associated with other ideas which are interesting, the problem, although complex and varied, is in principle comparatively plain. But there is an intermediate effect which is more mysterious, and more specifically an effect of beauty. It is found where sensible elements, by themselves indifferent, are so united as to please in combination. There is something unexpected in this phenomenon, so much so that those who cannot conceive its explanation often reassure themselves by denying its existence. To reduce beauty of form, however, to beauty of elements would not be easy, because the creation and variation of effect, by changing the relation of the simplest lines, offers too easy an experiment in reputation. And it would, moreover, follow to the comfort of the vulgar that all marble houses are equally beautiful.

To attribute beauty of form to expression is more plausible. If I take the meaningless short lines in the figure and arrange

them in the given ways, intended to represent the human face, there appear at once notably different æsthetic values. Two of the forms are differently grotesque and one approximately beautiful. Now these effects are due to the expression of the lines; not only because they make one think of fair or ugly faces, but because, it may be said, these faces would in reality be fair or ugly, according to their expression, according to the vital and moral associations of the different types.

Nevertheless, beauty of form cannot be reduced to expression without denying the existence of immediate æsthetic values altogether, and reducing them all to suggestions of moral good. For if the object expressed by the form, and from which the form derives its value, had itself beauty of form, we should not advance; we must come somewhere to the point where the expression is of something else than beauty; and this something else would of course be some practical or moral good. Moralists are fond of such an interpretation, and it is a very interesting one. It puts beauty in the same relation to morals in which morals stand to pleasure and pain; both would be intuitions, qualitatively new, but with the same materials; they would be new perspectives of the same object.

But this theory is actually inadmissible. Innumerable æsthetic effects, indeed all specific and unmixed ones, are direct transmutations of pleasures and pains; they express nothing extrinsic to themselves, much less moral excellences. The detached lines of our figure signify nothing, but they are not absolutely uninteresting; the straight line is the simplest and not the least beautiful of forms. To say that it owes its interest to the thought of the economy of travelling over the shortest road, or of other practical advantages, would betray a feeble hold on psychological reality. The impression of a straight line differs in a certain almost emotional way from that of a curve, as those of various curves do from one another. The quality of the sensation is different, like that of various colours or sounds. To attribute the character of these forms to association would be like explaining sea-sickness as the fear of shipwreck. There is a distinct quality and value, often a singular beauty, in these simple lines that is intrinsic in the perception of their form.

It would be pedantic, perhaps, anywhere but in a treatise on æsthetics, to deny to this quality the name of expression; we might commonly say that the circle has one expression and the oval another. But what does the circle express except circularity, or the oval except the nature of the ellipse? Such expression *expresses* nothing; it is really *im*pression. There may be analogy between it and other impressions; we may admit that odours, colours, and sounds correspond, and may mutually suggest one another; but this analogy is a superadded charm felt by very sensitive natures, and does not constitute the original value of the sensations. The common emotional tinge is rather what enables them to suggest one another, and what makes them comparable. Their expression, such as it is, is therefore due to the accident that both feelings have a kindred quality; and this quality has its effectiveness for sense independently of the perception of its recurrence in a different sphere. We shall accordingly take care to reserve the term "expression" for the suggestion of some other and assignable object, from which the expressive thing borrows an interest; and we shall speak of the intrinsic quality of forms as their emotional tinge or specific value.

§ 20. PHYSIOLOGY OF THE PERCEPTION OF FORM. The charm of a line evidently consists in the relation of its parts; in order to understand this interest in spatial relations, we must inquire how they are perceived.[1] If the eye had its sensitive surface, the retina, exposed directly to the light, we could never have a perception of form any more than in the nose or ear, which also perceive the object through media. When the perception is not through a medium, but direct, as in the case of the skin, we might get a notion of form, because each point of the object would excite a single point in the skin, and as the sensations in different parts of the skin differ in quality, a manifold of sense, in which discrimination of parts would be involved, could be presented to the mind. But when the perception is through a medium, a difficulty arises.

Any point, *a*, in the object will send a ray to every point, *a'*, *b'*, *c'*, of the sensitive surface; every point of the retina will therefore be similarly affected, since each will receive rays from every

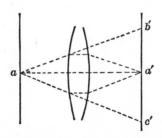

---

[1] The discussion is limited in this chapter to visible form; audible form is probably capable of a parallel treatment, but requires studies too technical for this place.

part of the object. If all the rays from one point of the object, *a*, are to be concentrated on a corresponding point of the retina, *a'*, which would then become the exclusive representative of *a*, we must have one or more refracting surfaces interposed, to gather the rays together. The presence of the lens, with its various coatings, has made representation of point by point possible for the eye. The absence of such an instrument makes the same sort of representation impossible to other senses, such as the nose, which does not smell in one place the effluvia of one part of the environment and in another place the effluvia of another, but smells indiscriminately the combination of all. Eyes without lenses like those possessed by some animals, undoubtedly give only a consciousness of diffused light, without the possibility of boundaries or divisions in the field of view. The abstraction of colour from form is therefore by no means an artificial one, since, by a simplification of the organ of sense, one may be perceived without the other.

But even if the lens enables the eye to receive a distributed image of the object, the manifold which consciousness would perceive would not be necessarily a manifold of parts juxtaposed in space. Each point of the retina might send to the brain a detached impression; these might be comparable, but not necessarily in their spatial position. The ear sends to the brain such a manifold of impressions (since the ear also has an apparatus by which various external differences in rapidity of vibrations are distributed into different parts of the organ). But this discriminated manifold is a manifold of pitches, not of positions. How does it happen that the manifold conveyed by the optic nerve appears in consciousness as spatial, and that the relation between its elements is seen as a relation of position?

An answer to this question has been suggested by various psychologists. The eye, by an instinctive movement, turns so as to bring every impression upon that point of the retina, near its centre, which has the acutest sensibility. A series of muscular sensations therefore always follows upon the conspicuous excitement of any outlying point. The object, as the eye brings it to the centre of vision, excites a series of points upon the retina; and the local sign, or peculiar quality of sensation, proper to each of these spots, is associated with that series of muscular feelings involved in turning the eyes. These feelings henceforth revive together; it is enough that a point in the periphery of the retina should receive a ray, for the mind to feel, together with that impression, the suggestion of a motion, and of the line of points that lies between the excited point and the centre of vision. A network of associations is thus formed, whereby the sensation of each retinal point is connected with all the others in a manner which is that of points in a plane. Every visible point becomes thus a point in a field, and has a felt radiation of lines of possible motion about it. Our notion of visual space has this origin, since the manifold of retinal impressions is distributed in a manner which serves as the type and exemplar of what we mean by a surface.

§ 21. VALUES OF GEOMETRICAL FIGURES. The reader will perhaps pardon these details and the strain they put on his attention, when he perceives how much they help us to understand the value of forms. The sense, then, of the position of any point consists in the tensions in the eye, that not only tends to bring that point to the centre of vision, but feels the suggestion of all the other points which are related to the given one in the web of visual experience. The definition of space as the possibility of motion is therefore an accurate and significant one, since the most direct and native perception of space we can have is the awakening of many tendencies to move our organs.

For example, if a circle is presented, the eye will fall upon its centre, as to the centre of gravity, as it were, of the balanced attractions of all the points; and there will be, in that position, an indifference and sameness of sensation, in whatever direction some accident moves the eye, that accounts very well for the emotional quality of the circle. It is a form which, although beautiful in its purity and simplicity, and wonderful in its continuity, lacks any stimulating quality, and is often ugly in the arts, especially when found in vertical surfaces where it is not always seen in perspective. For horizontal surfaces it is better because it is there always an ellipse to vision, and the ellipse has a less dull and stupefying effect. The eye can move easily, organize and subordinate its parts, and its relations to the environment are not similar in all directions. Small circles, like buttons, are not in the same danger of becoming ugly, because the eye considers them as points, and they diversify and help to divide surfaces, without appearing as surfaces themselves.

The straight line offers a curious object for analysis. It is not for the eye a very easy form to grasp. We bend it or we leave it. Unless it passes through the centre of vision, it is obviously a tangent to the points which have analogous relations to that centre. The local signs or tensions of the points in such a tangent vary in an unseizable progression; there is violence in keeping to it, and the effect is forced. This makes the dry and stiff quality of any long straight line, which the skilful Greeks avoided by the curves of their columns and entablatures, and the less economical barbarians by a profusion of interruptions and ornaments.

The straight line, when made the direct object of attention, is, of course, followed by the eye and not seen by the outlying parts of the retina in one eccentric position. The same explanation is good for this more common case, since the consciousness that the eye travels in a straight line consists in the surviving sense of the previous position, and in the manner in which the tensions of these various positions overlap. If the tensions change from moment to moment entirely, we have a broken, a fragmentary effect, as that of zigzag, where all is dropping and picking up again of associated motions; in the straight line, much prolonged, we have a gradual and inexorable rending of these tendencies to associated movements.

In the curves we call flowing and graceful, we have, on the contrary, a more natural and rhythmical set of movements in the optic muscles; and certain points in the various gyrations make rhymes and assonances, as it were, to the eye that reaches them. We find ourselves at every turn reawakening with a variation, the sense of the previous position. It is easy to understand by analogy with the superficially observed conditions of pleasure, that such rhythms and harmonies should be delightful. The deeper question of the physical basis of pleasure we have not intended to discuss. Suffice it that measure, in quantity, in intensity, and in time, must involve that physiological process, whatever it may be, the consciousness of which is pleasure.

§ 22. SYMMETRY. An important exemplification of these physiological principles is found in the charm of symmetry. When for any reason the eye is to be habitually directed to a single point, as to the opening of a gate or window, to an altar, a throne, a stage, or a fireplace, there will be violence and distraction caused by the tendency to look aside in the recurring necessity of looking forward, if the object is not so arranged that the tensions of eye are balanced, and the centre of gravity of vision lies in the point which one is obliged to keep in sight. In all such objects we therefore require bilateral symmetry. The necessity of vertical symmetry is not felt because the eyes and head do not so readily survey objects from top to bottom as from side to side. The inequality of the upper and lower parts does not generate the same tendency to motion, the same restlessness, as does the inequality of the right and left sides of an object in front of us. The comfort and economy that comes from muscular balance in the eye, is therefore in some cases the source of the value of symmetry.[1]

In other cases symmetry appeals to us through the charm of recognition and rhythm. When the eye runs over a façade, and finds the objects that attract it at equal intervals, an expectation, like the anticipation of an inevitable note or requisite word, arises in the mind, and its non-satisfaction involves a shock. This shock, if caused by the emphatic emergence of an interesting object, gives the effect of the picturesque; but when it comes with no compensation, it gives us the feeling of ugliness and imperfection—the defect which symmetry avoids. This kind of symmetry is accordingly in itself a negative merit, but often the condition of the greatest of all merits,—the permanent power to please. It contributes to that completeness which delights without stimulating, and to which our jaded senses return gladly, after all sorts of extravagances, as to a kind of domestic peace. The inwardness and solidity of this quiet beauty comes from the intrinsic character of the pleasure which makes it up. It is no adventitious charm; but the eye in its continual passage over the object finds always the same response, the same adequacy; and the very process of perception is made delightful by the object's fitness to be perceived. The parts, thus coalescing, form a single object, the unity and simplicity of which are based upon the rhythm and correspondence of its elements.

Symmetry is here what metaphysicians call a principle of individuation. By the emphasis which it lays upon the recurring elements, it cuts up the field into determinate units; all that lies between the beats is one interval, one individual. If there were no recurrent impressions, no corresponding points, the field of perception would remain a fluid continuum, without defined and recognizable divisions. The outlines of most things are symmetrical because we choose what symmetrical lines we find to be the boundaries of objects. Their symmetry is the condition of their unity, and their unity of their individuality and separate existence.

[1] The relation to stability also makes us sensitive to certain kinds of symmetry; but this is an adventitious consideration with which we are not concerned.

Experience, to be sure, can teach us to regard unsymmetrical objects as wholes, because their elements move and change together in nature; but this is a principle of individuation, *a posteriori*, founded on the association of recognized elements. These elements, to be recognized and seen to go together and form one thing, must first be somehow discriminated; and the symmetry, either of their parts, or of their position as wholes, may enable us to fix their boundaries and to observe their number. The category of unity, which we are so constantly imposing upon nature and its parts, has symmetry, then, for one of its instruments, for one of its bases of application.

If symmetry, then, is a principle of individuation and helps us to distinguish objects, we cannot wonder that it helps us to enjoy the perception. For our intelligence loves to perceive; water is not more grateful to a parched throat than a principle of comprehension to a confused understanding. Symmetry clarifies, and we all know that light is sweet. At the same time, we can see why there are limits to the value of symmetry. In objects, for instance, that are too small or too diffused for composition, symmetry has no value. In an avenue symmetry is stately and impressive, but in a large park, or in the plan of a city, or the side wall of a gallery it produces monotony in the various views rather than unity in any one of them. Greek temples, never being very large, were symmetrical on all their façades; Gothic churches were generally designed to be symmetrical only in the west front, and in the transepts, while the side elevation as a whole was eccentric. This was probably an accident, due to the demands of the interior arrangement; but it was a fortunate one, as we may see by contrasting its effect with that of our stations, exhibition buildings, and other vast structures, where symmetry is generally introduced even in the most extensive façades which, being too much prolonged for their height, cannot be treated as units. The eye is not able to take them in at a glance, and does not get the effect of repose from the balance of the extremes, while the mechanical sameness of the sections, surveyed in succession, makes the impression of an unmeaning poverty of resource.

Symmetry thus loses its value when it cannot, on account of the size of the object, contribute to the unity of our perception. The synthesis which it facilitates must be instantaneous. If the comprehension by which we unify our object is discursive, as, for instance, in conceiving the arrangement and numbering of the streets of New York, or the plan of the Escurial, the advantage of symmetry is an intellectual one; we can better imagine the relations of the parts, and draw a map of the whole in the fancy; but there is no advantage to direct perception, and therefore no added beauty. Symmetry is superfluous in those objects. Similarly animal and vegetable forms gain nothing by being symmetrically displayed, if the sense of their life and motion is to be given. When, however, these forms are used for mere decoration, not for the expression of their own vitality, then symmetry is again required to accentuate their unity and organization. This justifies the habit of conventionalizing natural forms, and the tendency of some kinds of hieratic art, like the Byzantine or Egyptian, to affect a rigid symmetry of posture. We can thereby increase the unity and force of the image without suggesting that individual life and mobility, which would interfere with the religious function of the object, as the symbol and embodiment of an impersonal faith.

§ 23. FORM THE UNITY OF A MANIFOLD. Symmetry is evidently a kind of unity in variety, where a whole is determined by the rhythmic repetition of similars. We have seen that it has a value where it is an aid to unification. Unity would thus appear to be the virtue of forms; but a moment's reflection will show us that unity cannot be absolute and be a form; a form is an aggregation, it must have elements, and the manner in which the elements are combined constitutes the character of the form. A perfectly simple perception, in which there was no consciousness of the distinction and relation of parts, would not be a perception of form; it would be a sensation. Physiologically these sensations may be aggregates and their values, as in the case of musical tones, may differ according to the manner in which certain elements, beats, vibrations, nervous processes, or what not, are combined; but for consciousness the result is simple, and the value is the pleasantness of a datum and not of a process. Form, therefore, does not appeal to the unattentive; they get from objects only a vague sensation which may in them awaken extrinsic associations; they do not stop to survey the parts or to appreciate their relation, and consequently are insensible to the various charms of various unifications; they can find in objects only the value of material or of function, not that of form.

Beauty of form, however, is what specifically appeals to an æsthetic nature; it is equally removed from the crudity of formless stimulation and from the emotional looseness of reverie and discursive thought. The indulgence in sentiment and suggestion, of which our time is fond, to the sacrifice of formal beauty, marks an absence of cultivation as real, if not as confessed, as that of the barbarian who revels in gorgeous confusion.

The synthesis, then, which constitutes form is an activity of the mind; the unity arises consciously, and is an insight into the relation of sensible elements separately perceived. It differs from sensation in the consciousness of the synthesis, and from expression in the homogeneity of the elements, and in their common presence to sense.

The variety of forms depends upon the character of the elements and on the variety of possible methods of unification. The elements may be all alike, and their only diversity be numerical. Their unity will then be merely the sense of their uniformity.[1] Or they may differ in kind, but so as to compel the mind to no particular order in their unification. Or they may finally be so constituted that they suggest inevitably the scheme of their unity; in this case there is organization in the object, and the synthesis of its parts is one and pre-determinate. We shall discuss these various forms in succession, pointing out the effects proper to each.

§ 24. MULTIPLICITY IN UNIFORMITY. The radical and typical case of the first kind of unity in variety is found in the perception of extension itself. This perception, if we look to its origin, may turn out to be primitive; no doubt the feeling of "crude extensity" is an original sensation; every inference, association, and distinction is a thing that looms up suddenly before the mind, and the nature and actuality of which is a datum of what—to indicate its irresistible immediacy and indescribability—we may well call sense. Forms are seen, and if we think of the origin of the perception, we may well call this vision a sensation. The distinction between a sensation of form, however, and one which is formless, regards the content and character, not the genesis of the perception. A distinction and association, or an inference, is a direct experience, a sensible fact; but it is the experience of a process, of a motion between two terms, and a consciousness of their coexistence and distinction; it is a feeling of relation. Now the sense of space is a feeling of this kind; the essence of it is the realization of a

[1] Cf. Fechner, *Vorschule der Aesthetik*, Erster Theil, S. 73, a passage by which the following classification of forms was first suggested.

variety of directions and of possible motions, by which the relation of point to point is vaguely but inevitably given. The perception of extension is therefore a perception of form, although
of the most rudimentary kind. It is merely *Auseinandersein*, and
we might call it the *materia prima* of form, were it not capable
of existing without further determination. For we can have the
sense of space without the sense of boundaries; indeed, this intuition is what tempts us to declare space infinite. Space would
have to consist of a finite number of juxtaposed blocks, if our
experience of extension carried with it essentially the realization
of limits.

The æsthetic effect of extensiveness is also entirely different
from that of particular shapes. Some things appeal to us by their
surfaces, others by the lines that limit those surfaces. And this
effect of surface is not necessarily an effect of material or colour;
the evenness, monotony, and vastness of a great curtain of colour
produce an effect which is that of the extreme of uniformity in
the extreme of multiplicity; the eye wanders over a fluid infinity of unrecognizable positions, and the sense of their number-
lessness and continuity is precisely the source of the emotion of
extent. The emotion is primary and has undoubtedly a physiological ground, while the idea of size is secondary and involves
associations and inferences. A small photograph of St. Peter's
gives the idea of size; as does a distant view of the same object.
But this is of course dependent on our realization of the distance, or of the scale of the representation. The value of size
becomes immediate only when we are at close quarters with the
object; then the surfaces really subtend a large angle in the field
of vision, and the sense of vastness establishes its standard, which
can afterwards be applied to other objects by analogy and contrast. There is also, to be sure, a moral and practical import in
the known size of objects, which, by association, determines their
dignity; but the pure sense of extension, based upon the attack
of the object upon the apperceptive resources of the eye, is the
truly æsthetic value which it concerns us to point out here, as
the most rudimentary example of form.

Although the effect of extension is not that of material, the
two are best seen in conjunction. Material must appear in some
form; but when its beauty is to be made prominent, it is well
that this form should attract attention as little as possible to
itself. Now, of all forms, absolute uniformity in extension is the
simplest and most allied to the material; it gives the latter only
just enough form to make it real and perceptible. Very rich and

beautiful materials therefore do well to assume this form. You will spoil the beauty you have by superimposing another; as if you make a statue of gold, or flute a jasper column, or bedeck a velvet cloak. The beauty of stuffs appears when they are plain. Even stone gives its specific quality best in great unbroken spaces of wall; the simplicity of the form emphasizes the substance. And again, the effect of extensity is never long satisfactory unless it is superinduced upon some material beauty; the dignity of great hangings would suffer if they were not of damask, but of cotton, and the vast smoothness of the sky would grow oppressive if it were not of so tender a blue.

§ 25. EXAMPLE OF THE STARS. Another beauty of the sky—the stars—offers so striking and fascinating an illustration of the effect of multiplicity in uniformity, that I am tempted to analyze it at some length. To most people, I fancy, the stars are beautiful; but if you asked why, they would be at a loss to reply, until they remembered what they had heard about astronomy, and the great size and distance and possible habitation of those orbs. The vague and illusive ideas thus aroused fall in so well with the dumb emotion we were already feeling, that we attribute this emotion to those ideas, and persuade ourselves that the power of the starry heavens lies in the suggestion of astronomical facts.

The idea of the insignificance of our earth and of the incomprehensible multiplicity of worlds is indeed immensely impressive; it may even be intensely disagreeable. There is something baffling about infinity; in its presence the sense of finite humility can never wholly banish the rebellious suspicion that we are being deluded. Our mathematical imagination is put on the rack by an attempted conception that has all the anguish of a nightmare and probably, could we but awake, all its laughable absurdity. But the obsession of this dream is an intellectual puzzle, not an æsthetic delight. It is not essential to our admiration. Before the days of Kepler the heavens declared the glory of the Lord; and we needed no calculation of stellar distances, no fancies about a plurality of worlds, no image of infinite spaces, to make the stars sublime.

Had we been taught to believe that the stars governed our fortunes, and were we reminded of fate whenever we looked at them, we should similarly tend to imagine that this belief was the source of their sublimity; and, if the superstition were dispelled, we should think the interest gone from the apparition. But experience would soon undeceive us, and prove to us that the sensuous character of the object was sublime in itself. Indeed, on account of that intrinsic sublimity the sky can be fitly chosen as a symbol for a sublime conception; the common quality in both makes each suggest the other. For that reason, too, the parable of the natal stars governing our lives is such a natural one to express our subjection to circumstances, and can be transformed by the stupidity of disciples into a literal tenet. In the same way, the kinship of the emotion produced by the stars with the emotion proper to certain religious moments makes the stars seem a religious object. They become, like impressive music, a stimulus to worship. But fortunately there are experiences which remain untouched by theory, and which maintain the mutual intelligence of men through the estrangements wrought by intellectual and religious systems. When the superstructures crumble, the common foundation of human sentience and imagination is exposed beneath.

The intellectual suggestion of the infinity of nature can, moreover, be awakened by other experiences which are by no means sublime. A heap of sand will involve infinity as surely as a universe of suns and planets. Any object is infinitely divisible and, when we press the thought, can contain as many worlds with as many winged monsters and ideal republics as can the satellites of Sirius. But the infinitesimal does not move us æsthetically; it can only awaken an amused curiosity. The difference cannot lie in the import of the idea, which is objectively the same in both cases. It lies in the different immediate effect of the crude images which give us the type and meaning of each; the crude image that underlies the idea of the infinitesimal is the dot, the poorest and most uninteresting of impressions; while the crude image that underlies the idea of infinity is space, multiplicity in uniformity, and this, as we have seen, has a powerful effect on account of the breadth, volume, and omnipresence of the stimulation. Every point in the retina is evenly excited, and the local signs of all are simultaneously felt. This equable tension, this balance and elasticity in the very absence of fixity, give the vague but powerful feeling that we wish to describe. Did not the infinite, by this initial assault upon our senses, awe us and overwhelm us, as solemn music might, the idea of it would be abstract and moral like that of the infinitesimal, and nothing but an amusing curiosity.

Nothing is objectively impressive; things are impressive only when they succeed in touching the sensibility of the observer, by finding the avenues to his brain and heart. The idea that the universe is a multitude of minute spheres circling, like specks of dust, in a dark and boundless void, might leave us cold and indifferent, if not bored and depressed, were it not that we identify this hypothetical scheme with the visible splendour, the poignant intensity, and the baffling number of the stars. So far is the object from giving value to the impression, that it is here, as it must always ultimately be, the impression that gives value to the object. For all worth leads us back to actual feeling somewhere, or else evaporates into nothing—into a word and a superstition.

Now, the starry heavens are very happily designed to intensify the sensations on which their beauties must rest. In the first place, the continuum of space is broken into points, numerous enough to give the utmost idea of multiplicity, and yet so distinct and vivid that it is impossible not to remain aware of their individuality. The variety of local signs, without becoming organized into forms, remains prominent and irreducible. This makes the object infinitely more exciting than a plane surface would be. In the second place, the sensuous contrast of the dark background,—blacker the clearer the night and the more stars we can see,—with the palpitating fire of the stars themselves, could not be exceeded by any possible device. This material beauty adds incalculably, as we have already pointed out, to the inwardness and sublimity of the effect. To realize the great importance of these two elements, we need but to conceive their absence, and observe the change in the dignity of the result.

Fancy a map of the heavens and every star plotted upon it, even those invisible to the naked eye: why would this object, as full of scientific suggestion surely as the reality, leave us so comparatively cold? Quite indifferent it might not leave us, for I have myself watched stellar photographs with almost inexhaustible wonder. The sense of multiplicity is naturally in no way diminished by the representation; but the poignancy of the sensation, the life of the light, are gone; and with the dulled impression the keenness of the emotion disappears. Or imagine the stars, undiminished in number, without losing any of their astronomical significance and divine immutability, marshalled in geometrical patterns; say in a Latin cross, with the words *In hoc signo vinces* in a scroll around them. The beauty of the illumination would be perhaps increased, and its import, practical, religious, and cosmic, would surely be a little plainer; but where would be the sublimity of the spectacle? Irretrievably lost: and lost because the form of the object would no longer tantalize us with its sheer multiplicity, and with the consequent over-powering sense of suspense and awe.

In a word, the infinity which moves us is the sense of multi-plicity in uniformity. Accordingly things which have enough multiplicity, as the lights of a city seen across water, have an effect similar to that of the stars, if less intense; whereas a star, if alone, because the multiplicity is lacking, makes a wholly dif-ferent impression. The single star is tender, beautiful, and mild; we can compare it to the humblest and sweetest of things:

> A violet by a mossy stone
> Half hidden from the eye,
> Fair as *a star when only one*
> *Is shining in the sky.*

It is, not only in fact but in nature, an attendant on the moon, associated with the moon, if we may be so prosaic here, not only by contiguity but also by similarity.

> Fairer than Phœbe's sapphire-regioned star
> Or vesper, amorous glow-worm of the sky.

The same poet can say elsewhere of a passionate lover:

> He arose
> Ethereal, flushed, and like a throbbing star,
> Amid the sapphire heaven's deep repose.

How opposite is all this from the cold glitter, the cruel and mysterious sublimity of the stars when they are many! With these we have no Sapphic associations; they make us think rather of Kant who could hit on nothing else to compare with his cate-gorical imperative, perhaps because he found in both the same baffling incomprehensibility and the same fierce actuality. Such ultimate feelings are sensations of physical tension.

§ 26. DEFECTS OF PURE MULTIPLICITY. This long analysis will be a sufficient illustration of the power of multiplicity in uni-formity; we may now proceed to point out the limitations in-herent in this form. The most obvious one is that of monotony; a file of soldiers or an iron railing is impressive in its way, but cannot long entertain us, nor hold us with that depth of develop-ing interest, with which we might study a crowd or a forest of trees.

The tendency of monotony is double, and in two directions deadens our pleasure. When the repeated impressions are acute, and cannot be forgotten in their endless repetition, their monotony becomes painful. The constant appeal to the same sense, the constant requirement of the same reaction, tires the system, and we long for change as for a relief. If the repeated stimulations are not very acute, we soon become unconscious of them; like the ticking of the clock, they become merely a factor in our bodily tone, a cause, as the case may be, of a diffused pleasure or unrest; but they cease to present a distinguishable object.

The pleasures, therefore, which a kindly but monotonous environment produces, often fail to make it beautiful, for the simple reason that the environment is not perceived. Likewise the hideousness of things to which we are accustomed—the blemishes of the landscape, the ugliness of our clothes or of our walls—does not oppress us, not so much because we do not see the ugliness as because we overlook the things. The beauties or defects of monotonous objects are easily lost, because the objects are themselves intermittent in consciousness. But it is of some practical importance to remark that this indifference of monotonous values is more apparent than real. The particular object ceases to be of consequence; but the congruity of its structure and quality with our faculties of perception remains, and its presence in our environment is still a constant source of vague irritation and friction, or of subtle and pervasive delight. And this value, although not associated with the image of the monotonous object, lies there in our mind, like all the vital and systemic feelings, ready to enhance the beauty of any object that arouses our attention, and meantime adding to the health and freedom of our life—making whatever we do a little easier and pleasanter for us. A grateful environment is a substitute for happiness. It can quicken us from without as a fixed hope and affection, or the consciousness of a right life, can quicken us from within. To humanize our surroundings is, therefore, a task which should interest the physicians both of soul and body.

But the monotony of multiplicity is not merely intrinsic in the form; what is perhaps even of greater consequence in the arts is the fact that its capacity for association is restricted. What is in itself uniform cannot have a great diversity of relations. Hence the dryness, the crisp definiteness and hardness, of those products of art which contain an endless repetition of the same elements. Their affinities are necessarily few; they are not fit for many uses, nor capable of expressing many ideas. The heroic couplet, now too much derided, is a form of this kind. Its compactness and inevitableness make it excellent for an epigram and adequate it for a satire, but its perpetual snap and unvarying rhythm are thin for an epic, and impossible for a song. The Greek colonnade, a form in many ways analogous, has similar limitations. Beautiful with a finished and restrained beauty, which our taste is hardly refined enough to appreciate, it is incapable of development. The experiments of Roman architecture sufficiently show it; the glory of which is their Roman frame rather than their Hellenic ornament.

When the Greeks themselves had to face the problem of larger and more complex buildings, in the service of a supernatural and hierarchical system, they transformed their architecture into what we call Byzantine, and St. Sophia took the place of the Parthenon. Here a vast vault was introduced, the colonnade disappeared, the architrave was rounded into an arch from column to column, the capitals of these were changed from concave to convex, and a thousand other changes in structure and ornament introduced flexibility and variety. Architecture could in this way, precisely because more vague and barbarous, better adapt itself to the conditions of the new epoch. Perfect taste is itself a limitation, not because it intentionally excludes any excellence, but because it impedes the wandering of the arts into those bypaths of caprice and grotesqueness in which, although at the sacrifice of formal beauty, interesting partial effects might still be discovered. And this objection applies with double force to the first crystallizations of taste, when tradition has carried us but a little way in the right direction. The authorized effects are then very simple, and if we allow no others, our art becomes wholly inadequate to the functions ultimately imposed upon it. Primitive arts might furnish examples, but the state of English poetry at the time of Queen Anne is a sufficient illustration of this possibility. The French classicism, of which the English school was an echo, was more vital and human, because it embodied a more native taste and a wider training.

§ 27. ÆSTHETICS OF DEMOCRACY. It would be an error to suppose that æsthetic principles apply only to our judgments of works of art or of those natural objects which we attend to chiefly on account of their beauty. Every idea which is formed in the human mind, every activity and emotion, has some relation, direct or indirect, to pain and pleasure. If, as is the case in all the more important instances, these fluid activities and emotions precipitate, as it were, in their evanescence certain psychical solids called ideas of things, then the concomitant pleasures are incorporated more or less in those concrete ideas and the things acquire an æsthetic colouring. And although this æsthetic colouring may be the last quality we notice in objects of practical interest, its influence upon us is none the less real, and often accounts for a great deal in our moral and practical attitude.

In the leading political and moral idea of our time, in the idea of democracy, I think there is a strong æsthetic ingredient, and the power of the idea of democracy over the imagination is an illustration of that effect of multiplicity in uniformity which we have been studying. Of course, nothing could be more absurd than to suggest that the French Revolution, with its immense implications, had an æsthetic preference for its basis; it sprang, as we know, from the hatred of oppression, the rivalry of classes, and the aspiration after a freer social and strictly moral organization. But when these moral forces were suggesting and partly realizing the democratic idea, this idea was necessarily vividly present to men's thoughts; the picture of human life which it presented was becoming familiar, and was being made the sanction and goal of constant endeavour. Nothing so much enhances a good as to make sacrifices for it. The consequence was that democracy, prized at first as a means to happiness and as an instrument of good government, was acquiring an intrinsic value; it was beginning to seem good in itself, in fact, the only intrinsically right and perfect arrangement. A utilitarian scheme was receiving an æsthetic consecration. That which was happening to democracy had happened before to the feudal and royalist systems; they too had come to be prized in themselves, for the pleasure men took in thinking of society organized in such an ancient, and thereby to their fancy, appropriate and beautiful manner. The practical value of the arrangement, on which, of course, it is entirely dependent for its origin and authority, was forgotten, and men were ready to sacrifice their welfare to their sense of propriety; that is, they allowed an æsthetic good to outweigh a practical one. That seems now a superstition, although, indeed, a very natural and even noble one. Equally natural and noble, but no less superstitious, is our own belief in the divine right of democracy. Its essential right is something purely æsthetic.

Such æsthetic love of uniformity, however, is usually disguised under some moral label: we call it the love of justice, perhaps because we have not considered that the value of justice also, in so far as it is not derivative and utilitarian, must be intrinsic, or, what is practically the same thing, æsthetic. But occasionally the beauties of democracy are presented to us undisguised. The

writings of Walt Whitman are a notable example. Never, perhaps, has the charm of uniformity in multiplicity been felt so
completely and so exclusively. Everywhere it greets us with a
passionate preference; not flowers but leaves of grass, not music
but drum-taps, not composition but aggregation, not the hero
but the average man, not the crisis but the vulgarest moment; and
by this resolute marshalling of nullities, by this effort to show
us everything as a momentary pulsation of a liquid and structure-
less whole, he profoundly stirs the imagination. We may wish to
dislike this power, but, I think, we must inwardly admire it. For
whatever practical dangers we may see in this terrible levelling,
our æsthetic faculty can condemn no actual effect; its privilege is
to be pleased by opposites, and to be capable of finding chaos
sublime without ceasing to make nature beautiful.

§ 28. Values of types and values of examples. It is time we
should return to the consideration of abstract forms. Nearest in
nature to the example of uniformity in multiplicity, we found
those objects, like a reversible pattern, that having some variety
of parts invite us to survey them in different orders, and so bring
into play in a marked manner the faculty of apperception.

There is in the senses, as we have seen, a certain form of stimulation, a certain measure and rhythm of waves with which the
æsthetic value of the sensation is connected. So when, in the
perception of the object, a notable contribution is made by
memory and mental habit, the value of the perception will be
due, not only to the pleasantness of the external stimulus, but
also to the pleasantness of the apperceptive reaction; and the
latter source of value will be more important in proportion as the
object perceived is more dependent, for the form and meaning
it presents, upon our past experience and imaginative trend, and
less on the structure of the external object.

Our apperception of form varies not only with our constitution, age, and health, as does the appreciation of sensuous values,
but also with our education and genius. The more indeterminate
the object, the greater share must subjective forces have in determining our perception; for, of course, every perception is in itself
perfectly specific, and can be called indefinite only in reference to
an abstract ideal which it is expected to approach. Every cloud
has just the outline it has, although we may call it vague, because we cannot classify its form under any geometrical or animal
species; it would be first definitely a whale, and then would become indefinite until we saw our way to calling it a camel. But

while in the intermediate stage, the cloud would be a form in the perception of which there would be little apperceptive activity, little reaction from the store of our experience, little sense of form; its value would be in its colour and transparency, and in the suggestion of lightness and of complex but gentle movement.

But the moment we said "Yes, very like a whale," a new kind of value would appear; the cloud could now be beautiful or ugly, not as a cloud merely, but as a whale. We do not speak now of the associations of the idea, as with the sea, or fishermen's yarns; that is an extrinsic matter of expression. We speak simply of the intrinsic value of the form of the whale, of its lines, its movement, its proportion. This is a more or less individual set of images which are revived in the act of recognition; this revival constitutes the recognition, and the beauty of the form is the pleasure of that revival. A certain musical phrase, as it were, is played in the brain; the awakening of that echo is the act of apperception and the harmony of the present stimulation with the form of that phrase; the power of this particular object to develope and intensify that generic phrase in the direction of pleasure, is the test of the formal beauty of this example. For these cerebral phrases have a certain rhythm; this rhythm can, by the influence of the stimulus that now reawakens it, be marred or enriched, be made more or less marked and delicate; and as this conflict or reinforcement comes, the object is ugly or beautiful in form.

Such an æsthetic value is thus dependent on two things. The first is the acquired character of the apperceptive form evoked; it may be a cadenza or a trill, a major or a minor chord, a rose or a violet, a goddess or a dairy-maid; and as one or another of these is recognized, an æsthetic dignity and tone is given to the object. But it will be noticed that in such mere recognition very little pleasure is found, or, what is the same thing, different æsthetic types in the abstract have little difference in intrinsic beauty. The great difference lies in their affinities. What will decide us to like or not to like the type of our apperception will be not so much what this type is, as its fitness to the context of our mind. It is like a word in a poem, more effective by its fitness than by its intrinsic beauty, although that is requisite too. We can be shocked at an incongruity of natures more than we can be pleased by the intrinsic beauty of each nature apart, so long, that is, as they remain abstract natures, objects recognized without being studied. The æsthetic dignity of the form, then, tells us the kind of beauty we are to expect, affects us by its welcome or unwelcome promise, but hardly gives us a positive pleasure in the beauty itself.

Now this is the first thing in the value of a form, the value of the type as such; the second and more important element is the relation of the particular impression to the form under which it is apperceived. This determines the value of the object as an example of its class. After our mind is pitched to the key and rhythm of a certain idea, say of a queen, it remains for the impression to fulfil, aggrandize, or enrich this form by a sympathetic embodiment of it. Then we have a queen that is truly royal. But if instead there is disappointment, if this particular queen is an ugly one, although perhaps she might have pleased as a witch, this is because the apperceptive form and the impression give a cerebral discord. The object is unideal, that is, the novel, external element is inharmonious with the revived and internal element by suggesting which the object has been apperceived.

§ 29. Origin of types. A most important thing, therefore, in the perception of form is the formation of types in our mind, with reference to which examples are to be judged. I say the formation of them, for we can hardly consider the theory that they are eternal as a possible one in psychology. The Platonic doctrine on that point is a striking illustration of an equivocation we mentioned in the beginning;[1] namely, that the import of an experience is regarded as a manifestation of its cause—the product of a faculty substituted for the description of its function. Eternal types are the instrument of æsthetic life, not its foundation. Take the æsthetic attitude, and you have for the moment an eternal idea; an idea, I mean, that you treat as an absolute standard, just as when you take the perceptive attitude you have an external object which you treat as an absolute existence. But the æsthetic, like the perceptive faculty, can be made an object of study in turn, and its theory can be sought; and then the eternal idea, like the external object, is seen to be a product of human nature, a symbol of experience, and an instrument of thought.

The question whether there are not, in external nature or in the mind of God, objects and eternal types, is indeed not settled, it is not even touched by this inquiry; but it is indirectly shown to be futile, because such transcendent realities, if they exist,

[1] See Introduction, p. 9.

can have nothing to do with our ideas of them. The Platonic idea of a tree may exist; how should I deny it? How should I deny that I might some day find myself outside the sky gazing at it, and feeling that I, with my mental vision, am beholding the plenitude of arboreal beauty, perceived in this world only as a vague essence haunting the multiplicity of finite trees? But what can that have to do with my actual sense of what a tree should be? Shall we take the Platonic myth literally, and say the idea is a memory of the tree I have already seen in heaven? How else establish any relation between that eternal object and the type in my mind? But why, in that case, this infinite variability of ideal trees? Was the Tree Beautiful an oak, or a cedar, an English or an American elm? My actual types are finite and mutually exclusive; that heavenly type must be one and infinite. The problem is hopeless.

Very simple, on the other hand, is the explanation of the existence of that type as a residuum of experience. Our idea of an individual thing is a compound and residuum of our several experiences of it; and in the same manner our idea of a class is a compound and residuum of our ideas of the particulars that compose it. Particular impressions have, by virtue of their intrinsic similarity or of the identity of their relations, a tendency to be merged and identified, so that many individual perceptions leave but a single blurred memory that stands for them all, because it combines their several associations. Similarly, when various objects have many common characteristics, the mind is incapable of keeping them apart. It cannot hold clearly so great a multitude of distinctions and relations as would be involved in naming and conceiving separately each grain of sand, or drop of water, each fly or horse or man that we have ever seen. The mass of our experience has therefore to be classified, if it is to be available at all. Instead of a distinct image to represent each of our original impressions, we have a general resultant—a composite photograph—of those impressions.

This resultant image is the idea of the class. It often has very few, if any, of the sensible properties of the particulars that underlie it, often an artificial symbol—the sound of a word—is the only element, present to all the instances, which the generic image clearly contains. For, of course, the reason why a name can represent a class of objects is that the name is the most conspicuous element of identity in the various experiences of objects in that class. We have seen many horses, but if we are not lovers of the animal, nor particularly keen observers, very likely we retain no clear image of all that mass of impressions except the reverberation of the sound "horse," which really or mentally has accompanied all those impressions. This sound, therefore, is the content of our general idea, and to it cling all the associations which constitute our sense of what the word means. But a person with a memory predominantly visual would probably add to this remembered sound a more or less detailed image of the animal; some particular horse in some particular attitude might possibly be recalled, but more probably some imaginative construction, some dream image, would accompany the sound. An image which reproduced no particular horse exactly, but which was a spontaneous fiction of the fancy, would serve, by virtue of its felt relations, the same purpose as the sound itself. Such a spontaneous image would be, of course, variable. In fact, no image can, strictly speaking, ever recur. But these percepts, as they are called, springing up in the mind like flowers from the buried seeds of past experience, would inherit all the powers of suggestion which are required by any instrument of classification.

These powers of suggestion have probably a cerebral basis. The new percept—the generic idea—repeats to a great extent, both in nature and localization, the excitement constituting the various original impressions; as the percept reproduces more or less of these it will be a more or less full and impartial representative of them. Not all the suggestions of a word or image are equally ripe. A generic idea or type usually presents to us a very inadequate and biassed view of the field it means to cover. As we reflect and seek to correct this inadequacy, the percept changes on our hands. The very consciousness that other individuals and other qualities fall under our concept, changes this concept, as a psychological presence, and alters its distinctness and extent. When I remember, to use a classical example, that the triangle is not isosceles, nor scalene, nor rectangular, but each and all of those, I reduce my percept to the word and its definition, with perhaps a sense of the general motion of the hand and eye by which we trace a three-cornered figure.

Since the production of a general idea is thus a matter of subjective bias, we cannot expect that a type should be the exact average of the examples from which it is drawn. In a rough way, it is the average; a fact that in itself is the strongest of arguments against the independence or priority of the general idea. The beautiful horse, the beautiful speech, the beautiful face, is always a medium between the extremes which our experience has offered. It is enough that a given characteristic should be generally present in our experience, for it to become an indispensable element of the ideal. There is nothing in itself beautiful or necessary in the shape of the human ear, or in the presence of nails on the fingers and toes; but the ideal of man, which the preposterous conceit of our judgment makes us set up as divine and eternal, requires these precise details; without them the human form would be repulsively ugly.

It often happens that the accidents of experience make us in this way introduce into the ideal, elements which, if they could be excluded without disgusting us, would make possible satisfactions greater than those we can now enjoy. Thus the taste formed by one school of art may condemn the greater beauties created by another. In morals we have the same phenomenon. A barbarous ideal of life requires tasks and dangers incompatible with happiness; a rude and oppressed conscience is incapable of regarding as good a state which excludes its own acrid satisfactions. So, too, a fanatical imagination cannot regard God as just unless he is represented as infinitely cruel. The purpose of education is, of course, to free us from these prejudices, and to develope our ideals in the direction of the greatest possible good. Evidently the ideal has been formed by the habit of perception; it is, in a rough way, that average form which we expect and most readily apperceive. The propriety and necessity of it is entirely relative to our experience and faculty of apperception. The shock of surprise, the incongruity with the formed percept, is the essence and measure of ugliness.

§ 30. THE AVERAGE MODIFIED IN THE DIRECTION OF PLEASURE. Nevertheless we do not form æsthetic ideals any more than other general types, entirely without bias. We have already observed that a percept seldom gives an impartial compound of the objects of which it is the generic image. This partiality is due to a variety of circumstances. One is the unequal accuracy of our observation. If some interest directs our attention to a particular quality of objects, that quality will be prominent in our percept; it may even be the only content clearly given in our general idea; and any object, however similar in other respects to those of the given class, will at once be distinguished as belonging to a different species if it lacks that characteristic on which our attention is particularly fixed. Our percepts are thus habitually biassed in the direction of practical interest, if practical interest does not indeed entirely govern their formation. In the same manner, our æsthetic ideals are biassed in the direction of æsthetic interest. Not all parts of an object are equally congruous with our perceptive faculty; not all elements are noted with the same pleasure. Those, therefore, which are agreeable are chiefly dwelt upon by the lover of beauty, and his percept will give an average of things with a great emphasis laid on that part of them which is beautiful. The ideal will thus deviate from the average in the direction of the observer's pleasure.

For this reason the world is so much more beautiful to a poet or an artist than to an ordinary man. Each object, as his æsthetic sense is developed, is perhaps less beautiful than to the uncritical eye; his taste becomes difficult, and only the very best gives him unalloyed satisfaction. But while each work of nature and art is thus apparently blighted by his greater demands and keener susceptibility, the world itself, and the various natures it contains, are to him unspeakably beautiful. The more blemishes he can see in men, the more excellence he sees in man, and the more bitterly he laments the fate of each particular soul, the more reverence and love he has for the soul in its ideal essence. Criticism and idealization involve each other. The habit of looking for beauty in everything makes us notice the shortcomings of things; our sense, hungry for complete satisfaction, misses the perfection it demands. But this demand for perfection becomes at the same time the nucleus of our observation; from every side a quick affinity draws what is beautiful together and stores it in the mind, giving body there to the blind yearnings of our nature. Many imperfect things crystallize into a single perfection. The mind is thus peopled by general ideas in which beauty is the chief quality; and these ideas are at the same time the types of things. The type is still a natural resultant of particular impressions; but the formation of it has been guided by a deep subjective bias in favour of what has delighted the eye.

This theory can be easily tested by asking whether, in the case where the ideal differs from the average form of objects, this variation is not due to the intrinsic pleasantness or impressiveness of the quality exaggerated. For instance, in the human form, the ideal differs immensely from the average. In many respects the extreme or something near it is the most beautiful. Xenophon describes the women of Armenia as καλλαὶ καί μεγάλαι, and we should still speak of one as fair and tall and of another as fair but little. Size is therefore, even where least requisite, a thing in which the ideal exceeds the average. And the reason—apart from associations of strength—is that unusual size makes things conspicuous. The first prerequisite of effect is impression, and size helps that; therefore in the æsthetic ideal the average will be modified by being enlarged, because that is a change in the direction of our pleasure, and size will be an element of beauty.[1]

Similarly the eyes, in themselves beautiful, will be enlarged also; and generally whatever makes by its sensuous quality, by its abstract form, or by its expression, a particular appeal to our attention and contribution to our delight, will count for more in the ideal type than its frequency would warrant. The generic image has been constructed under the influence of a selective attention, bent upon æsthetic worth.

To praise any object for approaching the ideal of its kind is therefore only a roundabout way of specifying its intrinsic merit and expressing its direct effect on our sensibility. If in referring to the ideal we were not thus analyzing the real, the ideal would be an irrelevant and unmeaning thing. We know what the ideal is because we observe what pleases us in the reality. If we allow the general notion to tyrannize at all over the particular impression and to blind us to new and unclassified beauties which the latter may contain, we are simply substituting words for feelings, and making a verbal classification pass for an æsthetic judgment. Then the sense of beauty is gone to seed. Ideals have their uses, but their authority is wholly representative. They stand for specific satisfactions, or else they stand for nothing at all.

In fact, the whole machinery of our intelligence, our general ideas and laws, fixed and external objects, principles, persons, and gods, are so many symbolic, algebraic expressions. They stand for experience; experience which we are incapable of retaining and surveying in its multitudinous immediacy. We should flounder hopelessly, like the animals, did we not keep ourselves afloat and direct our course by these intellectual devices. Theory helps us to bear our ignorance of fact.

The same thing happens, in a way, in other fields. Our armies are devices necessitated by our weakness; our property an encumbrance required by our need. If our situation were not precarious, these great engines of death and life would not be invented. And our intelligence is such another weapon against fate. We need not lament the fact, since, after all, to build these

[1] The contention of Burke that the beautiful is small is due to an arbitrary definition. By beautiful he means pretty and charming; agreeable as opposed to impressive. He only exaggerates the then usual opposition of the beautiful to the sublime.

various structures is, up to a certain point, the natural function of human nature. The trouble is not that the products are always subjective, but that they are sometimes unfit and torment the spirit which they exercise. The pathetic part of our situation appears only when we so attach ourselves to those necessary but imperfect fictions, as to reject the facts from which they spring and of which they seek to be prophetic. We are then guilty of that substitution of means for ends, which is called idolatry in religion, absurdity in logic, and folly in morals. In æsthetics the thing has no name, but is nevertheless very common; for it is found whenever we speak of what ought to please, rather than of what actually pleases.

§ 31. ARE ALL THINGS BEAUTIFUL? These principles lead to an intelligible answer to a question which is not uninteresting in itself and crucial in a system of æsthetics. Are all things beautiful? Are all types equally beautiful when we abstract from our practical prejudices? If the reader has given his assent to the foregoing propositions, he will easily see that, in one sense, we must declare that no object is essentially ugly. If impressions are painful, they are objectified with difficulty; the perception of a thing is therefore, under normal circumstances, when the senses are not fatigued, rather agreeable than disagreeable. And when the frequent perception of a class of objects has given rise to an apperceptive norm, and we have an ideal of the species, the recognition and exemplification of that norm will give pleasure, in proportion to the degree of interest and accuracy with which we have made our observations. The naturalist accordingly sees beauties to which the academic artist is blind, and each new environment must open to us, if we allow it to educate our perception, a new wealth of beautiful forms.

But we are not for this reason obliged to assert that all gradations of beauty and dignity are a matter of personal and accidental bias. The mystics who declare that to God there is no distinction in the value of things, and that only our human prejudice makes us prefer a rose to an oyster, or a lion to a monkey, have, of course, a reason for what they say. If we could strip ourselves of our human nature, we should undoubtedly find ourselves incapable of making these distinctions, as well as of thinking, perceiving, or willing in any way which is now possible to us. But how things would appear to us if we were not human is, to a man, a question of no importance. Even the mystic to whom the definite constitution of his own mind is so hateful, can only paralyze without transcending his faculties. A passionate negation, the motive of which, although morbid, is in spite of itself perfectly human, absorbs all his energies, and his ultimate triumph is to attain the absoluteness of indifference.

What is true of mysticism in general, is true also of its manifestation in æsthetics. If we could so transform our taste as to find beauty everywhere, because, perhaps, the ultimate nature of things is as truly exemplified in one thing as in another, we should, in fact, have abolished taste altogether. For the ascending series of æsthetic satisfactions we should have substituted a monotonous judgment of identity. If things are beautiful not by virtue of their differences but by virtue of an identical something which they equally contain, then there could be no discrimination in beauty. Like substance, beauty would be everywhere one and the same, and any tendency to prefer one thing to another would be a proof of finitude and illusion. When we try to make our judgments absolute, what we do is to surrender our natural standards and categories, and slip into another genus, until we lose ourselves in the satisfying vagueness of mere being.

Relativity to our partial nature is therefore essential to all our definite thoughts, judgments, and feelings. And when once the human bias is admitted as a legitimate, because for us a necessary, basis of preference, the whole wealth of nature is at once organized by that standard into a hierarchy of values. Everything is beautiful because everything is capable in some degree of interesting and charming our attention; but things differ immensely in this capacity to please us in the contemplation of them, and therefore they differ immensely in beauty. Could our nature be fixed and determined once for all in every particular, the scale of æsthetic values would become certain. We should not dispute about tastes, no longer because a common principle of preference could not be discovered, but rather because any disagreement would then be impossible.

As a matter of fact, however, human nature is a vague abstraction; that which is common to all men is the least part of their natural endowment. Æsthetic capacity is accordingly very unevenly distributed; and the world of beauty is much vaster and more complex to one man than to another. So long, indeed, as the distinction is merely one of development, so that we recognize in the greatest connoisseur only the refinement of the judgments of the rudest peasant, our æsthetic principle has not changed; we might say that, in so far, we had a common standard more or less widely applied. We might say so, because that standard would be an implication of a common nature more or less fully developed.

But men do not differ only in the degree of their susceptibility, they differ also in its direction. Human nature branches into opposed and incompatible characters. And taste follows this bifurcation. We cannot, except whimsically, say that a taste for music is higher or lower than a taste for sculpture. A man might be a musician and a sculptor by turns; that would only involve a perfectly conceivable enlargement in human genius. But the union thus effected would be an accumulation of gifts in the observer, not a combination of beauties in the object. The excellence of sculpture and that of music would remain entirely independent and heterogeneous. Such divergences are like those of the outer senses to which these arts appeal. Sound and colour have analogies only in their lowest depth, as vibrations and excitement; as they grow specific and objective, they diverge; and although the same consciousness perceives them, it perceives them as unrelated and uncombinable objects.

The ideal enlargement of human capacity, therefore, has no tendency to constitute a single standard of beauty. These standards remain the expression of diverse habits of sense and imagination. The man who combines the greatest range with the greatest endowment in each particular, will, of course, be the critic most generally respected. He will express the feelings of the greater number of men. The advantage of scope in criticism lies not in the improvement of our sense in each particular field; here the artist will detect the amateur's shortcomings. But no man is a specialist with his whole soul. Some latent capacity he has for other perceptions; and it is for the awakening of these, and their marshalling before him, that the student of each kind of beauty turns to the lover of them all.

The temptation, therefore, to say that all things are really equally beautiful arises from an imperfect analysis, by which the operations of the æsthetic consciousness are only partially disintegrated. The dependence of the *degrees* of beauty upon our nature is perceived, while the dependence of its *essence* upon our nature is still ignored. All things are not equally beautiful because the subjective bias that discriminates between them is the cause of their being beautiful at all. The principle of personal preference is the same as that of human taste; real and objective beauty, in contrast to a vagary of individuals, means only an affinity to a more prevalent and lasting susceptibility, a response to a more general and fundamental demand. And the keener discrimination, by which the distance between beautiful and ugly things is increased, far from being a loss of æsthetic insight, is a development of that faculty by the exercise of which beauty comes into the world.

§ 32. EFFECTS OF INDETERMINATE ORGANIZATION. It is the free exercise of the activity of apperception that gives so peculiar an interest to indeterminate objects, to the vague, the incoherent, the suggestive, the variously interpretable. The more this effect is appealed to, the greater wealth of thought is presumed in the observer, and the less mastery is displayed by the artist. A poor and literal mind cannot enjoy the opportunity for reverie and construction given by the stimulus of indeterminate objects; it lacks the requisite resources. It is nonplussed and annoyed, and turns away to simpler and more transparent things with a feeling of helplessness often turning into contempt. And, on the other hand, the artist who is not artist enough, who has too many irrepressible talents and too little technical skill, is sure to float in the region of the indeterminate. He sketches and never paints; he hints and never expresses; he stimulates and never informs. This is the method of the individuals and of the nations that have more genius than art.

The consciousness that accompanies this characteristic is the sense of profundity, of mighty significance. And this feeling is not necessarily an illusion. The nature of our materials—be they words, colours, or plastic matter—imposes a limit and bias upon our expression. The reality of experience can never be quite rendered through these media. The greatest mastery of technique will therefore come short of perfect adequacy and exhaustiveness; there must always remain a penumbra and fringe of suggestion if the most explicit representation is to communicate a truth. When there is real profundity,—when the living core of things is most firmly grasped,—there will accordingly be a felt inadequacy of expression, and an appeal to the observer to piece out our imperfections with his thoughts. But this should come only after the resources of a patient and well-learned art have been exhausted; else what is felt as depth is really confusion and incompetence. The simplest thing becomes unutterable, if we have forgotten how to speak. And a habitual indulgence in the inarticulate is a sure sign of the philosopher who has not learned to think, the poet who has not learned to write, the painter who has not learned to paint, and the impression that

has not learned to express itself—all of which are compatible
with an immensity of genius in the inexpressible soul.

Our age is given to this sort of self-indulgence, and on both
the grounds mentioned. Our public, without being really trained,
—for we appeal to too large a public to require training in it,—
is well informed and eagerly responsive to everything; it is ready
to work pretty hard, and do its share towards its own profit and
entertainment. It becomes a point of pride with it to understand
and appreciate everything. And our art, in its turn, does not
overlook this opportunity. It becomes disorganized, sporadic,
whimsical, and experimental. The crudity we are too distracted
to refine, we accept as originality, and the vagueness we are
too pretentious to make accurate, we pass off as sublimity. This
is the secret of making great works on novel principles, and of
writing hard books easily.

§ 33. EXAMPLE OF LANDSCAPE. An extraordinary taste for landscape compensates us for this ignorance of what is best and most
finished in the arts. The natural landscape is an indeterminate
object; it almost always contains enough diversity to allow the
eye a great liberty in selecting, emphasizing, and grouping its
elements, and it is furthermore rich in suggestion and in vague
emotional stimulus. A landscape to be seen has to be composed,
and to be loved has to be moralized. That is the reason why
rude or vulgar people are indifferent to their natural surroundings. It does not occur to them that the work-a-day world is
capable of æsthetic contemplation. Only on holidays, when they
add to themselves and their belongings some unusual ornament,
do they stop to watch the effect. The far more beautiful daily
aspects of their environment escape them altogether. When,
however, we learn to apperceive; when we grow fond of tracing
lines and developing vistas; when, above all, the subtler influences of places on our mental tone are transmuted into an
expressiveness in those places, and they are furthermore poetized
by our day-dreams, and turned by our instant fancy into so many
hints of a fairyland of happy living and vague adventure,—then
we feel that the landscape is beautiful. The forest, the fields, all
wild or rural scenes, are then full of companionship and entertainment.

This is a beauty dependent on reverie, fancy, and objectified
emotion. The promiscuous natural landscape cannot be enjoyed
in any other way. It has no real unity, and therefore requires
to have some form or other supplied by the fancy; which can

be the more readily done, in that the possible forms are many, and the constant changes in the object offer varying suggestions to the eye. In fact, psychologically speaking, there is no such thing as a landscape; what we call such is an infinity of different scraps and glimpses given in succession. Even a painted landscape, although it tends to select and emphasize some parts of the field, is composed by adding together a multitude of views. When this painting is observed in its turn, it is surveyed as a real landscape would be, and apperceived partially and piecemeal; although, of course, it offers much less wealth of material than its living original, and is therefore vastly inferior.

Only the extreme of what is called impressionism tries to give upon canvas one absolute momentary view; the result is that when the beholder has himself actually been struck by that aspect, the picture has an extraordinary force and emotional value—like the vivid power of recalling the past possessed by smells. But, on the other hand, such a work is empty and trivial in the extreme; it is the photograph of a detached impression, not followed, as it would be in nature, by many variations of itself. An object so unusual is often unrecognizable, if the vision thus unnaturally isolated has never happened to come vividly into our own experience. The opposite school—what might be called *discursive* landscape painting—collects so many glimpses and gives so fully the sum of our positive observations of a particular scene, that its work is sure to be perfectly intelligible and plain. If it seems unreal and uninteresting, that is because it is formless, like the collective object it represents, while it lacks that sensuous intensity and movement which might have made the reality stimulating.

The landscape contains, of course, innumerable things which have determinate forms; but if the attention is directed specifically to them, we have no longer what, by a curious limitation of the word, is called the love of nature. Not very long ago it was usual for painters of landscapes to introduce figures, buildings, or ruins to add some human association to the beauty of the place. Or, if wildness and desolation were to be pictured, at least one weary wayfarer must be seen sitting upon a broken column. He might wear a toga and then be Marius among the ruins of Carthage. The landscape without figures would have seemed meaningless; the spectator would have sat in suspense awaiting something, as at the theatre when the curtain rises on an empty stage. The indeterminateness of the suggestions of an unhumanized scene was then felt as a defect; now we feel it rather as an exaltation. We need to be free; our emotion suffices us; we do not ask for a description of the object which interests us as a part of ourselves. We should blush to say so simple and obvious a thing as that to us "the mountains are a feeling"; nor should we think of apologizing for our romanticism as Byron did:

> I love not man the less but nature more
> From these our interviews, in which I steal,
> From all I may be, or have been before,
> To mingle with the universe, and feel
> What I can ne'er express.

This ability to rest in nature unadorned and to find entertainment in her aspects, is, of course, a great gain. Æsthetic education consists in training ourselves to see the maximum of beauty. To see it in the physical world, which must continually be about us, is a great progress toward that marriage of the imagination with the reality which is the goal of contemplation.

While we gain this mastery of the formless, however, we should not lose the more necessary capacity of seeing form in those things which happen to have it. In respect to most of those things which are determinate as well as natural, we are usually in that state of æsthetic unconsciousness which the peasant is in in respect to the landscape. We treat human life and its environment with the same utilitarian eye with which he regards the field and mountain. That is beautiful which is expressive of convenience and wealth; the rest is indifferent. If we mean by love of nature æsthetic delight in the world in which we casually live (and what can be more *natural* than man and all his arts?), we may say that the absolute love of *nature* hardly exists among us. What we love is the stimulation of our own personal emotions and dreams; and landscape appeals to us, as music does to those who have no sense for musical form.

There would seem to be no truth in the saying that the ancients loved nature less than we. They loved landscape less— less, at least, in proportion to their love of the definite things it contained. The vague and changing effects of the atmosphere, the masses of mountains, the infinite and living complexity of forests, did not fascinate them. They had not that preponderant taste for the indeterminate that makes the landscape a favourite subject of contemplation. But love of nature, and comprehension of her, they had in a most eminent degree; in fact, they actually made explicit that objectification of our own soul in her, which for the romantic poet remains a mere vague and shifting suggestion. What are the celestial gods, the nymphs, the fauns, the dryads, but the definite apperceptions of that haunting spirit which we think we see in the sky, the mountains, and the woods? We may think that our vague intuition grasps the truth of what their childish imagination turned into a fable. But our belief, if it is one, is just as fabulous, just as much a projection of human nature into material things; and if we renounce all positive conception of quasi-mental principles in nature, and reduce our moralizing of her to a poetic expression of our own sensations, then can we say that our verbal and illusive images are comparable as representations of the life of nature to the precision, variety, humour, and beauty of the Greek mythology?

§ 34. EXTENSIONS TO OBJECTS USUALLY NOT REGARDED ÆSTHET-ICALLY. It may not be superfluous to mention here certain analogous fields where the human mind gives a series of unstable forms to objects in themselves indeterminate.[1] History, philosophy, natural as well as moral, and religion are evidently such fields. All theory is a subjective form given to an indeterminate material. The material is experience; and although each part of experience is, of course, perfectly definite in itself, and just that experience which it is, yet the recollection and relating together of the successive experiences is a function of the theoretical faculty. The systematic relations of things in time and space, and their dependence upon one another, are the work of our imagination. Theory can therefore never have the kind of truth which belongs to experience; as Hobbes has it, no discourse whatsoever can end in absolute knowledge of fact.

It is conceivable that two different theories should be equally true in respect to the same facts. All that is required is that they should be equally complete schemes for the relation and prediction of the realities they deal with. The choice between them would be an arbitrary one, determined by personal bias, for the object being indeterminate, its elements can be apperceived as forming all kinds of unities. A theory is a form of apperception,

[1] When we speak of things definite in themselves, we of course mean things made definite by some human act of definition. The senses are instruments that define and differentiate sensation; and the result of one operation is that definite object upon which the next operation is performed. The memory, for example, classifies in time what the senses may have classified in space. We are nowhere concerned with objects other than objects of human experience, and the epithets, definite and indefinite, refer necessarily to their relation to our various categories of perception and comprehension.

and in applying it to the facts, although our first concern is naturally the adequacy of our instrument of comprehension, we are also influenced, more than we think, by the ease and pleasure with which we think in its terms, that is, by its beauty.

The case of two alternative theories of nature, both exhaustive and adequate, may seem somewhat imaginary. The human mind is, indeed, not rich and indeterminate enough to drive, as the saying is, many horses abreast; it wishes to have one general scheme of conception only, under which it strives to bring everything. Yet the philosophers, who are the scouts of common sense, have come in sight of this possibility of a variety of methods of dealing with the same facts. As at the basis of evolution generally there are many variations, only some of which remain fixed, so at the origin of conception there are many schemes; these are simultaneously developed, and at most stages of thought divide the intelligence among themselves. So much is thought of on one principle—say mechanically—and so much on another—say teleologically. In those minds only that have a speculative turn, that is, in whom the desire for unity of comprehension outruns practical exigencies, does the conflict become intolerable. In them one or another of these theories tends to swallow all experience, but is commonly incapable of doing so.

The final victory of a single philosophy is not yet won, because none as yet has proved adequate to all experience. If ever unity should be attained, our unanimity would not indicate that, as the popular fancy conceives it, the truth had been discovered; it would only indicate that the human mind had found a definitive way of classifying its experience. Very likely, if man still retained his inveterate habit of hypostatizing his ideas, that definitive scheme would be regarded as a representation of the objective relations of things; but no proof that it was so would ever be found, nor even any hint that there were external objects, not to speak of relations between them. As the objects are hypostatized percepts, so the relations are hypostatized processes of the human understanding.

To have reached a final philosophy would be only to have formulated the typical and satisfying form of human apperception; the view would remain a theory, an instrument of comprehension and survey fitted to the human eye; it would be for ever utterly heterogeneous from fact, utterly unrepresentative of any of those experiences which it would artificially connect and weave into a pattern. Mythology and theology are the most striking illustrations of this human method of incorporating much diffuse experience into graphic and picturesque ideas; but steady reflection will hardly allow us to see anything else in the theories of science and philosophy. These, too, are creatures of our intelligence, and have their only being in the movement of our thought, as they have their only justification in their fitness to our experience.

Long before we can attain, however, the ideal unification of experience under one theory, the various fields of thought demand provisional surveys; we are obliged to reflect on life in a variety of detached and unrelated acts, since neither can the whole material of life be ever given while we still live, nor can that which is given be impartially retained in the human memory. When omniscience was denied us, we were endowed with versatility. The picturesqueness of human thought may console us for its imperfection.

History, for instance, which passes for the account of facts, is in reality a collection of apperceptions of an indeterminate material; for even the material of history is not fact, but consists of memories and words subject to ever-varying interpretation. No historian can be without bias, because the bias defines the history. The memory in the first place is selective; official and other records are selective, and often intentionally partial. Monuments and ruins remain by chance. And when the historian has set himself to study these few relics of the past, the work of his own intelligence begins. He must have some guiding interest. A history is not an indiscriminate register of every known event; a file of newspapers is not an inspiration of Clio. A history is a view of the fortunes of some institution or person; it traces the development of some interest. This interest furnishes the standard by which the facts are selected, and their importance gauged. Then, after the facts are thus chosen, marshalled, and emphasized, comes the indication of causes and relations; and in this part of his work the historian plunges avowedly into speculation, and becomes a philosophical poet. Everything will then depend on his genius, on his principles, on his passions,— in a word, on his apperceptive forms. And the value of history is similar to that of poetry, and varies with the beauty, power, and adequacy of the form in which the indeterminate material of human life is presented.

§ 35. FURTHER DANGERS OF INDETERMINATENESS. The fondness of a race or epoch for any kind of effect is a natural expression of temperament and circumstances, and cannot be blamed or easily corrected. At the same time we may stop to consider some of the disadvantages of a taste for the indeterminate. We shall be registering a truth and at the same time, perhaps, giving some encouragement to that rebellion which we may inwardly feel against this too prevalent manner. The indeterminate is by its nature ambiguous; it is therefore obscure and uncertain in its effect, and if used, as in many arts it often is, to convey a meaning, must fail to do so unequivocally. Where a meaning is not to be conveyed, as in landscape, architecture, or music, the illusiveness of the form is not so objectionable: although in all these objects the tendency to observe forms and to demand them is a sign of increasing appreciation. The ignorant fail to see the forms of music, architecture, and landscape, and therefore are insensible to relative rank and technical values in these spheres; they regard the objects only as so many stimuli to emotion, as soothing or enlivening influences. But the sensuous and associative values of these things—especially of music—are so great, that even without an appreciation of form considerable beauty may be found in them.

In literature, however, where the sensuous value of the words is comparatively small, indeterminateness of form is fatal to beauty, and, if extreme, even to expressiveness. For meaning is conveyed by the *form* and order of words, not by the words themselves, and no precision of meaning can be reached without precision of style. Therefore no respectable writer is voluntarily obscure in the structure of his phrases—that is an abuse reserved for the clowns of literary fashion. But a book is a larger sentence, and if it is formless it fails to mean anything, for the same reason that an unformed collection of words means nothing. The chapters and verses may have said something, as loose words may have a known sense and a tone; but the book will have brought no message.

In fact, the absence of form in composition has two stages: that in which, as in the works of Emerson, significant fragments are collected, and no system, no total thought, constructed out of them; and secondly, that in which, as in the writings of the Symbolists of our time, all the significance is kept back in the individual words, or even in the syllables that compose them. This mosaic of word-values has, indeed, a possibility of effect, for the absence of form does not destroy materials, but, as we have observed, rather allows the attention to remain fixed upon them; and for this reason absence of sense is a means of accentuating beauty of sound and verbal suggestion. But this example shows how the tendency to neglect structure in literature is a tendency to surrender the use of language as an instrument of thought. The descent is easy from ambiguity to meaninglessness.

The indeterminate in form is also indeterminate in value. It needs completion by the mind of the observer and as this completion differs, the value of the result must vary. An indeterminate object is therefore beautiful to him who can make it so, and ugly to him who cannot. It appeals to a few, and to them diversely. In fact, the observer's own mind is the storehouse from which the beautiful form has to be drawn. If the form is not there, it cannot be applied to the half-finished object; it is like asking a man without skill to complete another man's composition. The indeterminate object therefore requires an active and well-equipped mind, and is otherwise without value.

It is furthermore unprofitable even to the mind which takes it up; it stimulates that mind to action, but it presents it with no new object. We can respond only with those forms of apperception which we already are accustomed to. A formless object cannot *inform* the mind, cannot mould it to a new habit. That happens only when the data, by their clear determination, compel the eye and imagination to follow new paths and see new relations. Then we are introduced to a new beauty, and enriched to that extent. But the indeterminate, like music to the sentimental, is a vague stimulus. It calls forth at random such ideas and memories as may lie to hand, stirring the mind, but leaving it undisciplined and unacquainted with any new object. This stirring, like that of the pool of Bethesda, may indeed have its virtue. A creative mind, already rich in experience and observation, may, under the influence of such a stimulus, dart into a new thought, and give birth to that with which it is already pregnant; but the fertilizing seed came from elsewhere, from study and admiration of those definite forms which nature contains, or which art, in imitation of nature, has conceived and brought to perfection.

§ 36. Illusion of infinite perfection. The great advantage, then, of indeterminate organization is that it cultivates that spontaneity, intelligence, and imagination without which many important objects would remain unintelligible, and because unintelligible, uninteresting. The beauty of landscape, the forms of religion and science, the types of human nature itself, are due to this apperceptive gift. Without it we should have a chaos;

but its patient and ever-fresh activity carves out of the fluid material a great variety of forms. An object which stimulates us to this activity, therefore, seems often to be more sublime and beautiful than one which presents to us a single unchanging form, however perfect. There seems to be a life and infinity in the incomplete, which the determinate excludes by its own completeness and petrifaction. And yet the effort in this very activity is to reach determination; we can only see beauty in so far as we introduce form. The instability of the form can be no advantage to a work of art; the determinate keeps constantly what the indeterminate reaches only in those moments in which the observer's imagination is especially propitious. If we feel a certain disappointment in the monotonous limits of a definite form and its eternal, unsympathizing message, might we not feel much more the melancholy transiency of those glimpses of beauty which elude us in the indeterminate? Might not the torment and uncertainty of this contemplation, with the self-consciousness it probably involves, more easily tire us than the quiet companionship of a constant object? May we not prefer the unchangeable to the irrecoverable?

We may; and the preference is one which we should all more clearly feel, were it not for an illusion, proper to the romantic temperament, which lends a mysterious charm to things which are indefinite and indefinable. It is the suggestion of infinite perfection. In reality, perfection is a synonym of finitude. Neither in nature nor in the fancy can anything be perfect except by realizing a definite type, which excludes all variation, and contrasts sharply with every other possibility of being. There is no perfection apart from a form of apperception or type; and there are as many kinds of perfection as there are types or forms of apperception latent in the mind.

Now these various perfections are mutually exclusive. Only in a kind of æsthetic orgy—in the madness of an intoxicated imagination—can we confuse them. As the Roman emperor wished that the Roman people had but a single neck, to murder them at one blow, so we may sometimes wish that all beauties had but one form, that we might behold them together. But in the nature of things beauties are incompatible. The spring cannot coexist with the autumn, nor day with night; what is beautiful in a child is hideous in a man, and *vice versa;* every age, every country, each sex, has a peculiar beauty, finite and incommunicable; the better it is attained the more completely it excludes every other. The same is evidently true of schools of art, of styles and languages, and of every effect whatsoever. It exists by its finitude and is great in proportion to its determination.

But there is a loose and somewhat helpless state of mind in which while we are incapable of realizing any particular thought or vision in its perfect clearness and absolute beauty, we nevertheless feel its haunting presence in the background of consciousness. And one reason why the idea cannot emerge from that obscurity is that it is not alone in the brain; a thousand other ideals, a thousand other plastic tendencies of thought, simmer there in confusion; and if any definite image is presented in response to that vague agitation of our soul, we feel its inadequacy to our need in spite of, or perhaps on account of, its own particular perfection. We then say that the classic does not satisfy us, and that the "Grecian cloys us with his perfectness." We are not capable of that concentrated and serious attention to one thing at a time which would enable us to sink into its being, and enjoy the intrinsic harmonies of its form, and the bliss of its immanent particular heaven; we flounder in the vague, but at the same time we are full of yearnings, of half-thoughts and semi-visions, and the upward tendency and exaltation of our mood is emphatic and overpowering in proportion to our incapacity to think, speak, or imagine.

The sum of our incoherences has, however, an imposing volume and even, perhaps, a vague, general direction. We feel ourselves laden with an infinite burden; and what delights us most and seems to us to come nearest to the ideal is not what embodies any one possible form, but that which, by embodying none, suggests many, and stirs the mass of our inarticulate imagination with a pervasive thrill. Each thing, without being a beauty in itself, by stimulating our indeterminate emotion, seems to be a hint and expression of infinite beauty. That infinite perfection which cannot be realized, because it is self-contradictory, may be thus suggested, and on account of this suggestion an indeterminate effect may be regarded as higher, more significant, and more beautiful than any determinate one.

The illusion, however, is obvious. The infinite perfection suggested is an absurdity. What exists is a vague emotion, the objects of which, if they could emerge from the chaos of a confused imagination, would turn out to be a multitude of differently beautiful determinate things. This emotion of infinite perfection is the *materia prima—rudis indigestaque moles*—out of which attention, inspiration, and art can bring forth an infinity of particular perfections. Every æsthetic success, whether in contemplation or production, is the birth of one of these possibilities with which the sense of infinite perfection is pregnant. A work of art or an act of observation which remains indeterminate is, therefore, a failure, however much it may stir our emotion. It is a failure for two reasons. In the first place this emotion is seldom wholly pleasant; it is disquieting and perplexing; it brings a desire rather than a satisfaction. And in the second place, the emotion, not being embodied, fails to constitute the beauty of anything; and what we have is merely a sentiment, a consciousness that values are or might be there, but a failure to extricate those values, or to make them explicit and recognizable in an appropriate object.

These gropings after beauty have their worth as signs of æsthetic vitality and intimations of future possible accomplishment; but in themselves they are abortive, and mark the impotence of the imagination. Sentimentalism in the observer and romanticism in the artist are examples of this æsthetic incapacity. Whenever beauty is really seen and loved, it has a definite embodiment: the eye has precision, the work has style, and the object has perfection. The kind of perfection may indeed be new; and if the discovery of new perfections is to be called romanticism, then romanticism is the beginning of all æsthetic life. But if by romanticism we mean indulgence in confused suggestion and in the exhibition of turgid force, then there is evidently need of education, of attentive labour, to disentangle the beauties so vaguely felt, and give each its adequate embodiment. The breadth of our inspiration need not be lost in this process of clarification, for there is no limit to the number and variety of forms which the world may be made to wear; only, if it is to be appreciated as beautiful and not merely felt as unutterable, it must be seen as a kingdom of forms. Thus the works of Shakespeare give us a great variety, with a frequent marvellous precision of characterization, and the forms of his art are definite although its scope is great.

But by a curious anomaly, we are often expected to see the greatest expressiveness in what remains indeterminate, and in reality expresses nothing. As we have already observed, the sense of profundity and significance is a very detachable emotion; it can accompany a confused jumble of promptings quite as easily as it can a thorough comprehension of reality. The illusion of infinite perfection is peculiarly apt to produce this sensation. That illusion arises by the simultaneous awakening of many incipient thoughts and dim ideas; it stirs the depths of the mind

as a wind stirs the thickets of a forest; and the unusual consciousness of the life and longing of the soul, brought by that
gust of feeling, makes us recognize in the object a singular
power, a mysterious meaning.

But the feeling of significance signifies little. All we have in
this case is a potentiality of imagination; and only when this
potentiality begins to be realized in definite ideas, does a real
meaning, or any object which that meaning can mean, arise in
the mind. The highest æsthetic good is not that vague potentiality, nor that contradictory, infinite perfection so strongly desired;
it is the greatest number and variety of finite perfections. To
learn to see in nature and to enshrine in the arts the typical forms
of things; to study and recognize their variations; to domesticate
the imagination in the world, so that everywhere beauty can be
seen, and a hint found for artistic creation,—that is the goal of
contemplation. Progress lies in the direction of discrimination
and precision, not in that of formless emotion and reverie.

§ 37. ORGANIZED NATURE THE SOURCE OF APPERCEPTIVE FORMS;
EXAMPLE OF SCULPTURE. The form of the material world is in one
sense always perfectly definite, since the particles that compose
it are at each moment in a given relative position; but a world
that had no other form than that of such a constellation of
atoms would remain chaotic to our perception, because we
should not be able to survey it as a whole, or to keep our attention suspended evenly over its innumerable parts. According to
evolutionary theory, mechanical necessity has, however, brought
about a distribution and aggregation of elements such as, for
our purposes, constitutes individual things. Certain systems of
atoms move together as units; and these organisms reproduce
themselves and recur so often in our environment, that our
senses become accustomed to view their parts together. Their
form becomes a natural and recognizable one. An order and
sequence is established in our imagination by virtue of the order
and sequence in which the corresponding impressions have
come to our senses. We can remember, reproduce, and in re-
producing vary, by kaleidoscopic tricks of the fancy, the forms
in which our perceptions have come.

The mechanical organization of external nature is thus the
source of apperceptive forms in the mind. Did not sensation, by
a constant repetition of certain sequences, and a recurring
exactitude of mathematical relations, keep our fancy clear and
fresh, we should fall into an imaginative lethargy. Idealization

would degenerate into indistinctness, and, by the dulling of our memory, we should dream a world daily more poor and vague.

This process is periodically observable in the history of the arts. The way in which the human figure, for instance, is depicted, is an indication of the way in which it is apperceived. The arts give back only so much of nature as the human eye has been able to master. The most primitive stage of drawing and sculpture presents man with his arms and legs, his ten fingers and ten toes, branching out into mid-air; the apperception of the body has been evidently practical and successive, and the artist sets down what he knows rather than any of the particular perceptions that conveyed that knowledge. Those perceptions are merged and lost in the haste to reach the practically useful concept of the object. By a naïve expression of the same principle, we find in some Assyrian drawings the eye seen from the front introduced into a face seen in profile, each element being represented in that form in which it was most easily observed and remembered. The development of Greek sculpture furnishes a good example of the gradual penetration of nature into the mind, of the slowly enriched apperception of the object. The quasi-Egyptian stiffness melts away, first from the bodies of the minor figures, afterwards of those of the gods, and finally the face is varied, and the hieratic smile almost disappears.[1]

But this progress has a near limit; once the most beautiful and inclusive apperception reached, once the best form caught at its best moment, the artist seems to have nothing more to do. To reproduce the imperfections of individuals seems wrong, when beauty, after all, is the thing desired. And the ideal, as caught by the master's inspiration, is more beautiful than anything his pupils can find for themselves in nature. From its summit, the art therefore declines in one of two directions. It either becomes academic, forsakes the study of nature, and degenerates into empty convention, or else it becomes ignoble, forsakes beauty, and sinks into a tasteless and unimaginative technique. The latter was the course of sculpture in ancient times, the former, with moments of reawakening, has been its dreadful fate among the moderns.

This reawakening has come whenever there has been a return to nature, for a new form of apperception and a new ideal. Of

[1] In the Ægina marbles the wounded and dying warriors still wear this Buddha-like expression: their bodies, although conventional, show a great progress in observation, compared with the impossible Athena in the centre with her sacred feet in Egyptian profile and her owl-like visage.

this return there is continual need in all the arts; without it our apperceptions grow thin and worn, and subject to the sway of tradition and fashion. We continue to judge about beauty, but we give up looking for it. The remedy is to go back to the reality, to study it patiently, to allow new aspects of it to work upon the mind, sink into it, and beget there an imaginative offspring after their own kind. Then a new art can appear, which, having the same origin in admiration for nature which the old art had, may hope to attain the same excellence in a new direction.

In fact, one of the dangers to which a modern artist is exposed is the seduction of his predecessors. The gropings of our muse, the distracted experiments of our architecture, often arise from the attraction of some historical school; we cannot work out our own style because we are hampered by the beauties of so many others. The result is an eclecticism, which, in spite of its great historical and psychological interest, is without æsthetic unity or permanent power to please. Thus the study of many schools of art may become an obstacle to proficiency in any.

§ 38. Utility the principle of organization in nature. Utility (or, as it is now called, adaptation, and natural selection) organizes the material world into definite species and individuals. Only certain aggregations of matter are in equilibrium with the prevailing forces of the environment. Gravity, for instance, is in itself a chaotic force; it pulls all particles indiscriminately together without reference to the wholes into which the human eye may have grouped them. But the result is not chaos, because matter arranged in some ways is welded together by the very tendency which disintegrates it when arranged in other forms. These forms, selected by their congruity with gravity, are therefore fixed in nature, and become types. Thus the weight of the stones keeps the pyramid standing: here a certain shape has become a guarantee of permanence in the presence of a force in itself mechanical and undiscriminating. It is the utility of the pyramidal form—its fitness to stand—that has made it a type in building. The Egyptians merely repeated a process that they might have observed going on of itself in nature, who builds a pyramid in every hill, not indeed because she wishes to, or because pyramids are in any way an object of her action, but because she has no force which can easily dislodge matter that finds itself in that shape.

Such an accidental stability of structure is, in this moving world, a sufficient principle of permanence and individuality. The same mechanical principles, in more complex applications, insure the persistence of animal forms and prevent any permanent deviation from them. What is called the principle of self-preservation, and the final causes and substantial forms of the Aristotelian philosophy, are descriptions of the result of this operation. The tendency of everything to maintain and propagate its nature is simply the inertia of a stable juxtaposition of elements, which are not enough disturbed by ordinary accidents to lose their equilibrium; while the incidence of a too great disturbance causes that disruption we call death, or that variation of type, which, on account of its incapacity to establish itself permanently, we call abnormal. Nature thus organizes herself into recognizable species; and the æsthetic eye, studying her forms, tends, as we have already shown, to bring the type within even narrower limits than do the external exigencies of life.

§ 39. THE RELATION OF UTILITY TO BEAUTY. This natural harmony between utility and beauty, when its origin is not understood, is of course the subject of much perplexed and perplexing theory. Sometimes we are told that utility is itself the essence of beauty, that is, that our consciousness of the practical advantages of certain forms is the ground of our æsthetic admiration of them. The horse's legs are said to be beautiful because they are fit to run, the eye because it is made to see, the house because it is convenient to live in. An amusing application—which might pass for a *reductio ad absurdum*—of this dense theory is put by Xenophon into the mouth of Socrates. Comparing himself with a youth present at the same banquet, who was about to receive the prize of beauty, Socrates declares himself more beautiful and more worthy of the crown. For utility makes beauty, and eyes bulging out from the head like his are the most advantageous for seeing; nostrils wide and open to the air, like his, most appropriate for smell; and a mouth large and voluminous, like his, best fitted for both eating and kissing.[1]

Now since these things are, in fact, hideous, the theory that shows they *ought to be* beautiful, is vain and ridiculous. But that theory contains this truth: that had the utility of Socratic features been so great that men of all other type must have perished, Socrates would have been beautiful. He would have represented the human type. The eye would have been then ac-

[1] *Symposium* of Xenophon, V.

customed to that form, the imagination would have taken it as the basis of its refinements, and accentuated its naturally effective points. The beautiful does not depend on the useful; it is constituted by the imagination in ignorance and contempt of practical advantage; but it is not independent of the necessary, for the necessary must also be the habitual and consequently the basis of the type, and of all its imaginative variations.

There are, moreover, at a late and derivative stage in our æsthetic judgment, certain cases in which the knowledge of fitness and utility enters into our sense of beauty. But it does so very indirectly, rather by convincing us that we should tolerate what practical conditions have imposed on an artist, by arousing admiration of his ingenuity, or by suggesting the interesting things themselves with which the object is known to be connected. Thus a cottage-chimney, stout and tall, with the smoke floating from it, pleases because we fancy it to mean a hearth, a rustic meal, and a comfortable family. But that is all extraneous association. The most ordinary way in which utility affects us is negatively; if we know a thing to be useless and fictitious, the uncomfortable haunting sense of waste and trickery prevents all enjoyment, and therefore banishes beauty. But this is also an adventitious complication. The intrinsic value of a form is in no way affected by it.

Opposed to this utilitarian theory stands the metaphysical one that would make the beauty or intrinsic rightness of things the source of their efficiency and of their power to survive. Taken literally, as it is generally meant, this idea must, from our point of view, appear preposterous. Beauty and rightness are relative to our judgment and emotion; they in no sense exist in nature or preside over her. She everywhere appears to move by mechanical law. The types of things exist by what, in relation to our approbation, is mere chance, and it is our faculties that must adapt themselves to our environment and not our environment to our faculties. Such is the naturalistic point of view which we have adopted.

To say, however, that beauty is in some sense the ground of practical fitness, need not seem to us wholly unmeaning. The fault of the Platonists who say things of this sort is seldom that of emptiness. They have an intuition; they have sometimes a strong sense of the facts of consciousness. But they turn their discoveries into so many revelations, and the veil of the infinite and absolute soon covers their little light of specific truth. Some-

times, after patient digging, the student comes upon the treasure
of some simple fact, some common experience, beneath all their
mystery and unction. And so it may be in this case. If we make
allowances for the tendency to express experience in allegory
and myth, we shall see that the idea of beauty and rationality
presiding over nature and guiding her, as it were, for their own
greater glory, is a projection and a writing large of a psychological principle.

The mind that perceives nature is the same that understands
and enjoys her; indeed, these three functions are really elements
of one process. There is therefore in the mere perceptibility of
a thing a certain prophecy of its beauty; if it were not on the
road to beauty, if it had no approach to fitness to our faculties
of perception, the object would remain eternally unperceived.
The sense, therefore, that the whole world is made to be food
for the soul; that beauty is not only its own, but all things' excuse for being; that universal aspiration towards perfection is
the key and secret of the world,—that sense is the poetical reverberation of a psychological fact—of the fact that our mind is
an organism tending to unity, to unconsciousness of what is refractory to its action, and to assimilation and sympathetic transformation of what is kept within its sphere. The idea that nature
could be governed by an aspiration towards beauty is, therefore,
to be rejected as a confusion, but at the same time we must
confess that this confusion is founded on a consciousness of the
subjective relation between the perceptibility, rationality, and
beauty of things.

§ 40. UTILITY THE PRINCIPLE OF ORGANIZATION IN THE ARTS.
This subjective relation is, however, exceedingly loose. Most
things that are perceivable are not perceived so distinctly as to
be intelligible, nor so delightfully as to be beautiful. If our eye
had infinite penetration, or our imagination infinite elasticity,
this would not be the case; to see would then be to understand
and to enjoy. As it is, the degree of determination needed for
perception is much less than that needed for comprehension or
ideality. Hence there is room for hypothesis and for art. As
hypothesis organizes experiences imaginatively in ways in which
observation has not been able to do, so art organizes objects in
ways to which nature, perhaps, has never condescended.

The chief thing which the imitative arts add to nature is
permanence, the lack of which is the saddest defect of many

natural beauties. The forces which determine natural forms, therefore, determine also the forms of the imitative arts. But the non-imitative arts supply organisms different in kind from those which nature affords. If we seek the principle by which these objects are organized, we shall generally find that it is likewise utility. Architecture, for instance, has all its forms suggested by practical demands. Use requires our buildings to assume certain determinate forms; the mechanical properties of our materials, the exigency of shelter, light, accessibility, economy, and convenience, dictate the arrangements of our buildings.

Houses and temples have an evolution like that of animals and plants. Various forms arise by mechanical necessity, like the cave, or the shelter of overhanging boughs. These are perpetuated by a selection in which the needs and pleasures of man are the environment to which the structure must be adapted. Determinate forms thus establish themselves, and the eye becomes accustomed to them. The line of use, by habit of apperception, becomes the line of beauty. A striking example may be found in the pediment of the Greek temple and the gable of the northern house. The exigencies of climate determine these forms differently, but the eye in each case accepts what utility imposes. We admire height in one and breadth in the other, and we soon find the steep pediment heavy and the low gable awkward and mean.

It would be an error, however, to conclude that habit alone establishes the right proportion in these various types of building. We have the same intrinsic elements to consider as in natural forms. That is, besides the unity of type and correspondence of parts which custom establishes, there are certain appeals to more fundamental susceptibilities of the human eye and imagination. There is, for instance, the value of abstract form, determined by the pleasantness and harmony of implicated retinal or muscular tensions. Different structures contain or suggest more or less of this kind of beauty, and in that proportion may be called intrinsically better or worse. Thus artificial forms may be arranged in a hierarchy like natural ones, by reference to the absolute values of their contours and masses. Herein lies the superiority of a Greek to a Chinese vase, or of Gothic to Saracenic construction. Thus although every useful form is capable of proportion and beauty, when once its type is established, we cannot say that this beauty is always potentially equal; and an iron bridge, for instance, although it certainly possesses and daily acquires æsthetic interest, will probably never, on the average, equal a bridge of stone.

§ 41. FORM AND ADVENTITIOUS ORNAMENT. Beauty of form is the last to be found or admired in artificial as in natural objects. Time is needed to establish it, and training and nicety of perception to enjoy it. Motion or colour is what first interests a child in toys, as in animals; and the barbarian artist decorates long before he designs. The cave and wigwam are daubed with paint, or hung with trophies, before any pleasure is taken in their shape; and the appeal to the detached senses, and to associations of wealth and luxury, precedes by far the appeal to the perceptive harmonies of form. In music we observe the same gradation; first, we appreciate its sensuous and sentimental value; only with education can we enjoy its form. The plastic arts begin, therefore, with adventitious ornament and with symbolism. The æsthetic pleasure is in the richness of the material, the profusion of the ornament, the significance of the shape—in everything, rather than in the shape itself.

We have accordingly in works of art two independent sources of effect. The first is the useful form, which generates the type, and ultimately the beauty of form, when the type has been idealized by emphasizing its intrinsically pleasing traits. The second is the beauty of ornament, which comes from the excitement of the senses, or of the imagination, by colour, or by profusion or delicacy of detail. Historically, the latter is first developed, and applied to a form as yet merely useful. But the very presence of ornament attracts contemplation; the attention lavished on the object helps to fix its form in the mind, and to make us discriminate the less from the more graceful. The two kinds of beauty are then felt, and, yielding to that tendency to unity which the mind always betrays, we begin to subordinate and organize these two excellences. The ornament is distributed so as to emphasize the æsthetic essence of the form; to idealize it even more, by adding adventitious interests harmoniously to the intrinsic interest of the lines of structure.

There is here a great field, of course, for variety of combination and compromise. Some artists are fascinated by the decoration, and think of the structure merely as the background on which it can be most advantageously displayed. Others, of more austere taste, allow ornament only to emphasize the main lines of the design, or to conceal such inharmonious elements as nature or utility may prevent them from eliminating.[1] We may thus oscillate between decorative and structural motives, and only in one point, for each style, can we find the ideal equilibrium, in which the greatest strength and lucidity is combined with the greatest splendour.

A less subtle, but still very effective, combination is that hit upon by many oriental and Gothic architects, and found, also, by accident perhaps, in many buildings of the plateresque style; the ornament and structure are both presented with extreme emphasis, but locally divided; a vast rough wall, for instance, represents the one, and a profusion of mad ornament huddled around a central door or window represents the other.

Gothic architecture offers us in the pinnacle and flying buttress a striking example of the adoption of a mechanical feature, and its transformation into an element of beauty. Nothing could at first sight be more hopeless than the external half-arch propping the side of a pier, or the chimney-like weight of stones pressing it down from above; but a courageous acceptance of these necessities, and a submissive study of their form, revealed a new and strange effect: the bewildering and stimulating intricacy of masses suspended in mid-air; the profusion of line, variety of surface, and picturesqueness of light and shade. It needed but a little applied ornament judiciously distributed; a moulding in the arches; a florid canopy and statue amid the buttresses; a few grinning monsters leaning out of unexpected nooks; a leafy

[1] It is a superstition to suppose that a refined taste would necessarily find the actual and useful to be the perfect; to conceal structure is as legitimate as to emphasize it, and for the same reason. We emphasize in the direction of abstract beauty, in the direction of absolute pleasure; and we conceal or eliminate in the same direction. The most exquisite Greek taste, for instance, preferred to drape the lower part of the female figure, as in the Venus of Milo; also in men to shave the hair of the face and body, in order to maintain the purity and strength of the lines. In the one case we conceal structure, in the other we reveal it, modifying nature into greater sympathy with our faculties of perception. For, after all, it must be remembered that beauty, or pleasure to be given to the eye, is not a guiding principle in the world of nature or in that of the practical arts. The beauty is in nature a result of the functional adaptation of our senses and imagination to the mechanical products of our environment. This adaptation is never complete, and there is, accordingly, room for the fine arts, in which beauty is a result of the intentional adaptation of mechanical forms to the functions which our senses and imagination already have acquired. This watchful subservience to our æsthetic demands is the essence of fine art. Nature is the basis, but man is the goal.

budding of the topmost pinnacles; a piercing here and there of some little gallery, parapet, or turret into lacework against the sky—and the building became a poem, an inexhaustible emotion. Add some passing cloud casting its moving shadow over the pile, add the circling of birds about the towers, and you have an unforgettable type of beauty; not perhaps the noblest, sanest, or most enduring, but one for the existence of which the imagination is richer, and the world more interesting.

In this manner we accept the forms imposed upon us by utility, and train ourselves to apperceive their potential beauty. Familiarity breeds contempt only when it breeds inattention. When the mind is absorbed and dominated by its perceptions, it incorporates into them more and more of its own functional values, and makes them ultimately beautiful and expressive. Thus no language can be ugly to those who speak it well, no religion unmeaning to those who have learned to pour their life into its moulds.

Of course these forms vary in intrinsic excellence; they are by their specific character more or less fit and facile for the average mind. But the man and the age are rare who can choose their own path; we have generally only a choice between going ahead in the direction already chosen, or halting and blocking the path for others. The only kind of reform usually possible is reform from within; a more intimate study and more intelligent use of the traditional forms. Disaster follows rebellion against tradition or against utility, which are the basis and root of our taste and progress. But, within the given school, and as exponents of its spirit, we can adapt and perfect our works, if haply we are better inspired than our predecessors. For the better we know a given thing, and the more we perceive its strong and weak points, the more capable we are of idealizing it.

§ 42. FORM IN WORDS. The main effect of language consists in its meaning, in the ideas which it expresses. But no expression is possible without a presentation, and this presentation must have a form. This form of the instrument of expression is itself an element of effect, although in practical life we may overlook it in our haste to attend to the meaning it conveys. It is, moreover, a condition of the kind of expression possible, and often determines the manner in which the object suggested shall be apperceived. No word has the exact value of any other in the same or in another language.[1] But the intrinsic effect of language does not stop there. The single word is but a stage in the series of formations which constitute language, and which preserve for men the fruit of their experience, distilled and concentrated into a symbol.

This formation begins with the elementary sounds themselves, which have to be discriminated and combined to make recognizable symbols. The evolution of these symbols goes on spontaneously, suggested by our tendency to utter all manner of sounds, and preserved by the ease with which the ear discriminates these sounds when made. Speech would be an absolute and unrelated art, like music, were it not controlled by utility. The sounds have indeed no resemblance to the objects they symbolize; but before the system of sounds can represent the system of objects, there has to be a correspondence in the groupings of both. The structure of language, unlike that of music, thus becomes a mirror of the structure of the world as presented to the intelligence.

Grammar, philosophically studied, is akin to the deepest metaphysics, because in revealing the constitution of speech, it reveals the constitution of thought, and the hierarchy of those categories by which we conceive the world. It is by virtue of this parallel development that language has its function of expressing experience with exactness, and the poet—to whom language is an instrument of art—has to employ it also with a constant reference to meaning and veracity; that is, he must be a master of experience before he can become a true master of words. Nevertheless, language is primarily a sort of music, and the beautiful effects which it produces are due to its own structure, giving, as it crystallizes in a new fashion, an unforeseen form to experience.

Poets may be divided into two classes: the musicians and the psychologists. The first are masters of significant language as harmony; they know what notes to sound together and in

---

[1] Not only are words untranslatable when the exact object has no name in another language, as "home" or "mon ami," but even when the object is the same, the attitude toward it, incorporated in one word, cannot be rendered by another. Thus, to my sense, "bread" is as inadequate a translation of the human intensity of the Spanish "pan" as "Dios" is of the awful mystery of the English "God." This latter word does not designate an object at all, but a sentiment, a psychosis, not to say a whole chapter of religious history. English is remarkable for the intensity and variety of the colour of its words. No language, I believe, has so many words specifically poetic.

succession; they can produce, by the marshalling of sounds and
images, by the fugue of passion and the snap of wit, a thousand
brilliant effects out of old materials. The Ciceronian orator, the
epigrammatic, lyric, and elegiac poets, give examples of this art.
The psychologists, on the other hand, gain their effect not by
the intrinsic mastery of language, but by the closer adaptation of
it to things. The dramatic poets naturally furnish an illustration.

But however transparent we may wish to make our language,
however little we may call for its intrinsic effects, and direct
our attention exclusively to its expressiveness, we cannot avoid
the limitations of our particular medium. The character of the
tongue a man speaks, and the degree of his skill in speaking it,
must always count enormously in the æsthetic value of his compositions; no skill in observation, no depth of thought or feeling, but is spoiled by a bad style and enhanced by a good one.
The diversities of tongues and their irreducible æsthetic values,
begins with the very sound of the letters, with the mode of ut-
terance, and the characteristic inflections of the voice; notice,
for instance, the effect of the French of these lines of Alfred de
Musset,

> Jamais deux yeux plus doux n'ont du ciel le plus pur
> Sondé la profondeur et réfléchi l'azur.

and compare with its flute-like and treble quality the breadth,
depth, and volume of the German in this inimitable stanza of
Goethe's:

> Ueber allen Gipfeln
> Ist Ruh,
> In allen Wipfeln
> Spürest du
> Kaum einen Hauch;
> Die Vögelein schweigen im Walde.
> Warte nur, balde
> Ruhest du auch.

Even if the same tune could be played on both these vocal
instruments, the difference in their *timbre* would make the value
of the melody entirely distinct in each case.

§ 43. SYNTACTICAL FORM. The known impossibility of adequate
translation appears here at the basis of language. The other
diversities are superadded upon this diversity of sound. The
syntax is the next source of effect. What could be better than
Homer, or what worse than almost any translation of him? And
this holds even of languages so closely allied as the Indo-Euro-
pean, which, after all, have certain correspondences of syntax

and inflection. If there could be a language with other parts of speech than ours,—a language without nouns, for instance,—how would that grasp of experience, that picture of the world, which all our literature contains, be reproduced in it? Whatever beauties that language might be susceptible of, none of the effects produced on us, I will not say by poets, but even by nature itself, could be expressed in it.

Nor is such a language inconceivable. Instead of summarizing all our experiences of a thing by one word, its name, we should have to recall by appropriate adjectives the various sensations we had received from it; the objects we think of would be disintegrated, or, rather, would never have been unified. For "sun," they would say "high, yellow, dazzling, round, slowly moving," and the enumeration of these qualities (as we call them), without any suggestion of a unity at their source, might give a more vivid and profound, if more cumbrous, representation of the facts. But how could the machinery of such an imagination be capable of repeating the effects of ours, when the objects to us most obvious and real would be to those minds utterly indescribable?

The same diversity appears in the languages we ordinarily know, only in a lesser degree. The presence or absence of case-endings in nouns and adjectives, their difference of gender, the richness of inflections in the verbs, the frequency of particles and conjunctions,—all these characteristics make one language differ from another entirely in genius and capacity of expression. Greek is probably the best of all languages in melody, richness, elasticity, and simplicity; so much so, that in spite of its complex inflections, when once a vocabulary is acquired, it is more easy and natural for a modern than his ancestral Latin itself. Latin is the stiffer tongue; it is by nature at once laconic and grandiloquent, and the exceptional condensation and transposition of which it is capable make its effects entirely foreign to a modern, scarcely inflected, tongue. Take, for instance, these lines of Horace:

> me tabula sacer
> votiva paries indicat uvida
> suspendisse potenti
> vestimenta maris deo,

or these of Lucretius:

> Jamque caput quassans grandis suspirat arator
> Crebrius incassum magnum cecidisse laborem.

What conglomerate plebeian speech of our time could utter the stately grandeur of these Lucretian words, every one of which is noble, and wears the toga?

As a substitute for the inimitable interpenetration of the words in the Horatian strophe, we might have the external links of rhyme; and it seems, in fact, to be a justification of rhyme, that besides contributing something to melody and to the distribution of parts, it gives an artificial relationship to the phrases between which it obtains, which, but for it, would run away from one another in a rapid and irrevocable flux. In such a form as the sonnet, for instance, we have, by dint of assonance, a real unity forced upon the thought; for a sonnet in which the thought is not distributed appropriately to the structure of the verse, has no excuse for being a sonnet. By virtue of this inter-relation of parts, the sonnet, the *non plus ultra* of rhyme, is the most classic of modern poetical forms: much more classic in spirit than blank verse, which lacks almost entirely the power of synthesizing the phrase, and making the unexpected seem the inevitable.

This beauty given to the ancients by the syntax of their language, the moderns can only attain by the combination of their rhymes. It is a bad substitute perhaps, but better than the total absence of form, favoured by the atomic character of our words, and the flat juxtaposition of our clauses. The art which was capable of making a gem of every prose sentence,—the art which, carried, perhaps, to a pitch at which it became too conscious, made the phrases of Tacitus a series of cameos,—that art is inapplicable to our looser medium; we cannot give clay the finish and nicety of marble. Our poetry and speech in general, therefore, start out upon a lower level; the same effort will not, with this instrument, attain the same beauty. If equal beauty is ever attained, it comes from the wealth of suggestion, or the refinement of sentiment. The art of words remains hopelessly inferior. And what best proves this, is that when, as in our time, a reawakening of the love of beauty has prompted a refinement of our poetical language, we pass so soon into extravagance, obscurity, and affectation. Our modern languages are not susceptible of great formal beauty.

§ 44. LITERARY FORM. THE PLOT. The forms of composition in verse and prose which are practised in each language are further organizations of words, and have formal values. The most exacting of these forms and that which has been carried to the greatest perfection is the drama; but it belongs to rhetoric and poetics to investigate the nature of these effects, and we have here sufficiently indicated the principle which underlies them. The plot, which Aristotle makes, and very justly, the most important element in the effect of a drama, is the formal element of the drama as such: the ethos and sentiments are the expression, and the versification, music, and stage settings are the materials. It is in harmony with the romantic tendency of modern times that modern dramatists—Shakespeare as well as Molière, Calderon, and the rest—excel in ethos rather than in plot; for it is the evident characteristic of modern genius to study and enjoy expression,—the suggestion of the not-given,—rather than form, the harmony of the given.

Ethos is interesting mainly for the personal observations which it summarizes and reveals, or for the appeal to one's own actual or imaginative experience; it is portrait-painting, and enshrines something we love independently of the charm which at this moment and in this place it exercises over us. It appeals to our affections; it does not form them. But the plot is the synthesis of actions, and is a reproduction of those experiences from which our notion of men and things is originally derived; for character can never be observed in the world except as manifested in action.

Indeed, it would be more fundamentally accurate to say that a character is a symbol and mental abbreviation for a peculiar set of acts, than to say that acts are a manifestation of character. For the acts are the data, and the character the inferred principle, and a principle, in spite of its name, is never more than a description *a posteriori,* and a summary of what is subsumed under it. The plot, moreover, is what gives individuality to the play, and exercises invention; it is, as Aristotle again says, the most difficult portion of dramatic art, and that for which practice and training are most indispensable. And this plot, giving by its nature a certain picture of human experience, involves and suggests the ethos of its actors.

What the great characterizers, like Shakespeare, do, is simply to elaborate and develope (perhaps far beyond the necessities of the plot) the suggestion of human individuality which that plot contains. It is as if, having drawn from daily observation some knowledge of the tempers of our friends, we represented them saying and doing all manner of ultra-characteristic things, and in an occasional soliloquy laying bare, even more clearly than by any possible action, that character which their observed behaviour had led us to impute to them. This is an ingenious and fascinating invention, and delights us with the clear discovery of a hidden personality; but the serious and equable development of a plot has a more stable worth in its greater similarity to life, which allows us to see other men's minds through the medium of events, and not events through the medium of other men's minds.

§ 45. CHARACTER AS AN ÆSTHETIC FORM. We have just come upon one of the unities most coveted in our literature, and most valued by us when attained,—the portrait, the individuality, the character. The construction of a plot we call invention, but that of a character we dignify with the name of creation. It may therefore not be amiss, in finishing our discussion of form, to devote a few pages to the psychology of character-drawing. How does the unity we call a character arise, how is it described, and what is the basis of its effect?

We may set it down at once as evident that we have here a case of the type: the similarities of various persons are amalgamated, their differences cancelled, and in the resulting percept those traits emphasized which have particularly pleased or interested us. This, in the abstract, may serve for a description of the origin of an idea of character quite as well as of an idea of physical form. But the different nature of the material—the fact that a character is not a presentation to sense, but a rationalistic synthesis of successive acts and feelings, not combinable into any image—makes such a description much more unsatisfying in this case than in that of material forms. We cannot understand exactly how these summations and cancellings take place when we are not dealing with a visible object. And we may even feel that there is a wholeness and inwardness about the development of certain ideal characters, that makes such a treatment of them fundamentally false and artificial. The subjective element, the spontaneous expression of our own passion and will, here counts for so much, that the creation of an ideal character becomes a new and peculiar problem.

There is, however, a way of conceiving and delineating character which still bears a close resemblance to the process by which the imagination produces the type of any physical species. We may gather, for instance, about the nucleus of a word, designating some human condition or occupation, a number of detached observations. We may keep a note-book in our memory, or even in our pocket, with studious observations of the language, manners, dress, gesture, and history of the people we meet, classifying our statistics under such heads as innkeepers, soldiers, house-maids, governesses, adventuresses, Germans, Frenchmen, Italians, Americans, actors, priests, and professors. And then, when occasion offers, to describe, or to put into a book or a play, any one of these types, all we have to do is to look over our notes, to select according to the needs of the moment, and if we are skilful in reproduction, to obtain by that means a life-like image of the sort of person we wish to represent.

This process, which novelists and playwrights may go through deliberately, we all carry on involuntarily. At every moment experience is leaving in our minds some trait, some expression, some image, which will remain there attached to the name of a person, a class, or a nationality. Our likes and dislikes, our sum-mary judgments on whole categories of men, are nothing but the distinct survival of some such impression. These traits have vivacity. If the picture they draw is one-sided and inadequate, the sensation they recall may be vivid, and suggestive of many other aspects of the thing. Thus the epithets in Homer, although they are often far from describing the essence of the object— γλαυκῶπις ᾿Αθήνη, εὐκνήμιδες ᾿Αχαιοί—seem to recall a sensation, and to give vitality to the narrative. By bringing you, through one sense, into the presence of the object, they give you that same hint of further discovery, that same expectation of experience, which we have at the sight of whatever we call real.

The graphic power of this method of observation and aggrega-tion of characteristic traits is thus seen to be great. But it is not by this method that the most famous or most living charac-ters have been conceived. This method gives the average, or at most the salient, points of the type, but the great characters of poetry—a Hamlet, a Don Quixote, an Achilles—are no averages, they are not even a collection of salient traits common to certain classes of men. They seem to be persons; that is, their actions and words seem to spring from the inward nature of an individual soul. Goethe is reported to have said that he conceived the character of his Gretchen entirely without observation of origi-nals. And, indeed, he would probably not have found any. His creation rather is the original to which we may occasionally think we see some likeness in real maidens. It is the fiction here that is the standard of naturalness. And on this, as on so many occasions, we may repeat the saying that poetry is truer than history. Perhaps no actual maid ever spoke and acted so natu-rally as this imaginary one.

If we think there is any paradox in these assertions, we should reflect that the standard of naturalness, individuality, and truth is in us. A real person seems to us to have character and consistency when his behaviour is such as to impress a definite and simple image upon our mind. In themselves, if we could count all their undiscovered springs of action, all men have character and consistency alike: all are equally fit to be types. But their characters are not equally intelligible to us, their behaviour is not equally deducible, and their motives not equally appreciable. Those who appeal most to us, either in themselves or by the emphasis they borrow from their similarity to other individuals, are those we remember and regard as the centres around which variations oscillate. These men are natural: all others are more or less eccentric.

§ 46. IDEAL CHARACTERS. The standard of naturalness being thus subjective, and determined by the laws of our imagination, we can understand why a spontaneous creation of the mind can be more striking and living than any reality, or any abstraction from realities. The artist can invent a form which, by its adaptation to the imagination, lodges there, and becomes a point of reference for all observations, and a standard of naturalness and beauty. A type may be introduced to the mind suddenly, by the chance presentation of a form that by its intrinsic impressiveness and imaginative coherence, acquires that pre-eminence which custom, or the mutual reinforcement of converging experiences, ordinarily gives to empirical percepts.

This method of originating types is what we ordinarily describe as artistic creation. The name indicates the suddenness, originality, and individuality of the conception thus attained. What we call idealization is often a case of it. In idealization proper, however, what happens is the elimination of individual eccentricities; the result is abstract, and consequently meagre. This meagreness is often felt to be a greater disadvantage than the accidental and picturesque imperfection of real individuals, and the artist therefore turns to the brute fact, and studies and reproduces that with indiscriminate attention, rather than lose strength and individuality in the presentation of an insipid type. He seems forced to a choice between an abstract beauty and an unlovely example.

But the great and masterful presentations of the ideal are somehow neither the one nor the other. They present ideal beauty with just that definiteness with which nature herself sometimes presents it. When we come in a crowd upon an incomparably beautiful face, we know it immediately as an embodiment of the ideal; while it contains the type,—for if it did not we should find it monstrous and grotesque,—it clothes that type in a peculiar splendour of form, colour, and expression. It has an individuality. And just so the imaginary figures of poetry and plastic art may have an individuality given them by the happy affinities of their elements in the imagination. They are not idealizations, they are spontaneous variations, which can arise in the mind quite as easily as in the world. They spring up in

> The wreathèd trellis of a working brain;
> . . . With all the gardner fancy e'er could feign
> Who, breeding flowers, will never breed the same.

Imagination, in a word, generates as well as abstracts; it observes, combines, and cancels; but it also dreams. Spontaneous syntheses arise in it which are not mathematical averages of the images it receives from sense; they are effects of diffused excitements left in the brain by sensations. These excitements vary constantly in their various renewals, and occasionally take such a form that the soul is surprised by the inward vision of an unexampled beauty. If this inward vision is clear and steady, we have an æsthetic inspiration, a vocation to create; and if we can also command the technique of an appropriate art, we shall hasten to embody that inspiration, and realize an ideal. This ideal will be gradually recognized as supremely beautiful for the same reason that the object, had it been presented in the real world, would have been recognized as supremely beautiful; because while embodying a known type of form,—being, that is, a proper man, animal, or vegetable,— it possessed in an extraordinary degree those direct charms which most subjugate our attention.

Imaginary forms then differ in dignity and beauty not according to their closeness to fact or type in nature, but according to the ease with which the normal imagination reproduces the synthesis they contain. To add wings to a man has always been a natural fancy; because man can easily imagine himself to fly, and the idea is delightful to him. The winged man is therefore a form generally recognized as beautiful; although it can happen, as it did to Michael Angelo, that our appreciation of the actual form of the human body should be too keen and overmastering to allow us to relish even so charming and imaginative an extravagance. The centaur is another beautiful monster. The imagination can easily follow the synthesis of the dream in which horse and man melted into one, and first gave the glorious suggestion of their united vitality.

The same condition determines the worth of imaginary personalities. From the gods to the characters of comedy, all are, in proportion to their beauty, natural and exhilarating expressions of possible human activity. We sometimes remould visible forms into imaginary creatures; but our originality in this respect is meagre compared with the profusion of images of action which arise in us, both asleep and awake; we constantly dream of new situations, extravagant adventures, and exaggerated passions. Even our soberer thoughts are very much given to following the possible fortunes of some enterprise, and foretasting the satisfactions of love and ambition. The mind is therefore particularly sensitive to pictures of action and character; we are easily induced to follow the fortunes of any hero, and share his sentiments.

Our will, as Descartes said in a different context, is infinite, while our intelligence is finite; we follow experience pretty closely in our ideas of things, and even the furniture of fairyland bears a sad resemblance to that of earth; but there is no limit to the elasticity of our passion; and we love to fancy ourselves kings and beggars, saints and villains, young and old, happy and unhappy. There seems to be a boundless capacity of development in each of us, which the circumstances of life determine to a narrow channel; and we like to revenge ourselves in our reveries for this imputed limitation, by classifying ourselves with all that we are not, but might so easily have been. We are full of sympathy for every manifestation of life, however unusual; and even the conception of infinite knowledge and happiness—than which nothing could be more removed from our condition or more unrealizable to our fancy—remains eternally interesting to us.

The poet, therefore, who wishes to delineate a character need not keep a note-book. There is a quicker road to the heart—if he has the gift to find it. Probably his readers will not themselves have kept note-books, and his elaborate observations will only be effective when he describes something which they also happen to have noticed. The typical characters describable by the empirical method are therefore few: the miser, the lover, the old nurse, the ingénue, and the other types of traditional comedy. Any greater specification would appeal only to a small audience for a short time, because the characteristics depicted would no longer exist to be recognized. But whatever experience a poet's hearers may have had, they are men. They will have certain imaginative capacities to conceive and admire those forms of character and action which, although never actually found, are felt by each man to express what he himself might and would have been, had circumstances been more favourable.

The poet has only to study himself, and the art of expressing his own ideals, to find that he has expressed those of other people. He has but to enact in himself the part of each of his personages, and if he possesses that pliability and that definiteness of imagination which together make genius, he may express for his fellows those inward tendencies which in them have remained painfully dumb. He will be hailed as master of the human soul. He may know nothing of men, he may have almost no experience; but his creations will pass for models of naturalness, and for types of humanity. Their names will be in every one's mouth, and the lives of many generations will be enriched by the vision, one might almost say by the friendship, of these imaginary beings. They have individuality without having reality, because individuality is a thing acquired in the mind by the congeries of its impressions. They have power, also, because that depends on the appropriateness of a stimulus to touch the springs of reaction in the soul. And they of course have beauty, because in them is embodied the greatest of our imaginative delights,— that of giving body to our latent capacities, and of wandering, without the strain and contradiction of actual existence, into all forms of possible being.

§ 47. THE RELIGIOUS IMAGINATION. The greatest of these creations have not been the work of any one man. They have been the slow product of the pious and poetic imagination. Starting from some personification of nature or some memory of a great man, the popular and priestly tradition has refined and developed the ideal; it has made it an expression of men's aspiration and a counterpart of their need. The devotion of each tribe, shrine, and psalmist has added some attribute to the god or some parable to his legend; and thus, around the kernel of some original divine function, the imagination of a people has gathered every possible expression of it, creating a complete and beautiful personality, with its history, its character, and its gifts. No poet has ever equalled the perfection or significance of these religious creations. The greatest characters of fiction are uninteresting and unreal compared with the conceptions of the gods; so much so that men have believed that their gods have objective reality.

The forms men see in dreams might have been a reason for believing in vague and disquieting ghosts; but the belief in individual and well-defined divinities, with which the visions of the dreams might be identified, is obviously due to the intrinsic coherence and impressiveness of the conception of those deities. The vision would never have suggested the legend and attributes of the god; but when the figure of the god was once imaginatively conceived, and his name and aspect fixed in the imagination, it would be easy to recognize him in any hallucination, or to interpret any event as due to his power. These manifestations, which constitute the evidence of his actual existence, can be regarded as manifestations of him, rather than of a vague, unknown power, only when the imagination already possesses a vivid picture of him, and of his appropriate functions. This picture is the work of a spontaneous fancy.

No doubt, when the belief is once specified, and the special and intelligible god is distinguished in the night and horror of the all-pervading natural power, the belief in his reality helps to concentrate our attention on his nature, and thus to develope and enrich our idea. The belief in the reality of an ideal personality brings about its further idealization. Had it ever occurred to any Greek seer to attribute events to the influence of Achilles, or to offer sacrifices to him in the heat of the enthusiasm kindled by the thought of his beauty and virtue, the legend of Achilles, now become a god, would have grown and deepened; it would have been moralized like the legend of Hercules, or naturalized like that of Persephone, and what is now but a poetic character of extraordinary force and sublimity would have become the adored patron of generation after generation, and a manifestation of the divine man.

Achilles would then have been as significant and unforgettable a figure as Apollo or his sister, as Zeus, Athena, and the other greater gods. If ever, while that phase of religion lasted, his character had been obscured and his features dimmed, he would have been recreated by every new votary: poets would never have tired of singing his praises, or sculptors of rendering his form. When, after the hero had been the centre and subject of so much imaginative labour, the belief in his reality lapsed, to be transferred to some other conception of cosmic power, he would have remained an ideal of poetry and art, and a formative influence

of all cultivated minds. This he is still, like all the great creations of avowed fiction, but he would have been immensely more
so, had belief in his reality kept the creative imagination con-
tinuously intent upon his nature.

The reader can hardly fail to see that all this applies with
equal force to the Christian conception of the sacred personalities. Christ, the Virgin Mary, and the saints may have been
exactly what our imagination pictures them to be; that is
entirely possible; nor can I see that it is impossible that the conceptions of other religions might themselves have actual counter-
parts somewhere in the universe. That is a question of faith and
empirical evidence with which we are not here concerned. But
however descriptive of truth our conceptions may be, they have
evidently grown up in our minds by an inward process of development. The materials of history and tradition have been
melted and recast by the devout imagination into those figures
in the presence of which our piety lives.

That is the reason why the reconstructed logical gods of the
metaphysicians are always an offence and a mockery to the religious consciousness. There is here, too, a bare possibility that
some one of these absolutes may be a representation of the
truth; but the method by which this representation is acquired
is violent and artificial; while the traditional conception of God
is the spontaneous embodiment of passionate contemplation and
long experience.

As the God of religion differs from that of metaphysics, so
does the Christ of tradition differ from that of our critical historians. Even if we took the literal narrative of the Gospels and
accepted it as all we could know of Christ, without allowing
ourselves any imaginative interpretation of the central figure, we
should get an ideal of him, I will not say very different from that
of St. Francis or St. Theresa, but even from that of the English
prayer-book. The Christ men have loved and adored is an ideal
of their own hearts, the construction of an ever-present personality, living and intimately understood, out of the fragments
of story and doctrine connected with a name. This subjective
image has inspired all the prayers, all the conversions, all the
penances, charities, and sacrifices, as well as half the art of the
Christian world.

The Virgin Mary, whose legend is so meagre, but whose power
over the Catholic imagination is so great, is an even clearer illustration of this inward building up of an ideal form. Everything
is here spontaneous sympathetic expansion of two given events:

the incarnation and the crucifixion. The figure of the Virgin, found in these mighty scenes, is gradually clarified and developed, until we come to the thought on the one hand of her freedom from original sin, and on the other to that of her universal maternity. We thus attain the conception of one of the noblest of conceivable rôles and of one of the most beautiful of characters. It is a pity that a foolish iconoclasm should so long have deprived the Protestant mind of the contemplation of this ideal.

Perhaps it is a sign of the average imaginative dulness or fatigue of certain races and epochs that they so readily abandon these supreme creations. For, if we are hopeful, why should we not believe that the best we can fancy is also the truest; and if we are distrustful in general of our prophetic gifts, why should we cling only to the most mean and formless of our illusions? From the beginning to the end of our perceptive and imaginative activity, we are synthesizing the material of experience into unities the independent reality of which is beyond proof, nay, beyond the possibility of a shadow of evidence. And yet the life of intelligence, like the joy of contemplation, lies entirely in the formation and inter-relation of these unities. This activity yields us all the objects with which we can deal, and endows them with the finer and more intimate part of their beauty. The most perfect of these forms, judged by its affinity to our powers and its stability in the presence of our experience, is the one with which we should be content; no other kind of veracity could add to its value.

The greatest feats of synthesis which the human mind has yet accomplished will, indeed, be probably surpassed and all ideals yet formed be superseded, because they were not based upon enough experience, or did not fit that experience with adequate precision. It is also possible that changes in the character of the facts, or in the powers of intelligence, should necessitate a continual reconstruction of our world. But unless human nature suffers an inconceivable change, the chief intellectual and æsthetic value of our ideas will always come from the creative action of the imagination.

PART IV

EXPRESSION

§ 48. EXPRESSION DEFINED. We have found in the beauty of material and form the objectification of certain pleasures connected with the process of direct perception, with the formation, in the one case of a sensation, or quality, in the other of a synthesis of sensations or qualities. But the human consciousness is not a perfectly clear mirror, with distinct boundaries and clear-cut images, determinate in number and exhaustively perceived. Our ideas half emerge for a moment from the dim continuum of vital feeling and diffused sense, and are hardly fixed before they are changed and transformed, by the shifting of attention and the perception of new relations, into ideas of really different objects. This fluidity of the mind would make reflection impossible, did we not fix in words and other symbols certain abstract contents; we thus become capable of recognizing in one perception the repetition of another, and of recognizing in certain recurrences of impressions a persistent object. This discrimination and classification of the contents of consciousness is the work of perception and understanding, and the pleasures that accompany these activities make the beauty of the sensible world.

But our hold upon our thoughts extends even further. We not only construct visible unities and recognizable types, but remain aware of their affinities to what is not at the time perceived; that is, we find in them a certain tendency and quality, not original to them, a meaning and a tone, which upon investigation we shall see to have been the proper characteristics of other objects and feelings, associated with them once in our experience. The hushed reverberations of these associated feelings continue in the brain, and by modifying our present reaction, colour the image upon which our attention is fixed. The quality thus acquired by objects through association is what we call their expression. Whereas in form or material there is one object with its emotional effect, in expression there are two, and the emotional effect belongs to the character of the second or suggested

119

one. Expression may thus make beautiful by suggestion things in themselves indifferent, or it may come to heighten the beauty which they already possess.

Expression is not always distinguishable in consciousness from the value of material or form, because we do not always have a distinguishable memory of the related idea which the expressiveness implies. When we have such a memory, as at the sight of some once frequented garden, we clearly and spontaneously attribute our emotion to the memory and not to the present fact which it beautifies. The revival of a pleasure and its embodiment in a present object which in itself might have been indifferent, is here patent and acknowledged.

The distinctness of the analysis may indeed be so great as to prevent the synthesis; we may so entirely pass to the suggested object, that our pleasure will be embodied in the memory of that, while the suggestive sensation will be overlooked, and the expressiveness of the present object will fail to make it beautiful. Thus the mementos of a lost friend do not become beautiful by virtue of the sentimental associations which may make them precious. The value is confined to the images of the memory; they are too clear to let any of that value escape and diffuse itself over the rest of our consciousness, and beautify the objects which we actually behold. We say explicitly: I value this trifle for its associations. And so long as this division continues, the worth of the thing is not for us æsthetic.

But a little dimming of our memory will often make it so. Let the images of the past fade, let them remain simply as a halo and suggestion of happiness hanging about a scene; then this scene, however empty and uninteresting in itself, will have a deep and intimate charm; we shall be pleased by its very vulgarity. We shall not confess so readily that we value the place for its associations; we shall rather say: I am fond of this landscape; it has for me an ineffable attraction. The treasures of the memory have been melted and dissolved, and are now gilding the object that supplants them; they are giving this object expression.

Expression then differs from material or formal value only as habit differs from instinct—in its origin. Physiologically, they are both pleasurable radiations of a given stimulus; mentally, they are both values incorporated in an object. But an observer, looking at the mind historically, sees in the one case the survival of an experience, in the other the reaction of an innate disposition. This experience, moreover, is generally rememberable, and then the extrinsic source of the charm which expression gives becomes evident even to the consciousness in which it arises. A word, for instance, is often beautiful simply by virtue of its meaning and associations; but sometimes this expressive beauty is added to a musical quality in the world itself. In all expression we may thus distinguish two terms: the first is the object actually presented, the word, the image, the expressive thing; the second is the object suggested, the further thought, emotion, or image evoked, the thing expressed.

These lie together in the mind, and their union constitutes expression. If the value lies wholly in the first term, we have no beauty of expression. The decorative inscriptions in Saracenic monuments can have no beauty of expression for one who does not read Arabic; their charm is wholly one of material and form. Or if they have any expression, it is by virtue of such thoughts as they might suggest, as, for instance, of the piety and oriental sententiousness of the builders and of the aloofness from us of all their world. And even these suggestions, being a wandering of our fancy rather than a study of the object, would fail to arouse a pleasure which would be incorporated in the present image. The scroll would remain without expression, although its presence might have suggested to us interesting visions of other things. The two terms would be too independent, and the intrinsic values of each would remain distinct from that of the other. There would be no visible expressiveness, although there might have been discursive suggestions.

Indeed, if expression were constituted by the external relation of object with object, everything would be expressive equally, indeterminately, and universally. The flower in the crannied wall would express the same thing as the bust of Cæsar or the *Critique of Pure Reason*. What constitutes the individual expressiveness of these things is the circle of thoughts allied to each in a given mind; my words, for instance, express the thoughts which they actually arouse in the reader; they may express more to one man than to another, and to me they may have expressed more or less than to you. My thoughts remain unexpressed, if my words do not arouse them in you, and very likely your greater wisdom will find in what I say the manifestation of a thousand principles of which I never dreamed. Expression depends upon the union of two terms, one of which must be furnished by the imagination; and a mind cannot furnish what it does not possess. The expressiveness of everything accordingly increases with the intelligence of the observer.

But for expression to be an element of beauty, it must, of course, fulfil another condition. I may see the relations of an object, I may understand it perfectly, and may nevertheless regard it with entire indifference. If the pleasure fails, the very substance and protoplasm of beauty is wanting. Nor, as we have seen, is even the pleasure enough; for I may receive a letter full of the most joyous news, but neither the paper, nor the writing, nor the style, need seem beautiful to me. Not until I confound the impressions, and suffuse the symbols themselves with the emotions they arouse, and find joy and sweetness in the very words I hear, will the expressiveness constitute a beauty; as when they sing, *Gloria in excelsis Deo.*

The value of the second term must be incorporated in the first; for the beauty of expression is as inherent in the object as that of material or form, only it accrues to that object not from the bare act of perception, but from the association with it of further processes, due to the existence of former impressions. We may conveniently use the word "expressiveness" to mean all the capacity of suggestion possessed by a thing, and the word "expression" for the æsthetic modification which that expressiveness may cause in it. Expressiveness is thus the power given by experience to any image to call up others in the mind; and this expressiveness becomes an æsthetic value, that is, becomes expression, when the value involved in the associations thus awakened are incorporated in the present object.

§ 49. THE ASSOCIATIVE PROCESS. The purest case in which an expressive value could arise might seem to be that in which both terms were indifferent in themselves, and what pleased was the activity of relating them. We have such a phenomenon in mathematics, and in any riddle, puzzle, or play with symbols. But such pleasures fall without the æsthetic field in the absence of any objectification; they are pleasures of exercise, and the objects involved are not regarded as the substances in which those values inhere. We think of more or less interesting problems or calculations, but it never occurs to the mathematician to establish a hierarchy of forms according to their beauty. Only by a metaphor could he say that $(a + b)^2 = a^2 + 2ab + b^2$ was a more beautiful formula than $2 + 2 = 4$. Yet in proportion as such conceptions become definite and objective in the mind, they approach æsthetic values, and the use of æsthetic epithets in describing them becomes more constant and literal.

The beauties of abstract music are but one step beyond such

mathematical relations—they are those relations presented in a sensible form, and constituting an imaginable object. But, as we see clearly in this last case, when the relation and not the terms constitute the object, we have, if there is beauty at all, a beauty of form, not of expression; for the more mathematical the charm of music is, the more form and the less expression do we see in it. In fact, the sense of relation is here the essence of the object itself, and the activity of passing from term to term, far from taking us beyond our presentation to something extrinsic, constitutes that presentation. The pleasure of this relational activity is therefore the pleasure of conceiving a determined form, and nothing could be more thoroughly a formal beauty.

And we may here insist upon a point of fundamental importance; namely, that the process of association enters consciousness as directly, and produces as simple a sensation, as any process in any organ. The pleasures and pains of cerebration, the delight and the fatigue of it, are felt exactly like bodily impressions; they have the same directness, although not the same localization. Their seat is not open to our daily observation, and therefore we leave them disembodied, and fancy they are peculiarly spiritual and intimate to the soul. Or we try to think that they flow by some logical necessity from the essences of objects simultaneously in our mind. We involve ourselves in endless perplexities in trying to deduce excellence and beauty, unity and necessity, from the describable qualities of things; we repeat the rationalistic fiction of turning the notions which we abstract from the observation of facts into the powers that give those facts character and being.

We have, for instance, in the presence of two images a sense of their incongruity; and we say that the character of the images causes this emotion; whereas in dreams we constantly have the most rapid transformations and patent contradictions without any sense of incongruity at all; because the brain is dozing and the necessary shock and mental inhibition are avoided. Add this stimulation, and the incongruity returns. Had such a shock never been felt, we should not know what incongruity meant; no more than without eyes we should know the meaning of blue or yellow.

In saying this, we are not really leaning upon physiological theory. The appeal to our knowledge of the brain facilitates the conception of the immediacy of our feelings of relation; but the immediacy would be apparent to a sharp introspection. We do not need to think of the eye or skin to feel that light and heat are ultimate data; no more do we need to think of cerebral excitements to see that right and left, before and after, good and bad, one and two, like and unlike, are irreducible feelings. The categories are senses without organs, or with organs unknown. Just as the discrimination of our feelings of colour and sound might never have been distinct and constant, had we not come upon the organs that seem to convey and control them; so perhaps our classification of our inner sensations will never be settled until their respective organs are discovered; for psychology has always been physiological, without knowing it. But this truth remains—quite apart from physical conceptions, not to speak of metaphysical materialism—that whatever the historical conditions of any state of mind may be said to be, it exists, when it does exist, immediately and absolutely; each of its distinguishable parts might conceivably have been absent from it; and its character, as well as its existence, is a mere datum of sense.

The pleasure that belongs to the consciousness of relations is therefore as immediate as any other; indeed, our emotional consciousness is always single, but we treat it as a resultant of many and even of conflicting feelings because we look at it historically with a view to comprehending it, and distribute it into as many factors as we find objects or causes to which to attribute it. The pleasure of association is an immediate feeling, which we account for by its relation to a feeling in the past, or to cerebral structure modified by a former experience; just as memory itself, which we explain by a reference to the past, is a peculiar complication of present consciousness.

§ 50. Kinds of value in the second term. These reflections may make less surprising to us what is the most striking fact about the philosophy of expression; namely, that the value acquired by the expressive thing is often of an entirely different kind from that which the thing expressed possesses. The expression of physical pleasure, of passion, or even of pain, may constitute beauty and please the beholder. Thus the value of the second term may be physical, or practical, or even negative; and it may be transmuted, as it passes to the first term, into a value at once positive and æsthetic. The transformation of practical values into æsthetic has often been noted, and has even led to the theory that beauty is utility seen at arm's length; a premonition of pleasure and prosperity, much as smell is a premonition of taste. The transformation of negative values into positive has naturally attracted even more attention, and given rise to various theories of the comic, tragic, and sublime. For these three species of æsthetic good seem to please us by the suggestion of evil; and the problem arises how a mind can be made happier by having suggestions of unhappiness stirred within it; an unhappiness it cannot understand without in some degree sharing in it. We must now turn to the analysis of this question.

The expressiveness of a smile is not discovered exactly through association of images. The child smiles (without knowing it) when he feels pleasure; and the nurse smiles back; his own pleasure is associated with her conduct, and her smile is therefore expressive of pleasure. The fact of his pleasure at her smile is the ground of his instinctive belief in her pleasure in it. For this reason the circumstances expressive of happiness are not those that are favourable to it in reality, but those that are congruous with it in idea. The green of spring, the bloom of youth, the variability of childhood, the splendour of wealth and beauty, all these are symbols of happiness, not because they have been known to accompany it in fact,—for they do not, any more than their opposites,—but because they produce an image and echo of it in us æsthetically. We believe those things to be happy which it makes us happy to think of or to see; the belief in the blessedness of the supreme being itself has no other foundation. Our joy in the thought of omniscience makes us attribute joy to the possession of it, which it would in fact perhaps be very far from involving or even allowing.

The expressiveness of forms has a value as a sign of the life that actually inhabits those forms only when they resemble our own body; it is then probable that similar conditions of body involve, in them and in us, similar emotions; and we should not long continue to regard as the expression of pleasure an attitude that we know, by experience in our own person, to accompany pain. Children, indeed, may innocently torture animals, not having enough sense of analogy to be stopped by the painful suggestions of their writhings; and, although in a rough way we soon correct these crying misinterpretations by a better classification of experience, we nevertheless remain essentially subject to the same error. We cannot escape it, because the method which involves it is the only one that justifies belief in objective consciousness at all. Analogy of bodies helps us to distribute and classify the life we conceive about us; but what leads us to conceive it is the direct association of our own feeling with images of things, an association which precedes any clear representation of our own gestures and attitude. I know that smiles mean pleasure before I have caught myself smiling in the glass; they mean pleasure because they give it.

Since these æsthetic effects include some of the most moving and profound beauties, philosophers have not been slow to turn the unanalyzed paradox of their formation into a principle, and to explain by it the presence and necessity of evil. As in the tragic and the sublime, they have thought, the sufferings and dangers to which a hero is exposed seem to add to his virtue and dignity, and to our sacred joy in the contemplation of him, so the sundry evils of life may be elements in the transcendent glory of the whole. And once fired by this thought, those who pretend to justify the ways of God to man have, naturally, not stopped to consider whether so edifying a phenomenon was not a hasty illusion. They have, indeed, detested any attempt to explain it rationally, as tending to obscure one of the moral laws of the universe. In venturing, therefore, to repeat such an attempt, we should not be too sanguine of success; for we have to encounter not only the intrinsic difficulties of the problem, but also a wide-spread and arrogant metaphysical prejudice.

For the sake of greater clearness we may begin by classifying the values that can enter into expression; we shall then be better able to judge by what combinations of them various well-known effects and emotions are produced. The intrinsic value of the first term can be entirely neglected, since it does not contribute to expression. It does, however, contribute greatly to the beauty of the expressive object. The first term is the source of stimulation, and the acuteness and pleasantness of this determine to a great extent the character and sweep of the associations that will be aroused. Very often the pleasantness of the medium will counterbalance the disagreeableness of the import, and expressions, in themselves hideous or inappropriate, may be excused for the sake of the object that conveys them. A beautiful voice will redeem a vulgar song, a beautiful colour and texture an unmeaning composition. Beauty in the first term—beauty of sound, rhythm, and image—will make any thought whatever poetic, while no thought whatever can be so without that immediate beauty of presentation.[1]

[1] Curiously enough, common speech here reverses our use of terms, because it looks at the matter from the practical instead of from the æsthetic point of view, regarding (very unpsychologically) the thought as the source of the image, not the image as the source of the thought. People call the words the expression of the thought: whereas for the observer, the hearer (and generally for the speaker, too), the words are the datum and the thought is their expressiveness—that which they suggest.

§ 51. ÆSTHETIC VALUE IN THE SECOND TERM. That the noble associations of any object should embellish that object is very comprehensible. Homer furnishes us with a good illustration of the constant employment of this effect. The first term, one need hardly say, leaves with him little to be desired. The verse is beautiful. Sounds, images, and composition conspire to stimulate and delight. This immediate beauty is sometimes used to clothe things terrible and sad; there is no dearth of the tragic in Homer. But the tendency of his poetry is nevertheless to fill the outskirts of our consciousness with the trooping images of things no less fair and noble than the verse itself. The heroes are virtuous. There is none of importance who is not admirable in his way. The palaces, the arms, the horses, the sacrifices, are always excellent. The women are always stately and beautiful. The ancestry and the history of every one are honourable and good. The whole Homeric world is clean, clear, beautiful, and providential, and no small part of the perennial charm of the poet is that he thus immerses us in an atmosphere of beauty; a beauty not concentrated and reserved for some extraordinary sentiment, action, or person, but permeating the whole and colouring the common world of soldiers and sailors, war and craft, with a marvellous freshness and inward glow. There is nothing in the associations of life in this world or in another to contradict or disturb our delight. All is beautiful, and beautiful through and through.

Something of this quality meets us in all simple and idyllic compositions. There is, for instance, a popular demand that stories and comedies should "end well." The hero and heroine must be young and handsome; unless they die,—which is another matter,—they must not in the end be poor. The landscape in the play must be beautiful; the dresses pretty; the plot without serious mishap. A pervasive presentation of pleasure must give warmth and ideality to the whole. In the proprieties of social life we find the same principle; we study to make our surroundings, manner, and conversation suggest nothing but what is pleasing. We hide the ugly and disagreeable portion of our lives, and do not allow the least hint of it to come to light upon festive and public occasions. Whenever, in a word, a thoroughly pleasing effect is found, it is found by the expression, as well as presentation, of what is in itself pleasing—and when this effect is to be produced artificially, we attain it by the suppression of all expression that is not suggestive of something good.

If our consciousness were exclusively æsthetic, this kind of expression would be the only one allowed in art or prized in nature. We should avoid as a shock or an insipidity, the suggestion of anything not intrinsically beautiful. As there would be no values not æsthetic, our pleasure could never be heightened by any other kind of interest. But as contemplation is actually a luxury in our lives, and things interest us chiefly on passionate and practical grounds, the accumulation of values too exclusively æsthetic produces in our minds an effect of closeness and artificiality. So selective a diet cloys, and our palate, accustomed to much daily vinegar and salt, is surfeited by such unmixed sweet.

Instead we prefer to see through the medium of art—through the beautiful first term of our expression—the miscellaneous world which is so well known to us—perhaps so dear, and at any rate so inevitable, an object. We are more thankful for this presentation of the unlovely truth in a lovely form, than for the like presentation of an abstract beauty; what is lost in the purity of the pleasure is gained in the stimulation of our attention, and in the relief of viewing with æsthetic detachment the same things that in practical life hold tyrannous dominion over our souls. The beauty that is associated only with other beauty is therefore a sort of æsthetic dainty; it leads the fancy through a fairyland of lovely forms, where we must forget the common objects of our interest. The charm of such an idealization is undeniable; but the other important elements of our memory and will cannot long be banished. Thoughts of labour, ambition, lust, anger, confusion, sorrow, and death must needs mix with our contemplation and lend their various expressions to the objects with which in experience they are so closely allied. Hence the incorporation in the beautiful of values of other sorts, and the comparative rareness in nature or art of expressions the second term of which has only æsthetic value.

§ 52. Practical value in the same. More important and frequent is the case of the expression of utility. This is found whenever the second term is the idea of something of practical advantage to us, the premonition of which brings satisfaction; and this satisfaction prompts an approval of the presented object. The tone of our consciousness is raised by the foretaste of a success; and this heightened pleasure is objectified in the present image, since the associated image to which the satisfaction properly belongs often fails to become distinct. We do not conceive clearly what this practical advantage will be; but the vague sense that an advantage is there, that something desirable has been done, accompanies the presentation, and gives it expression.

The case that most resembles that of which we have been just speaking, is perhaps that in which the second term is a piece of interesting information, a theory, or other intellectual datum. Our interest in facts and theories, when not æsthetic, is of course practical; it consists in their connexion with our interests, and in the service they can render us in the execution of our designs. Intellectual values are utilitarian in their origin but æsthetic in their form, since the advantage of knowledge is often lost sight of, and ideas are prized for their own sake. Curiosity can become a disinterested passion, and yield intimate and immediate satisfaction like any other impulse.

When we have before us, for instance, a fine map, in which the line of coast, now rocky, now sandy, is clearly indicated, together with the windings of the rivers, the elevations of the land, and the distribution of the population, we have the simultaneous suggestion of so many facts, the sense of mastery over so much reality, that we gaze at it with delight, and need no practical motive to keep us studying it, perhaps for hours together. A map is not naturally thought of as an æsthetic object; it is too exclusively expressive. The first term is passed over as a mere symbol, and the mind is filled either with imaginations of the landscape the country would really offer, or with thoughts about its history and inhabitants. These circumstances prevent the ready objectification of our pleasure in the map itself. And yet, let the tints of it be a little subtle, let the lines be a little delicate, and the masses of land and sea somewhat balanced, and we really have a beautiful thing; a thing the charm of which consists almost entirely in its meaning, but which nevertheless pleases us in the same way as a picture or a graphic symbol might please. Give the symbol a little intrinsic worth of form, line, and colour, and it attracts like a magnet all the values of the things it is known to symbolize. It becomes beautiful in its expressiveness.

Hardly different from this example is that of travel or of reading; for in these employments we get many æsthetic pleasures, the origin of which is in the satisfaction of curiosity and intelligence. When we say admiringly of anything that it is characteristic, that it embodies a whole period or a whole man, we are absorbed by the pleasant sense that it offers innumerable avenues of approach to interesting and important things. The less we are able to specify what these are, the more beautiful will the object be that expresses them. For if we could specify them, the felt value would disintegrate, and distribute itself among the ideas of the suggested things, leaving the expressive object bare of all interest, like the letters of a printed page.

The courtiers of Philip the Second probably did not regard his rooms at the Escurial as particularly interesting, but simply as small, ugly, and damp. The character which we find in them and which makes us regard them as eminently expressive of whatever was sinister in the man, probably did not strike them. They knew the king, and had before them words, gestures, and acts enough in which to read his character. But all these living facts are wanting to our experience; and it is the suggestion of them in their unrealizable vagueness that fills the apartments of the monarch with such pungent expression. It is not otherwise with all emphatic expressiveness—moonlight and castle moats, minarets and cypresses, camels filing through the desert—such images get their character from the strong but misty atmosphere of sentiment and adventure which clings about them. The profit of travel, and the extraordinary charm of all visible relics of antiquity, consists in the acquisition of images in which to focus a mass of discursive knowledge, not otherwise felt together. Such images are concrete symbols of much latent experience, and the deep roots of association give them the same hold upon our attention which might be secured by a fortunate form or splendid material.

§ 53. Cost as an element of effect. There is one consideration which often adds much to the interest with which we view an object, but which we might be virtuously inclined not to admit among æsthetic values. I mean cost. Cost is practical value expressed in abstract terms, and from the price of anything we can often infer what relation it has to the desires and efforts of mankind. There is no reason why cost, or the circumstances which are its basis, should not, like other practical values, heighten the tone of consciousness, and add to the pleasure with which we view an object. In fact, such is our daily experience; for great as is the sensuous beauty of gems, their rarity and price adds an expression of distinction to them, which they would never have if they were cheap.

The circumstance that makes the appreciation of cost often unæsthetic is the abstractness of that quality. The price of an object is an algebraic symbol, it is a conventional term, invented to facilitate our operations, which remains arid and unmeaning if we stop with it and forget to translate it again at the end into its concrete equivalent. The commercial mind dwells in that intermediate limbo of symbolized values; the calculator's senses are muffled by his intellect and by his habit of abbreviated thinking. His mental process is a reckoning that loses sight of its original values, and is over without reaching any concrete image. Therefore the knowledge of cost, when expressed in terms of money, is incapable of contributing to æsthetic effect, but the reason is not so much that the suggested value is not æsthetic, as that no real value is suggested at all. No object of any kind is presented to the mind by the numerical expression. If we reinterpret our price, however, and translate it back into the facts which constitute it, into the materials employed, their original place and quality, and the labour and art which transformed them into the present thing, then we add to the æsthetic value of the object, by the expression which we find in it, not of its price in money, but of its human cost. We have now the consciousness of the real values which it represents, and these values, sympathetically present to the fancy, increase our present interest and admiration.

I believe economists count among the elements of the value of an object the rarity of its material, the labour of its manufacture, and the distance from which it is brought. Now all these qualities, if attended to in themselves, appeal greatly to the imagination. We have a natural interest in what is rare and affects us with unusual sensations. What comes from a far country carries our thoughts there, and gains by the wealth and picturesqueness of its associations. And that on which human labour has been spent, especially if it was a labour of love, and is apparent in the product, has one of the deepest possible claims to admiration. So that the standard of cost, the most vulgar of all standards, is such only when it remains empty and abstract. Let the thoughts wander back and consider the elements of value, and our appreciation, from being verbal and commercial, becomes poetic and real.

We have in this one more example of the manner in which practical values, when suggested by and incorporated in any object, contribute to its beauty. Our sense of what lies behind, unlovely though that background may be, gives interest and poignancy to that which is present; our attention and wonder are engaged, and a new meaning and importance is added to such intrinsic beauty as the presentation may possess.

§ 54. THE EXPRESSION OF ECONOMY AND FITNESS. The same principle explains the effect of evident cleanliness, security, economy, and comfort. This Dutch charm hardly needs explanation; we are conscious of the domesticity and neatness which pleases us in it. There are few things more utterly discomforting to our minds than waste: it is a sort of pungent extract and quintessence of folly. The visible manifestation of it is therefore very offensive; and that of its absence very reassuring. The force of our approval of practical fitness and economy in things rises into an appreciation that is half-æsthetic, and which becomes wholly so when the fit form becomes fixed in a type, to the lines of which we are accustomed; so that the practical necessity of the form is heightened and concentrated into the æsthetic propriety of it.

The much-praised expression of function and truth in architectural works reduces itself to this principle. The useful contrivance at first appeals to our practical approval; while we admire its ingenuity, we cannot fail to become gradually accustomed to its presence, and to register with attentive pleasure the relation of its parts. Utility, as we have pointed out in its place, is thus the guiding principle in the determination of forms.

The recurring observation of the utility, economy, and fitness of the traditional arrangement in buildings or other products of art, re-enforces this formal expectation with a reflective approval. We are accustomed, for instance, to sloping roofs; the fact that they were necessary has made them familiar, and the fact that they are familiar has made them objects of study and of artistic enjoyment. If at any moment, however, the notion of condemning them passes through the mind,—if we have visions of the balustrade against the sky,—we revert to our homely image with kindly loyalty, when we remember the long months of rain and snow, and the comfortless leaks to be avoided. The thought of a glaring, practical unfitness is enough to spoil our pleasure in any form, however beautiful intrinsically, while the sense of practical fitness is enough to reconcile us to the most awkward and rude contrivances.

This principle is, indeed, not a fundamental, but an auxiliary one; the expression of utility modifies effect, but does not constitute it. There would be a kind of superstitious haste in the notion that what is convenient and economical is necessarily and by miracle beautiful. The uses and habits of one place and society require works which are or may easily become intrinsically beautiful; the uses and habits of another make these beautiful works impossible. The beauty has a material and formal basis that we have already studied; no fitness of design will make a building of ten equal storeys as beautiful as a pavilion or a finely proportioned tower; no utility will make a steamboat as beautiful as a sailing vessel. But the forms once established, with their various intrinsic characters, the fitness we know to exist in them will lend them some added charm, or their unfitness will disquiet us, and haunt us like a conscientious qualm. The other interests of our lives here mingle with the purely æsthetic, to enrich or to embitter it.

If Sybaris is so sad a name to the memory—and who is without some Sybaris of his own?—if the image of it is so tormenting and in the end so disgusting, this is not because we no longer think its marbles bright, its fountains cool, its athletes strong, or its roses fragrant; but because, mingled with all these supreme beauties, there is the ubiquitous shade of Nemesis, the sense of a vacant will and a suicidal inhumanity. The intolerableness of this moral condition poisons the beauty which continues to be felt. If this beauty did not exist, and was not still desired, the tragedy would disappear and Jehovah would be deprived of the worth of his victim. The sternness of moral forces lies precisely in this, that the sacrifices morality imposes upon us are real, that the things it renders impossible are still precious.

We are accustomed to think of prudence as estranging us only from low and ignoble things; we forget that utility and the need of system in our lives is a bar also to the free flights of the spirit. The highest instincts tend to disorganization as much as the lowest, since order and benefit is what practical morality everywhere insists upon, while sanctity and genius are as rebellious as vice. The constant demands of the heart and the belly can allow man only an incidental indulgence in the pleasures of the eye and the understanding. For this reason, utility keeps close watch over beauty, lest in her wilfulness and riot she should offend against our practical needs and ultimate happiness. And when the conscience is keen, this vigilance of the practical imagination over the speculative ceases to appear as an eventual and external check. The least suspicion of luxury, waste, impurity, or cruelty is then a signal for alarm and insurrection. That which emits this *sapor hœreticus* becomes so initially horrible, that naturally no beauty can ever be discovered in it; the senses and imagination are in that case inhibited by the conscience.

For this reason, the doctrine that beauty is essentially nothing but the expression of moral or practical good appeals to persons of predominant moral sensitiveness, not only because they wish it were the truth, but because it largely describes the experience of their own minds, somewhat warped in this particular. It will further be observed that the moralists are much more able to condemn than to appreciate the effects of the arts. Their taste is delicate without being keen, for the principle on which they judge is one which really operates to control and extend æsthetic effects; it is a source of expression and of certain *nuances* of satisfaction; but it is foreign to the stronger and more primitive æsthetic values to which the same persons are comparatively blind.

§ 55. THE AUTHORITY OF MORALS OVER ÆSTHETICS. The extent to which æsthetic goods should be sacrificed is, of course, a moral question; for the function of practical reason is to compare, combine, and harmonize all our interests, with a view to attaining the greatest satisfactions of which our nature is capable. We must expect, therefore, that virtue should place the same restraint upon all our passions—not from superstitious aversion to any one need, but from an equal concern for them all. The consideration to be given to our æsthetic pleasures will depend upon their greater or less influence upon our happiness; and as this influence varies in different ages and countries, and with different individuals, it will be right to let æsthetic demands count for more or for less in the organization of life.

We may, indeed, according to our personal sympathies, prefer one type of creature to another. We may love the martial, or the angelic, or the political temperament. We may delight to find in others that balance of susceptibilities and enthusiasms which we feel in our own breast. But no moral precept can require one species or individual to change its nature in order to resemble another, since such a requirement can have no power or authority over those on whom we would impose it. All that morality can require is the inward harmony of each life: and if we still abhor the thought of a possible being who should be happy without love, or knowledge, or beauty, the aversion we feel is not moral but instinctive, not rational but human. What revolts us is not the want of excellence in that other creature, but his want of affinity to ourselves. Could we survey the whole universe, we might indeed assign to each species a moral dignity proportionate to its general beneficence and inward wealth; but such an absolute standard, if it exists, is incommunicable to us; and we are reduced to judging of the excellence of every nature by its relation to the human.

All these matters, however, belong to the sphere of ethics, nor should we give them here even a passing notice, but for the influence which moral ideas exert over æsthetic judgments. Our sense of practical benefit not only determines the moral value of beauty, but sometimes even its existence as an æsthetic good. Especially in the right *selection* of effects, these considerations have weight. Forms in themselves pleasing may become disagreeable when the practical interests then uppermost in the mind cannot, without violence, yield a place to them. Thus too much eloquence in a diplomatic document, or in a familiar letter, or in a prayer, is an offence not only against practical sense, but also against taste. The occasion has tuned us to a certain key of sentiment, and deprived us of the power to respond to other stimuli.

If things of moment are before us, we cannot stop to play with symbols and figures of speech. We cannot attend to them with pleasure, and therefore they lose the beauty they might elsewhere have had. They are offensive, not in themselves,—for nothing is intrinsically ugly,—but by virtue of our present demand for something different. A prison as gay as a bazaar, a church as dumb as a prison, offend by their failure to support by their æsthetic quality the moral emotion with which we approach them. The arts must study their occasions; they must stand modestly aside until they can slip in fitly into the interstices of life. This is the consequence of the superficial stratum on which they flourish; their roots, as we have seen, are not deep in the world, and they appear only as unstable, superadded activities, employments of our freedom, after the work of life is done and the terror of it is allayed. They must, therefore, fit their forms, like parasites, to the stouter growths to which they cling.

Herein lies the greatest difficulty and nicety of art. It must not only create things abstractly beautiful, but it must conciliate all the competitors these may have to the attention of the world, and must know how to insinuate their charms among the objects of our passion. But this subserviency and enforced humility of beauty is not without its virtue and reward. If the æsthetic habit lie under the necessity of respecting and observing our passions, it possesses the privilege of soothing our griefs. There is no situation so terrible that it may not be relieved by the momentary pause of the mind to contemplate it æsthetically.

Grief itself becomes in this way not wholly pain; a sweetness is added to it by our reflection. The saddest scenes may lose their bitterness in their beauty. This ministration makes, as it were, the piety of the Muses, who succour their mother, Life, and repay her for their nurture by the comfort of their continual presence. The æsthetic world is limited in its scope; it must submit to the control of the organizing reason, and not trespass upon more useful and holy ground. The garden must not encroach upon the corn-fields; but the eye of the gardener may transform the corn-fields themselves by dint of loving observation into a garden of a soberer kind. By finding grandeur in our disasters, and merriment in our mishaps, the æsthetic sense thus mollifies both, and consoles us for the frequent impossibility of a serious and perfect beauty.

§ 56. NEGATIVE VALUES IN THE SECOND TERM. All subjects, even the most repellent, when the circumstances of life thrust them before us, can thus be observed with curiosity and treated with art. The calling forth of these æsthetic functions softens the violence of our sympathetic reaction. If death, for instance, did not exist and did not thrust itself upon our thoughts with painful importunity, art would never have been called upon to soften and dignify it, by presenting it in beautiful forms and surrounding it with consoling associations. Art does not seek out the pathetic, the tragic, and the absurd; it is life that has imposed them upon our attention, and enlisted art in their service, to make the contemplation of them, since it is inevitable, at least as tolerable as possible.

The agreeableness of the presentation is thus mixed with the horror of the thing; and the result is that while we are saddened by the truth we are delighted by the vehicle that conveys it to us. The mixture of these emotions constitutes the peculiar flavour and poignancy of pathos. But because unlovely objects and feelings are often so familiar as to be indifferent or so momentous as to be alone in the mind, we are led into the confusion of supposing that beauty depends upon them for its æsthetic value; whereas the truth is that only by the addition of positive beauties can these evil experiences be made agreeable to contemplation.

There is, in reality, no such paradox in the tragic, comic, and sublime, as has been sometimes supposed. We are not pleased by virtue of the suggested evils, but in spite of them; and if ever the charm of the beautiful presentation sinks so low, or the vividness of the represented evil rises so high, that the balance is in favour of pain, at that very moment the whole object becomes horrible, passes out of the domain of art, and can be justified only by its scientific or moral uses. As an æsthetic value it is destroyed; it ceases to be a benefit; and the author of it, if he were not made harmless by the neglect that must soon overtake him, would have to be punished as a malefactor who adds to the burden of mortal life. For the sad, the ridiculous, the grotesque, and the terrible, unless they become æsthetic goods, remain moral evils.

We have, therefore, to study the various æsthetic, intellectual, and moral compensations by which the mind can be brought to contemplate with pleasure a thing which, if experienced alone, would be the cause of pain. There is, to be sure, a way of avoiding this inquiry. We might assert that since all moderate excitement is pleasant, there is nothing strange in the fact that the representation of evil should please; for the experience is evil by virtue of the pain it gives; but it gives pain only when felt with great intensity. Observed from afar, it is a pleasing impression; it is vivid enough to interest, but not acute enough to wound. This simple explanation is possible in all those cases where æsthetic effect is gained by the inhibition of sympathy.

The term "evil" is often a conventional epithet; a conflagration may be called an evil, because it usually involves loss and suffering; but if, without caring for a loss and suffering we do not share, we are delighted by the blaze, and still say that what pleases us is an evil, we are using this word as a conventional appellation, not as the mark of a felt value. We are not pleased by an evil; we are pleased by a vivid and exciting sensation, which is a good, but which has for objective cause an event which may indeed be an evil to others, but about the consequences of which we are not thinking at all. There is, in this sense, nothing in all nature, perhaps, which is not an evil; nothing which is not unfavourable to some interest, and does not involve some infinitesimal or ultimate suffering in the universe of life.

But when we are ignorant or thoughtless, this suffering is to us as if it did not exist. The pleasures of drinking and walking are not tragic to us, because we may be poisoning some bacillus or crushing some worm. To an omniscient intelligence such acts may be tragic by virtue of the insight into their relations to conflicting impulses; but unless these impulses are present to the same mind, there is no consciousness of tragedy. The child that, without understanding of the calamity, should watch a shipwreck from the shore, would have a simple emotion of pleasure as from a jumping jack; what passes for tragic interest is often nothing but this. If he understood the event, but was entirely without sympathy, he would have the æsthetic emotion of the careless tyrant, to whom the notion of suffering is no hindrance to the enjoyment of the lyre. If the temper of his tyranny were purposely cruel, he might add to that æsthetic delight the luxury of *Schadenfreude;* but the pathos and horror of the sight could only appeal to a man who realized and shared the sufferings he beheld.

A great deal of brutal tragedy has been endured in the world because the rudeness of the representation, or of the public, or of both, did not allow a really sympathetic reaction to arise. We all smile when Punch beats Judy in the puppet show. The treatment and not the subject is what makes a tragedy. A parody of *Hamlet* or of *King Lear* would not be a tragedy; and these tragedies themselves are not wholly such, but by the strain of wit and nonsense they contain are, as it were, occasional parodies on themselves. By treating a tragic subject bombastically or satirically we can turn it into an amusement for the public; they will not feel the griefs which we have been careful to harden them against by arousing in them contrary emotions. A work, nominally a work of art, may also appeal to non-æsthetic feelings by its political bias, brutality, or obscenity. But if an effect of true pathos is sought, the sympathy of the observer must be aroused; we must awaken in him the emotion we describe. The intensity of the impression must not be so slight that its painful quality is not felt; for it is this very sense of pain, mingling with the æsthetic excitement of the spectacle, that gives it a tragic or pathetic colouring.

We cannot therefore rest in the assertion that the slighter degree of excitement is pleasant, when a greater degree of the same would be disagreeable; for that principle does not express the essence of the matter, which is that we must be aware of the evil, and conscious of it as such, absorbed more or less in the experience of the sufferer, and consequently suffering ourselves, before we can experience the essence of tragic emotion. This emotion must therefore be complex; it must contain an element of pain overbalanced by an element of pleasure; in our delight there must be a distinguishable touch of shrinking and sorrow; for it is this conflict and rending of our will, this fascination by what is intrinsically terrible or sad, that gives these turbid feelings their depth and pungency.

§ 57. INFLUENCE OF THE FIRST TERM IN THE PLEASING EXPRESSION OF EVIL. A striking proof of the compound nature of tragic effects can be given by a simple experiment. Remove from any drama—say from *Othello*—the charm of the medium of presentation; reduce the tragedy to a mere account of the facts and of the words spoken, such as our newspapers almost daily contain; and the tragic dignity and beauty is entirely lost. Nothing remains but a disheartening item of human folly, which may still excite curiosity, but which will rather defile than purify the mind that considers it. A French poet has said:

> Il n'est de vulgaire chagrin
> Que celui d'une âme vulgaire.

The counterpart of this maxim is equally true. There is no noble sorrow except in a noble mind, because what is noble is the reaction upon the sorrow, the attitude of the man in its presence, the language in which he clothes it, the associations with which he surrounds it, and the fine affections and impulses which shine through it. Only by suffusing some sinister experience with this moral light, as a poet may do who carries that light within him, can we raise misfortune into tragedy and make it better for us to remember our lives than to forget them.

There are times, although rare, when men are noble in the very moment of passion: when that passion is not unqualified, but already mastered by reflection and levelled with truth. Then the experience is itself the tragedy, and no poet is needed to make it beautiful in representation, since the sufferer has been an artist himself, and has moulded what he has endured. But usually these two stages have to be successive: first we suffer, afterwards we sing. An interval is necessary to make feeling presentable, and subjugate it to that form in which alone it is beautiful.

This form appeals to us in itself, and without its aid no subject-matter could become an æsthetic object. The more terrible the experience described, the more powerful must the art be which is to transform it. For this reason prose and literalness are more tolerable in comedy than in tragedy; any violent passion, any overwhelming pain, if it is not to make us think of a demonstration in pathology, and bring back the smell of ether, must be rendered in the most exalted style. Metre, rhyme, melody, the widest flights of allusion, the highest reaches of fancy, are there in place. For these enable the mind swept by the deepest cosmic harmonies, to endure and absorb the shrill notes which would be intolerable in a poorer setting.

The sensuous harmony of words, and still more the effects of rhythm, are indispensable at this height of emotion. Evolutionists have said that violent emotion naturally expresses itself in rhythm. That is hardly an empirical observation, nor can the expressiveness of rhythms be made definite enough to bear specific association with complex feelings. But the suspension and rush of sound and movement have in themselves a strong effect; we cannot undergo them without profound excitement; and this, like martial music, nerves us to courage and, by a sort of intoxication, bears us along amid scenes which might otherwise be sickening. The vile effect of literal and disjointed renderings of suffering, whether in writing or acting, proves how necessary is the musical quality to tragedy—a fact Aristotle long ago set forth. The afflatus of rhythm, even if it be the pomp of the Alexandrine, sublimates the passion, and clarifies its mutterings into poetry. This breadth and rationality are necessary to art, which is not skill merely, but skill in the service of beauty.

§ 58. MIXTURE OF OTHER EXPRESSIONS, INCLUDING THAT OF TRUTH. To the value of these sensuous and formal elements must be added the continual suggestion of beautiful and happy things, which no tragedy is sombre enough to exclude. Even if we do not go so far as to intersperse comic scenes and phrases into a pathetic subject,—a rude device, since the comic passages themselves need that purifying which they are meant to effect,—we must at least relieve our theme with pleasing associations. For this reason we have palaces for our scene, rank, beauty, and virtue in our heroes, nobility in their passions and in their fate, and altogether a sort of glorification of life without which tragedy would lose both in depth of pathos—since things so precious are destroyed— and in subtlety of charm, since things so precious are manifested.

Indeed, one of the chief charms that tragedies have is the suggestion of what they might have been if they had not been tragedies. The happiness which glimmers through them, the hopes, loves, and ambitions of which it is made, these things fascinate us, and win our sympathy; so that we are all the more willing to suffer with our heroes, even if we are at the same time all the more sensitive to their suffering. Too wicked a character or too unrelieved a situation revolts us for this reason. We do not find enough expression of good to make us endure the expression of the evil.

A curious exception to this rule, which, however, admirably illustrates the fundamental principle of it, is where by the diversity of evils represented the mind is relieved from painful absorption in any of them. There is a scene in *King Lear*, where the horror of the storm is made to brood over at least four miseries, that of the king, of the fool, of Edgar in his real person, and of Edgar in his assumed character. The vividness of each of these portrayals, with its different note of pathos, keeps the mind detached and free, forces it to compare and reflect, and thereby to universalize the spectacle. Yet even here, the beautiful effect is not secured without some touches of good. How much is not gained by the dumb fidelity of the fool, and by the sublime humanity of Lear, when he says, "Art cold? There is a part of me is sorry for thee yet."

Yet all these compensations would probably be unavailing but for another which the saddest things often have,—the compensation of being true. Our practical and intellectual nature is deeply interested in truth. What describes fact appeals to us for that reason; it has an inalienable interest. However unpleasant truth may prove, we long to know it, partly perhaps because experience has shown us the prudence of this kind of intellectual courage, and chiefly because the consciousness of ignorance and the dread of the unknown is more tormenting than any possible discovery. A primitive instinct makes us turn the eyes full on any object that appears in the dim borderland of our field of vision—and this all the more quickly, the more terrible that object threatens to be.

This physical thirst for seeing has its intellectual extension. We covet truth, and to attain it, amid all accidents, is a supreme satisfaction. Now this satisfaction the representation of evil can also afford. Whether we hear the account of some personal accident, or listen to the symbolic representation of the inherent tragedy of life, we crave the same knowledge; the desire for truth makes us welcome eagerly whatever comes in its name. To be sure, the relief of such instruction does not of itself constitute an æsthetic pleasure: the other conditions of beauty remain to be fulfilled. But the satisfaction of so imperious an intellectual instinct insures our willing attention to the tragic object, and strengthens the hold which any beauties it may possess will take upon us. An intellectual value stands ready to be transmuted into an æsthetic one, if once its discursiveness is lost, and it is left hanging about the object as a vague sense of dignity and meaning.

To this must be added the specific pleasure of recognition, one of the keenest we have, and the sentimental one of nursing our own griefs and dignifying them by assimilation to a less inglorious representation of them. Here we have truth on a small scale; conformity in the fiction to incidents of our personal experience. Such correspondences are the basis of much popular appreciation of trivial and undigested works that appeal to some momentary phase of life or feeling, and disappear with it. They have the value of personal stimulants only; they never achieve beauty. Like the souvenirs of last season's gayeties, or the diary of an early love, they are often hideous in themselves in proportion as they are redolent with personal associations. But however hopelessly mere history or confession may fail to constitute a work of art, a work of art that has an historical warrant, either literal or symbolical, gains the support of that vivid interest we have in facts. And many tragedies and farces, that to a mind without experience of this sublunary world might seem monstrous and disgusting fictions, may come to be forgiven and even perhaps preferred over all else, when they are found to be a sketch from life.

Truth is thus the excuse which ugliness has for being. Many people, in whom the pursuit of knowledge and the indulgence in sentiment have left no room for the cultivation of the æsthetic sense, look in art rather for this expression of fact or of passion than for the revelation of beauty. They accordingly produce and admire works without intrinsic value. They employ the procedure of the fine arts without an eye to what can give pleasure in the effect. They invoke rather the *a priori* interest which men are expected to have in the subject-matter, or in the theories and moral implied in the presentation of it. Instead of using the allurements of art to inspire wisdom, they require an appreciation of wisdom to make us endure their lack of art.

Of course, the instruments of the arts are public property and any one is free to turn them to new uses. It would be an interesting development of civilization if they should now be employed only as methods of recording scientific ideas and personal confessions. But the experiment has not succeeded and can hardly succeed. There are other simpler, clearer, and more satisfying ways of expounding truth. A man who is really a student of history or philosophy will never rest with the vague and

partial oracles of poetry, not to speak of the inarticulate suggestions of the plastic arts. He will at once make for the principles
which art cannot express, even if it can embody them, and
when those principles are attained, the works of art, if they had
no other value than that of suggesting them, will lapse from
his mind. Forms will give place to formulas as hieroglyphics have
given place to the letters of the alphabet.

If, on the other hand, the primary interest is really in beauty,
and only the confusion of a moral revolution has obscured for
a while the vision of the ideal, then as the mind regains its
mastery over the world, and digests its new experience, the
imagination will again be liberated, and create its forms by its
inward affinities, leaving all the weary burden, archæological,
psychological, and ethical, to those whose business is not to delight. But the sudden inundation of science and sentiment which
has made the mind of the nineteenth century so confused, by
overloading us with materials and breaking up our habits of
apperception and our ideals, has led to an exclusive sense of the
value of expressiveness, until this has been almost identified with
beauty. This exaggeration can best prove how the expression of
truth may enter into the play of æsthetic forces, and give a value
to representations which, but for it, would be repulsive.

§ 59. THE LIBERATION OF SELF. Hitherto we have been considering those elements of a pathetic presentation which may miti-
gate our sympathetic emotion, and make it on the whole
agreeable. These consist in the intrinsic beauties of the medium
of presentation, and in the concomitant manifestation of various
goods, notably of truth. The mixture of these values is perhaps
all we have in mildly pathetic works, in the presence of which
we are tolerably aware of a sort of balance and compensation
of emotions. The sorrow and the beauty, the hopelessness and
the consolation, mingle and merge into a kind of joy which has
its poignancy, indeed, but which is far too passive and peniten-
tial to contain the louder and sublimer of our tragic moods. In
these there is a wholeness, a strength, and a rapture, which still
demands an explanation.

Where this explanation is to be found may be guessed from
the following circumstance. The pathetic is a quality of the
object, at once lovable and sad, which we accept and allow to
flow in upon the soul; but the heroic is an attitude of the will,
by which the voices of the outer world are silenced, and a
moral energy, flowing from within, is made to triumph over

them. If we fail, therefore, to discover, by analysis of the object, anything which could make it sublime, we must not be surprised at our failure. We must remember that the object is always but a portion of our consciousness: that portion which has enough coherence and articulation to be recognized as permanent and projected into the outer world. But consciousness remains one, in spite of this diversification of its content, and the object is not really independent, but is in constant relation to the rest of the mind, in the midst of which it swims like a bubble on a dark surface of water.

The æsthetic effect of objects is always due to the total emotional value of the consciousness in which they exist. We merely attribute this value to the object by a projection which is the ground of the apparent objectivity of beauty. Sometimes this value may be inherent in the process by which the object itself is perceived; then we have sensuous and formal beauty; sometimes the value may be due to the incipient formation of other ideas, which the perception of this object evokes; then we have beauty of expression. But among the ideas with which every object has relation there is one vaguest, most comprehensive, and most powerful one, namely, the idea of self. The impulses, memories, principles, and energies which we designate by that word baffle enumeration; indeed, they constantly fade and change into one another; and whether the self is anything, everything, or nothing depends on the aspect of it which we momentarily fix, and especially on the definite object with which we contrast it.

Now, it is the essential privilege of beauty to so synthesize and bring to a focus the various impulses of the self, so to suspend them to a single image, that a great peace falls upon that perturbed kingdom. In the experience of these momentary harmonies we have the basis of the enjoyment of beauty, and of all its mystical meanings. But there are always two methods of securing harmony: one is to unify all the given elements, and another is to reject and expunge all the elements that refuse to be unified. Unity by inclusion gives us the beautiful; unity by exclusion, opposition, and isolation gives us the sublime. Both are pleasures: but the pleasure of the one is warm, passive, and pervasive; that of the other cold, imperious, and keen. The one identifies us with the world, the other raises us above it.

There can be no difficulty in understanding how the expression of evil in the object may be the occasion of this heroic reaction of the soul. In the first place, the evil may be felt; but at the same time the sense that, great as it may be in itself,

it cannot touch us, may stimulate extraordinarily the consciousness of our own wholeness. This is the sublimity which Lucretius
calls "sweet" in the famous lines in which he so justly analyzes
it. We are not pleased because another suffers an evil, but because, seeing it is an evil, we see at the same time our own
immunity from it. We might soften the picture a little, and perhaps make the principle even clearer by so doing. The shipwreck
observed from the shore does not leave us wholly unmoved; we
suffer, also, and if possible, would help. So, too, the spectacle
of the erring world must sadden the philosopher even in the
Acropolis of his wisdom; he would, if it might be, descend from
his meditation and teach. But those movements of sympathy are
quickly inhibited by despair of success; impossibility of action is
a great condition of the sublime. If we could count the stars,
we should not weep before them. While we think we can change
the drama of history, and of our own lives, we are not awed
by our destiny. But when the evil is irreparable, when our life
is lived, a strong spirit has the sublime resource of standing at
bay and of surveying almost from the other world the vicissitudes
of this.

The more intimate to himself the tragedy he is able to look
back upon with calmness, the more sublime that calmness is,
and the more divine the ecstasy in which he achieves it. For the
more of the accidental vesture of life we are able to strip ourselves of, the more naked and simple is the surviving spirit; the
more complete its superiority and unity, and, consequently, the
more unqualified its joy. There remains little in us, then, but
that intellectual essence, which several great philosophers have
called eternal and identified with the Divinity.

A single illustration may help to fix these principles in the
mind. When Othello has discovered his fatal error, and is resolved to take his own life, he stops his groaning, and addresses
the ambassadors of Venice thus:

> Speak of me as I am: nothing extenuate,
> Nor set down aught in malice: then, must you speak
> Of one that loved, not wisely, but too well;
> Of one not easily jealous, but, being wrought,
> Perplexed in the extreme; of one whose hand,
> Like the base Indian, threw a pearl away
> Richer than all his tribe; of one whose subdued eyes,
> Albeit unusèd to the melting mood,
> Drop tears as fast as the Arabian trees
> Their medicinal gum. Set you down this:
> And say, besides, that in Aleppo once

When a malignant and a turbaned Turk
Beat a Venetian, and traduced the state,
I took by the throat the circumcisèd dog,
And smote him, thus.

There is a kind of criticism that would see in all these allusions, figures of speech, and wandering reflections, an unnatural rendering of suicide. The man, we might be told, should have muttered a few broken phrases, and killed himself without this pomp of declamation, like the jealous husbands in the daily papers. But the conventions of the tragic stage are more favourable to psychological truth than the conventions of real life. If we may trust the imagination (and in imagination lies, as we have seen, the test of propriety), this is what Othello would have felt. If he had not expressed it, his dumbness would have been due to external hindrances, not to the failure in his mind of just such complex and rhetorical thoughts as the poet has put into his mouth. The height of passion is naturally complex and rhetorical. Love makes us poets, and the approach of death should make us philosophers. When a man knows that his life is over, he can look back upon it from a universal standpoint. He has nothing more to live for, but if the energy of his mind remains unimpaired, he will still wish to live, and, being cut off from his personal ambitions, he will impute to himself a kind of vicarious immortality by identifying himself with what is eternal. He speaks of himself as he is, or rather as he was. He sums himself up, and points to his achievement. This I have been, says he, this I have done.

This comprehensive and impartial view, this synthesis and objectification of experience, constitutes the liberation of the soul and the essence of sublimity. That the hero attains it at the end consoles us, as it consoles him, for his hideous misfortunes. Our pity and terror are indeed purged; we go away knowing that, however tangled the net may be in which we feel ourselves caught, there is liberation beyond, and an ultimate peace.

§ 60. THE SUBLIME INDEPENDENT OF THE EXPRESSION OF EVIL. So natural is the relation between the vivid conception of great evils, and that self-assertion of the soul which gives the emotion of the sublime, that the sublime is often thought to depend upon the terror which these conceived evils inspire. To be sure, that terror would have to be inhibited and subdued, otherwise we should have a passion too acute to be incorporated in any object; the sublime would not appear as an æsthetic quality in things, but remain merely an emotional state in the subject. But this subdued and objectified terror is what is commonly regarded as the essence of the sublime, and so great an authority as Aristotle would seem to countenance some such definition. The usual cause of the sublime is here confused, however, with the sublime itself. The suggestion of terror makes us withdraw into ourselves: there with the supervening consciousness of safety or indifference comes a rebound, and we have that emotion of detachment and liberation in which the sublime really consists.

Thoughts and actions are properly sublime, and visible things only by analogy and suggestion when they induce a certain moral emotion; whereas beauty belongs properly to sensible things, and can be predicated of moral facts only by a figure of rhetoric. What we objectify in beauty is a sensation. What we objectify in the sublime is an act. This act is necessarily pleasant, for if it were not the sublime would be a bad quality and one we should rather never encounter in the world. The glorious joy of self-assertion in the face of an uncontrollable world is indeed so deep and entire, that it furnishes just that transcendent element of worth for which we were looking when we tried to understand how the expression of pain could sometimes please. It can please, not in itself, but because it is balanced and annulled by positive pleasures, especially by this final and victorious one of detachment. If the expression of evil seems necessary to the sublime, it is so only as a condition of this moral reaction.

We are commonly too much engrossed in objects and too little centred in ourselves and our inalienable will, to see the sublimity of a pleasing prospect. We are then enticed and flattered, and won over to a commerce with these external goods, and the consummation of our happiness would lie in the perfect comprehension and enjoyment of their nature. This is the office of art and love; and its partial fulfilment is seen in every perception of beauty. But when we are checked in this sympathetic endeavour after unity and comprehension; when we come upon a great evil or an irreconcilable power, we are driven to seek our happiness by the shorter and heroic road; then we recognize the hopeless foreignness of what lies before us, and stiffen ourselves against it. We thus for the first time reach the sense of our possible separation from our world, and of our abstract stability; and with this comes the sublime.

But although experience of evil is the commonest approach

to this attitude of mind, and we commonly become philosophers only after despairing of instinctive happiness, yet there is nothing impossible in the attainment of detachment by other channels. The immense is sublime as well as the terrible; and mere infinity of the object, like its hostile nature, can have the effect of making the mind recoil upon itself. Infinity, like hostility, removes us from things, and makes us conscious of our independence. The simultaneous view of many things, innumerable attractions felt together, produce equilibrium and indifference, as effectually as the exclusion of all. If we may call the liberation of the self by the consciousness of evil in the world, the Stoic sublime, we may assert that there is also an Epicurean sublime, which consists in liberation by equipoise. Any wide survey is sublime in that fashion. Each detail may be beautiful. We may even be ready with a passionate response to its appeal. We may think we covet every sort of pleasure, and lean to every kind of vigorous, impulsive life. But let an infinite panorama be suddenly unfolded; the will is instantly paralyzed, and the heart choked. It is impossible to desire everything at once, and when all is offered and approved, it is impossible to choose everything. In this suspense, the mind soars into a kind of heaven, benevolent but unmoved.

This is the attitude of all minds to which breadth of interest or length of years has brought balance and dignity. The sacerdotal quality of old age comes from this same sympathy in disinterestedness. Old men full of hurry and passion appear as fools, because we understand that their experience has not left enough mark upon their brain to qualify with the memory of other goods any object that may be now presented. We cannot venerate any one in whom appreciation is not divorced from desire. And this elevation and detachment of the heart need not follow upon any great disappointment; it is finest and sweetest where it is the gradual fruit of many affections now merged and mellowed into a natural piety. Indeed, we are able to frame our idea of the Deity on no other model.

When the pantheists try to conceive all the parts of nature as forming a single being, which shall contain them all and yet have absolute unity, they find themselves soon denying the existence of the world they are trying to deify; for nature, reduced to the unity it would assume in an omniscient mind, is no longer nature, but something simple and impossible, the exact opposite of the real world. Such an opposition would constitute the liberation of the divine mind from nature, and its existence as a self-conscious individual. The effort after comprehensiveness of view reduces things to unity, but this unity stands out in opposition to the manifold phenomena which it transcends, and rejects as unreal.

Now this destruction of nature, which the metaphysicians since Parmenides have so often repeated (nature nevertheless surviving still), is but a theoretical counterpart and hypostasis of what happens in every man's conscience when the comprehensiveness of his experience lifts him into thought, into abstraction. The sense of the sublime is essentially mystical: it is the transcending of distinct perception in favour of a feeling of unity and volume. So in the moral sphere, we have the mutual cancelling of the passions in the breast that includes them all, and their final subsidence beneath the glance that comprehends them. This is the Epicurean approach to detachment and perfection; it leads by systematic acceptance of instinct to the same goal which the stoic and the ascetic reach by systematic rejection of instinct. It is thus possible to be moved to that self-enfranchisement which constitutes the sublime, even when the object contains no expression of evil.

This conclusion supports that part of our definition of beauty which declares that the values beauty contains are all positive; a definition which we should have had to change if we had found that the sublime depended upon the suggestion of evil for its effect. But the sublime is not the ugly, as some descriptions of it might lead us to suppose; it is the supremely, the intoxicatingly beautiful. It is the pleasure of contemplation reaching such an intensity that it begins to lose its objectivity, and to declare itself, what it always fundamentally was, an inward passion of the soul. For while in the beautiful we find the perfection of life by sinking into the object, in the sublime we find a purer and more inalienable perfection by defying the object altogether. The surprised enlargement of vision, the sudden escape from our ordinary interests and the identification of ourselves with something permanent and superhuman, something much more abstract and inalienable than our changing personality, all this carries us away from the blurred objects before us, and raises us into a sort of ecstasy.

In the trite examples of the sublime, where we speak of the vast mass, strength, and durability of objects, or of their sinister aspect, as if we were moved by them on account of our own danger, we seem to miss the point. For the suggestion of our own danger would produce a touch of fear; it would be a prac-

tical passion, or if it could by chance be objectified enough to become æsthetic, it would merely make the object hateful and repulsive, like a mangled corpse. The object is sublime when we
forget our danger, when we escape from ourselves altogether, and
live as it were in the object itself, energizing in imitation of its
movement, and saying, "Be thou me, impetuous one!" This passage into the object, to live its life, is indeed a characteristic of all
perfect contemplation. But when in thus translating ourselves we
rise and play a higher personage, feeling the exhilaration of a
life freer and wilder than our own, then the experience is one of
sublimity. The emotion comes not from the situation we observe,
but from the powers we conceive; we fail to sympathize with the
struggling sailors because we sympathize too much with the wind
and waves. And this mystical cruelty can extend even to ourselves; we can so feel the fascination of the cosmic forces that
engulf us as to take a fierce joy in the thought of our own
destruction. We can identify ourselves with the abstractest essence
of reality, and, raised to that height, despise the human accidents
of our own nature. Lord, we say, though thou slay me, yet will
I trust in thee. The sense of suffering disappears in the sense of
life and the imagination overwhelms the understanding.

§ 61. THE COMIC. Something analogous takes place in the
other spheres where an æsthetic value seems to arise out of suggestions of evil, in the comic, namely, and the grotesque. But
here the translation of our sympathies is partial, and we are
carried away from ourselves only to become smaller. The larger
humanity, which cannot be absorbed, remains ready to contradict
the absurdity of our fiction. The excellence of comedy lies in the
invitation to wander along some by-path of the fancy, among
scenes not essentially impossible, but not to be actually enacted
by us on account of the fixed circumstances of our lives. If the
picture is agreeable, we allow ourselves to dream it true. We
forget its relations; we forbid the eye to wander beyond the
frame of the stage, or the conventions of the fiction. We indulge
an illusion which deepens our sense of the essential pleasantness
of things.

So far, there is nothing in comedy that is not delightful, except, perhaps, the moment when it is over. But fiction, like all
error or abstraction, is necessarily unstable; and the awakening
is not always reserved for the disheartening moment at the end.
Everywhere, when we are dealing with pretension or mistake, we
come upon sudden and vivid contradictions; changes of view,

transformations of apperception which are extremely stimulating to the imagination. We have spoken of one of these: when the sudden dissolution of our common habits of thought lifts us into a mystical contemplation, filled with the sense of the sublime; when the transformation is back to common sense and reality, and away from some fiction, we have a very different emotion. We feel cheated, relieved, abashed, or amused, in proportion as our sympathy attaches more to the point of view surrendered or to that attained.

The disintegration of mental forms and their redintegration is the life of the imagination. It is a spiritual process of birth and death, nutrition and generation. The strongest emotions accompany these changes, and vary infinitely with their variations. All the qualities of discourse, wit, eloquence, cogency, absurdity, are feelings incidental to this process, and involved in the juxtapositions, tensions, and resolutions of our ideas. Doubtless the last explanation of these things would be cerebral; but we are as yet confined to verbal descriptions and classifications of them, which are always more or less arbitrary.

The most conspicuous headings under which comic effects are gathered are perhaps incongruity and degradation. But clearly it cannot be the logical essence of incongruity or degradation that constitutes the comic; for then contradiction and deterioration would always amuse. Amusement is a much more directly physical thing. We may be amused without any idea at all, as when we are tickled, or laugh in sympathy with others by a contagious imitation of their gestures. We may be amused by the mere repetition of a thing at first not amusing. There must therefore be some nervous excitement on which the feeling of amusement directly depends, although this excitement may most often coincide with a sudden transition to an incongruous or meaner image. Nor can we suppose that particular ideational excitement to be entirely dissimilar to all others; wit is often hardly distinguishable from brilliancy, as humour from pathos. We must, therefore, be satisfied with saying vaguely that the process of ideation involves various feelings of movement and relation,—feelings capable of infinite gradation and complexity, and ranging from sublimity to tedium and from pathos to uncontrollable merriment.

Certain crude and obvious cases of the comic seem to consist of little more than a shock of surprise: a pun is a sort of jack-in-the-box, popping from nowhere into our plodding thoughts. The liveliness of the interruption, and its futility, often please;

dulce est desipere in loco; and yet those who must endure the society of inveterate jokers know how intolerable this sort of scintillation can become. There is something inherently vulgar about it; perhaps because our train of thought cannot be very entertaining in itself when we are so glad to break in upon it with irrelevant nullities. The same undertone of disgust mingles with other amusing surprises, as when a dignified personage slips and falls, or some disguise is thrown off, or those things are mentioned and described which convention ignores. The novelty and the freedom please, yet the shock often outlasts the pleasure, and we have cause to wish we had been stimulated by something which did not involve this degradation. So, also, the impossibility in plausibility which tickles the fancy in Irish bulls, and in wild exaggerations, leaves an uncomfortable impression, a certain aftertaste of foolishness.

The reason will be apparent if we stop to analyze the situation. We have a prosaic background of common sense and everyday reality; upon this background an unexpected idea suddenly impinges. But the thing is a futility. The comic accident falsifies the nature before us, starts a wrong analogy in the mind, a suggestion that cannot be carried out. In a word, we are in the presence of an absurdity; and man, being a rational animal, can like absurdity no better than he can like hunger or cold. A pinch of either may not be so bad, and he will endure it merrily enough if you repay him with abundance of warm victuals; so, too, he will play with all kinds of nonsense for the sake of laughter and good fellowship and the tickling of his fancy with a sort of caricature of thought. But the qualm remains, and the pleasure is never perfect. The same exhilaration might have come without the falsification, just as repose follows more swiftly after pleasant than after painful exertions.

Fun is a good thing, but only when it spoils nothing better. The best place for absurdity is in the midst of what is already absurd—then we have the play of fancy without the sense of ineptitude. Things amuse us in the mouth of a fool that would not amuse us in that of a gentleman; a fact which shows how little incongruity and degradation have to do with our pleasure in the comic. In fact, there is a kind of congruity and method even in fooling. The incongruous and the degraded displease us even there, as by their nature they must at all times. The shock which they bring may sometimes be the occasion of a subsequent pleasure, by attracting our attention, or by stimulating passions, such as scorn, or cruelty, or self-satisfaction (for there is a good

deal of malice in our love of fun); but the incongruity and
degradation, as such, always remain unpleasant. The pleasure
comes from the inward rationality and movement of the fiction,
not from its inconsistency with anything else. There are a great
many topsy-turvy worlds possible to our fancy, into which we
like to drop at times. We enjoy the stimulation and the shaking
up of our wits. It is like getting into a new posture, or hearing
a new song.

Nonsense is good only because common sense is so limited.
For reason, after all, is one convention picked out of a thousand.
We love expansion, not disorder, and when we attain freedom
without incongruity we have a much greater and a much purer
delight. The excellence of wit can dispense with absurdity. For
on the same prosaic background of common sense, a novelty
might have appeared that was not absurd, that stimulated the
attention quite as much as the ridiculous, without so baffling
the intelligence. This purer and more thoroughly delightful
amusement comes from what we call wit.

§ 62. Wit. Wit also depends upon transformation and substitution of ideas. It has been said to consist in quick association
by similarity. The substitution must here be valid, however, and
the similarity real, though unforeseen. Unexpected justness
makes wit, as sudden incongruity makes pleasant foolishness. It
is characteristic of wit to penetrate into hidden depths of things,
to pick out there some telling circumstance or relation, by noting
which the whole object appears in a new and clearer light.
Wit often seems malicious because analysis in discovering common traits and universal principles assimilates things at the
poles of being; it can apply to cookery the formulas of theology,
and find in the human heart a case of the fulcrum and lever. We
commonly keep the departments of experience distinct; we think
the different principles hold in each and that the dignity of
spirit is inconsistent with the explanation of it by physical analogy, and the meanness of matter unworthy of being an illustration of moral truths. Love must not be classed under physical
cravings, nor faith under hypnotization. When, therefore, an
original mind overleaps these boundaries, and recasts its categories, mixing up our old classifications, we feel that the values
of things are also confused. But these depended upon a deeper
relation, upon their response to human needs and aspirations.
All that can be changed by the exercise of intelligence is our
sense of the unity and homogeneity of the world. We may come

to hold an object of thought in less isolated respect, and another in less hasty derision; but the pleasures we derive from all, or our total happiness and wonder, will hardly be diminished. For this reason the malicious or destructive character of intelligence must not be regarded as fundamental. Wit belittles one thing and dignifies another; and its comparisons are as often flattering as ironical.

The same process of mind that we observed in wit gives rise to those effects we call charming, brilliant, or inspired. When Shakespeare says,

> Come and kiss me, *sweet and twenty,*
> Youth's a stuff will not endure,

the fancy of the phrase consists in a happy substitution, a merry way of saying something both true and tender. And where could we find a more exquisite charm? So, to take a weightier example, when St. Augustine says the virtues of the pagans were *splendid vices,* we have—at least if we catch the full meaning—a pungent assimilation of contrary things, by force of a powerful principle; a triumph of theory, the boldness of which can only be matched by its consistency. In fact, a phrase could not be more brilliant, or better condense one theology and two civilizations. The Latin mind is particularly capable of this sort of excellence. Tacitus alone could furnish a hundred examples. It goes with the power of satirical and bitter eloquence, a sort of scornful rudeness of intelligence, that makes for the core of a passion or of a character, and affixes to it a more or less scandalous label. For in our analytical zeal it is often possible to condense and abstract too much. Reality is more fluid and elusive than reason, and has, as it were, more dimensions than are known even to the latest geometry. Hence the understanding, when not suffused with some glow of sympathetic emotion or some touch of mysticism, gives but a dry, crude image of the world. The quality of wit inspires more admiration than confidence. It is a merit we should miss little in any one we love.

The same principle, however, can have more sentimental embodiments. When our substitutions are brought on by the excitement of generous emotion, we call wit inspiration. There is the same finding of new analogies, and likening of disparate things; there is the same transformation of our apperception. But the brilliancy is here not only penetrating, but also exalting. For instance:

Peace, peace, he is not dead, he doth not sleep,
He hath awakened from the dream of life:
'Tis we that wrapped in stormy visions keep
With phantoms an unprofitable strife.

There is here paradox, and paradox justified by reflection. The poet analyzes, and analyzes without reserve. The dream, the storm, the phantoms, and the unprofitableness could easily make a satirical picture. But the mood is transmuted; the mind takes an upward flight, with a sense of liberation from the convention it dissolves, and of freer motion in the vagueness beyond. The disintegration of our ideal here leads to mysticism, and because of this effort towards transcendence, the brilliancy becomes sublime.

§ 63. HUMOUR. A different mood can give a different direction to the same processes. The sympathy by which we reproduce the feeling of another, is always very much opposed to the æsthetic attitude to which the whole world is merely a stimulus to our sensibility. In the tragic, we have seen how the sympathetic feeling, by which suffering is appreciated and shared, has to be overlaid by many incidental æsthetic pleasures, if the resulting effect is to be on the whole good. We have also seen how the only way in which the ridiculous can be kept within the sphere of the æsthetically good is abstracting it from its relations, and treating it as an independent and curious stimulus; we should stop laughing and begin to be annoyed if we tried to make sense out of our absurdity. The less sympathy we have with men the more exquisite is our enjoyment of their folly: satirical delight is closely akin to cruelty. Defect and mishap stimulate our fancy, as blood and tortures excite in us the passions of the beast of prey. The more this inhuman attitude yields to sympathy and reason, the less are folly and error capable of amusing us. It would therefore seem impossible that we should be pleased by the foibles or absurdities of those we love. And in fact we never enjoy seeing our own persons in a satirical light, or any one else for whom we really feel affection. Even in farces, the hero and heroine are seldom made ridiculous, because that would jar upon the sympathy with which we are expected to regard them. Nevertheless, the essence of what we call humour is that amusing weaknesses should be combined with an amicable humanity. Whether it be in the way of ingenuity, or oddity, or drollery, the humorous person must have an absurd side, or be placed in an absurd situation. Yet this comic aspect, at which we ought to wince, seems to endear the character all the more. This is a parallel case to that of tragedy, where the depth of the woe we sympathize with seems to add to our satisfaction. And the explanation of the paradox is the same. We do not enjoy the expression of evil, but only the pleasant excitements that come with it; namely, the physical stimulus and the expression of good. In tragedy, the misfortunes help to give the impression of truth, and to bring out the noble qualities of the hero, but are in themselves depressing, so much so that over-sensitive people cannot enjoy the beauty of the representation. So also in humour, the painful suggestions are felt as such, and need to be overbalanced by agreeable elements. These come from both directions, from the æsthetic and the sympathetic reaction. On the one hand there is the sensuous and merely perceptive stimulation, the novelty, the movement, the vivacity of the spectacle. On the other hand, there is the luxury of imaginative sympathy, the mental assimilation of another congenial experience, the expansion into another life.

The juxtaposition of these two pleasures produces just that tension and complication in which the humorous consists. We are satirical, and we are friendly at the same time. The consciousness of the friendship gives a regretful and tender touch to the satire, and the sting of the satire makes the friendship a trifle humble and sad. Don Quixote is mad; he is old, useless, and ridiculous, but he is the soul of honour, and in all his laughable adventures we follow him like the ghost of our better selves. We enjoy his discomfitures too much to wish he had been a perfect Amadis; and we have besides a shrewd suspicion that he is the only kind of Amadis there can ever be in this world. At the same time it does us good to see the courage of his idealism, the ingenuity of his wit, and the simplicity of his goodness. But how shall we reconcile our sympathy with his dream and our perception of its absurdity? The situation is contradictory. We are drawn to some different point of view, from which the comedy may no longer seem so amusing. As humour becomes deep and really different from satire, it changes into pathos, and passes out of the sphere of the comic altogether. The mischances that were to amuse us as scoffers now grieve us as men, and the value of the representation depends on the touches of beauty and seriousness with which it is adorned.

§ 64. THE GROTESQUE. Something analogous to humour can appear in plastic forms, when we call it the grotesque. This is an interesting effect produced by such a transformation of an ideal type as exaggerates one of its elements or combines it with other types. The real excellence of this, like that of all fiction, consists in re-creation; in the formation of a thing which nature has not, but might conceivably have offered. We call these inventions comic and grotesque when we are considering their divergence from the natural rather than their inward possibility. But the latter constitutes their real charm; and the more we study and develope them, the better we understand it. The incongruity with the conventional type then disappears, and what was impossible and ridiculous at first takes its place among recognized ideals. The centaur and the satyr are no longer grotesque; the type is accepted. And the grotesqueness of an individual has essentially the same nature. If we like the inward harmony, the characteristic balance of his features, we are able to disengage this individual from the class into which we were trying to force him; we can forget the expectation which he was going to disappoint. The ugliness then disappears, and only the reassertion of the old habit and demand can make us regard him as in any way extravagant.

What appears as grotesque may be intrinsically inferior or superior to the normal. That is a question of its abstract material and form. But until the new object impresses its form on our imagination, so that we can grasp its unity and proportion, it appears to us as a jumble and distortion of other forms. If this confusion is absolute, the object is simply null; it does not exist æsthetically, except by virtue of materials. But if the confusion is not absolute, and we have an inkling of the unity and character in the midst of the strangeness of the form, then we have the grotesque. It is the half-formed, the perplexed, and the suggestively monstrous.

The analogy to the comic is very close, as we can readily conceive that it should be. In the comic we have this same juxtaposition of a new and an old idea, and if the new is not futile and really inconceivable, it may in time establish itself in the mind, and cease to be ludicrous. Good wit is novel truth, as the good grotesque is novel beauty. But there are natural conditions of organization, and we must not mistake every mutilation for the creation of a new form. The tendency of nature to establish well-marked species of animals shows what various combinations are most stable in the face of physical forces, and there is a fitness also for survival in the mind, which is determined by the relation of any form to our fixed method of perception. New things are therefore generally bad because, as has been well said, they are incapable of becoming old. A thousand originalities are produced by defect of faculty, for one that is produced by genius. For in the pursuit of beauty, as in that of truth, an infinite number of paths lead to failure, and only one to success.

§ 65. THE POSSIBILITY OF FINITE PERFECTION. If these observations have any accuracy, they confirm this important truth,—that no æsthetic value is really founded on the experience or the suggestion of evil. This conclusion will doubtless seem the more interesting if we think of its possible extension to the field of ethics and of the implied vindication of the ideals of moral perfection as something essentially definable and attainable. But without insisting on an analogy to ethics, which might be misleading, we may hasten to state the principle which emerges from our analysis of expression. Expressiveness may be found in any one thing that suggests another, or draws from association with that other any of its emotional colouring. There may, therefore, of course, be an expressiveness of evil; but this expressiveness will not have any æsthetic value. The description or suggestion of suffering may have a worth as science or discipline, but can never in itself enhance any beauty. Tragedy and comedy please in spite of this expressiveness and not by virtue of it; and except for the pleasures they give, they have no place among the fine arts. Nor have they, in such a case, any place in human life at all; unless they are instruments of some practical purpose and serve to preach a moral, or achieve a bad notoriety. For ugly things can attract attention, although they cannot keep it; and the scandal of a new horror may secure a certain vulgar admiration which follows whatever is momentarily conspicuous, and which is attained ever by crime. Such admiration, however, has nothing æsthetic about it, and is only made possible by the bluntness of our sense of beauty.

The effect of the pathetic and comic is therefore never pure; since the expression of some evil is mixed up with those elements by which the whole appeals to us. These elements we have seen to be the truth of the presentation, which involves the pleasures of recognition and comprehension, the beauty of the medium, and the concomitant expression of things intrinsically good. To these sources all the æsthetic value of comic and tragic is due; and the sympathetic emotion which arises from the spectacle of evil must never be allowed to overpower these pleasures of contemplation, else the entire object becomes distasteful and loses its excuse for being. Too exclusive a relish for the comic and pathetic is accordingly a sign of bad taste and of comparative insensibility to beauty.

This situation has generally been appreciated in the practice of the arts, where effect is perpetually studied; but the greatest care has not always succeeded in avoiding the dangers of the pathetic, and history is full of failures due to bombast, caricature, and unmitigated horror. In all these the effort to be expressive has transgressed the conditions of pleasing effect. For the creative and imitative impulse is indiscriminate. It does not consider the eventual beauty of the effect, but only the blind instinct of self-expression. Hence an untrained and not naturally sensitive mind cannot distinguish or produce anything good. This critical incapacity has always been a cause of failure and a just ground for ridicule; but it remained for some thinkers of our time—a time of little art and much undisciplined production —to erect this abuse into a principle and declare that the essence of beauty is to express the artist and not to delight the world. But the conditions of effect, and the possibility of pleasing, are the only criterion of what is capable and worthy of expression. Art exists and has value by its adaptation to these universal conditions of beauty.

Nothing but the good of life enters into the texture of the beautiful. What charms us in the comic, what stirs us in the sublime and touches us in the pathetic, is a glimpse of some good; imperfection has value only as an incipient perfection. Could the labours and sufferings of life be reduced, and a better harmony between man and nature be established, nothing would be lost to the arts; for the pure and ultimate value of the comic is discovery, of the pathetic, love, of the sublime, exaltation; and these would still subsist. Indeed, they would all be increased; and it has ever been, accordingly, in the happiest and most prosperous moments of humanity, when the mind and the world were knit into a brief embrace, that natural beauty has been best perceived, and art has won its triumphs. But it sometimes happens, in moments less propitious, that the soul is subdued to what it works in, and loses its power of idealization and hope. By a pathetic and superstitious self-depreciation, we then punish ourselves for the imperfection of nature. Awed by the magnitude of a reality that we can no longer conceive as free from evil, we try to assert that its evil also is a good; and we poison the very essence of the good to make its extension universal. We confuse the causal connexion of those things in nature which we call good or evil by an adventitious denomination, with the logical opposition between good and evil themselves; because one generation makes room for another, we say death is necessary to life; and because the causes of sorrow and joy are so mingled in this world, we cannot conceive how, in a better world, they might be disentangled.

This incapacity of the imagination to reconstruct the conditions of life and build the frame of things nearer to the heart's desire is very fatal to a steady loyalty to what is noble and fine. We surrender ourselves to a kind of miscellaneous appreciation, without standard or goal; and calling every vexatious apparition by the name of beauty, we become incapable of discriminating its excellence or feeling its value. We need to clarify our ideals, and enliven our vision of perfection. No atheism is so terrible as the absence of an ultimate ideal, nor could any failure of power be more contrary to human nature than the failure of moral imagination, or more incompatible with healthy life. For we have faculties, and habits, and impulses. These are the basis of our demands. And these demands, although variable, constitute an ever-present intrinsic standard of value by which we feel and judge. The ideal is immanent in them; for the ideal means that environment in which our faculties would find their freest employment, and their most congenial world. Perfection would be nothing but life under those conditions. Accordingly our consciousness of the ideal becomes distinct in proportion as we advance in virtue and in proportion to the vigour and definiteness with which our faculties work. When the vital harmony is complete, when the *act* is *pure*, faith in perfection passes into vision. That man is unhappy indeed, who in all his life has had no glimpse of perfection, who in the ecstasy of love, or in the delight of contemplation, has never been able to say: It is attained. Such moments of inspiration are the source of the arts, which have no higher function than to renew them.

A work of art is indeed a monument to such a moment, the memorial to such a vision; and its charm varies with its power of recalling us from the distractions of common life to the joy of a more natural and perfect activity.

§ 66. THE STABILITY OF THE IDEAL. The perfection thus revealed is relative to our nature and faculties; if it were not, it could have no value for us. It is revealed to us in brief moments, but it is not for that reason an unstable or fantastic thing. Human attention inevitably flickers; we survey things in succession, and our acts of synthesis and our realization of fact are only occasional.

This is the tenure of all our possessions; we are not uninterruptedly conscious of ourselves, our physical environment, our ruling passions, or our deepest conviction. What wonder, then, that we are not constantly conscious of that perfection which is the implicit ideal of all our preferences and desires? We view it only in parts, as passion or perception successively directs our attention to its various elements. Some of us never try to conceive it in its totality. Yet our whole life is an act of worship to this unknown divinity; every heartfelt prayer is offered before one or another of its images.

This ideal of perfection varies, indeed, but only with the variations of our nature of which it is the counterpart and entelechy. There is perhaps no more frivolous notion than that to which Schopenhauer has given a new currency, that a good, once attained, loses all its value. The instability of our attention, the need of rest and repair in our organs, makes a round of objects necessary to our minds; but we turn from a beautiful thing, as from a truth or a friend, only to return incessantly, and with increasing appreciation. Nor do we lose all the benefit of our achievements in the intervals between our vivid realizations of what we have gained. The tone of the mind is permanently raised; and we live with that general sense of steadfastness and resource, which is perhaps the kernel of happiness. Knowledge, affection, religion, and beauty are not less constant influences in a man's life because his consciousness of them is intermittent. Even when absent, they fill the chambers of the mind with a kind of fragrance. They have a continual efficacy, as well as a perennial worth.

There are, indeed, other objects of desire that if attained leave nothing but restlessness and dissatisfaction behind them. These are the objects pursued by fools. That such objects ever attract us is a proof of the disorganization of our nature, which drives us in contrary directions and is at war with itself. If we had attained anything like steadiness of thought or fixity of character, if we knew ourselves, we should know also our inalienable satisfactions. To say that all goods become worthless in possession is either a piece of superficial satire that intentionally denies the normal in order to make the abnormal seem more shocking, or else it is a confession of frivolity, a confession that, as an idiot never learns to distinguish reality amid the phantasms of his brain, so we have never learned to distinguish true goods amid our extravagances of whim and passion. That true goods exist is nevertheless a fact of moral experience. "A thing of beauty is a joy for ever"; a great affection, a clear thought, a profound and well-tried faith, are eternal possessions. And this is not merely a fact, to be asserted upon the authority of those who know it by experience. It is a psychological necessity. While we retain the same senses, we must get the same impressions from the same objects; while we keep our instincts and passions, we must pursue the same goods; while we have the same powers of imagination, we must experience the same delight in their exercise. Age brings about, of course, variation in all these particulars, and the susceptibility of two individuals is never exactly similar. But the eventual decay of our personal energies does not destroy the natural value of objects, so long as the same will embodies itself in other minds, and human nature subsists in the world. The sun is not now unreal because each one of us in succession, and all of us in the end, must close our eyes upon it; and yet the sun exists for us only because we perceive it. The ideal has the same conditions of being, but has this advantage over the sun, that we cannot know if its light is ever destined to fail us.

There is then a broad foundation of identity in our nature, by virtue of which we live in a common world, and have an art and a religion in common. That the ideal should be constant within these limits is as inevitable as that it should vary beyond them. And so long as we exist and recognize ourselves individually as persons or collectively as human, we must recognize also our immanent ideal, the realization of which would constitute perfection for us. That ideal cannot be destroyed except in proportion as we ourselves perish. An absolute perfection, independent of human nature and its variations, may interest the metaphysician; but the artist and the man will be satisfied with a perfection that is inseparable from the consciousness of mankind, since it is at once the natural vision of the imagination, and the rational goal of the will.

§ 67. CONCLUSION. We have now studied the sense of beauty in what seem to be its fundamental manifestations, and in some of the more striking complications which it undergoes. In surveying so broad a field we stand in need of some classification and subdivision; and we have chosen the familiar one of matter, form, and expression, as least likely to lead us into needless artificiality. But artificiality there must always be in the discursive description of anything given in consciousness. Psychology attempts what is perhaps impossible, namely, the anatomy of life. Mind is a fluid; the lights and shadows that flicker through it have no real boundaries, and no possibility of permanence. Our whole classification of mental facts is borrowed from the physical conditions or expressions of them. The very senses are distinguished because of the readiness with which we can isolate their outer organs. Ideas can be identified only by identifying their objects. Feelings are recognized by their outer expression, and when we try to recall an emotion, we must do so by recalling the circumstances in which it occurred.

In distinguishing, then, in our sense of beauty, an appreciation of sensible material, one of abstract form, and another of associated values, we have been merely following the established method of psychology, the only one by which it is possible to analyze the mind. We have distinguished the elements of the object, and treated the feeling as if it were composed of corresponding parts. The worlds of nature and fancy, which are the object of æsthetic feeling, can be divided into parts in space and time. We can then distinguish the material of things from the various forms it may successively assume; we can distinguish, also, the earlier and the later impressions made by the same object; and we can ascertain the coexistence of one impression with another, or with the memory of others. But æsthetic feeling itself has no parts, and this physiology of its causes is not a description of its proper nature.

Beauty as we feel it is something indescribable: what it is or what it means can never be said. By appealing to experiment and memory we can show that this feeling varies as certain things vary in the objective conditions; that it varies with the frequency, for instance, with which a form has been presented, or with the associates which that form has had in the past. This will justify a description of the feeling as composed of the various contributions of these objects. But the feeling itself knows nothing of composition nor contributions. It is an affection of the soul, a consciousness of joy and security, a pang, a dream, a pure pleasure. It suffuses an object without telling why; nor has it any need to ask the question. It justifies itself and the vision it gilds; nor is there any meaning in seeking for a cause of it, in this inward sense. Beauty exists for the same reason that the object which is beautiful exists, or the world in which that object lies, or we that look upon both. It is an experience: there is nothing more to say about it. Indeed, if we look at things teleologically, and as they ultimately justify themselves to the heart, beauty is of all things what least calls for explanation. For matter and space and time and principles of reason and of evolution, all are ultimately brute, unaccountable data. We may describe what actually is, but it might have been otherwise, and the mystery of its being is as baffling and dark as ever.

But we,—the minds that ask all questions and judge of the validity of all answers,—we are not ourselves independent of this world in which we live. We sprang from it, and our relations in it determine all our instincts and satisfactions. This final questioning and sense of mystery is an unsatisfied craving which nature has her way of stilling. Now we only ask for reasons when we are surprised. If we had no expectations we should have no surprises. And what gives us expectation is the spontaneous direction of our thought, determined by the structure of our brain and the effects of our experience. If our spontaneous thoughts came to run in harmony with the course of nature, if our expectations were then continually fulfilled, the sense of mystery would vanish. We should be incapable of asking why the world existed or had such a nature, just as we are now little inclined to ask why anything is right, but mightily disinclined to give up asking why anything is wrong.

This satisfaction of our reason, due to the harmony between our nature and our experience, is partially realized already. The sense of beauty is its realization. When our senses and imagination find what they crave, when the world so shapes itself or so moulds the mind that the correspondence between them is perfect, then perception is pleasure, and existence needs no apology. The duality which is the condition of conflict disappears. There is no inward standard different from the outward fact with which that outward fact may be compared. A unification of this kind is the goal of our intelligence and of our affection, quite as much as of our æsthetic sense; but we have in those departments fewer examples of success. In the heat of speculation or of love there may come moments of equal perfection, but they are very unstable. The reason and the heart remain deeply unsatisfied. But the eye finds in nature, and in some supreme achievements of art, constant and fuller satisfaction. For the eye is quick, and seems to have been more docile to the education of life than the heart or the reason of man, and able sooner to adapt itself to the reality. Beauty therefore seems to be the clearest manifestation of perfection, and the best evidence of its possibility. If perfection is, as it should be, the ultimate justification of being, we may understand the ground of the moral dignity of beauty. Beauty is a pledge of the possible conformity between the soul and nature, and consequently a ground of faith in the supremacy of the good.

INDEX

Achilles, 110, 115

Æsthetic feeling, its importance, 3
speculation, causes of its neglect,
3-4
theory, its uses, 6

Æsthetics, Use of the word, 12

Angels, 36, 112

Apperception, 61 *et seq.*

Arabic inscriptions as ornament, 121

Architecture, Effects of Gothic, 102-
103
governed by use, 100

Aristotelian forms, 97

Aristotle, 108, 239

Associative process, 122 *et seq.*

Augustine, Saint, quoted, 154

Beauty a value, 11 *et seq.*
as felt is indescribable, 163
a justification of things, 164
defined, 31 *et seq.*
verbal definitions quoted, 11

Beethoven, 28

Breathing related to the sense of
beauty, 37

Burke, 78, note

Byron, quoted, 85

Byzantine architecture, 69

Calderon, 108

Centaurs, 113, 157

Character as an æsthetic form, 109
et seq.

Characters, Ideal, 111 *et seq.*

Charles V.'s palace at the Alhambra,
28

Christ, the various ideas of his
nature, 116

Circle, its æsthetic quality, 57

Classicism, French and English, 69

Colonnades, 69

Colour, 46 *et seq.*
its analogy to other sensations,
47
possibility of an abstract art of
colour, 48

Comic, The, 150 *et seq.*

Conscience, its representative character, 22

Cost as an element of effect, 130
et seq.

Couplet, The, 68

Criticism, Use of the word, 11

Definite and indefinite, meaning of
the terms, 86, note

Degradation not what pleases in the
comic, 151 *et seq.*

Democracy, æsthetics of it, 69 *et seq.*

Descartes, 12, 113

Disinterestedness not the differentia
of æsthetic pleasure, 24 *et seq.*

Don Quixote, 110, 156

Economy and fitness, 132 *et seq.*

Emerson, 89

Epicurean æsthetics, 8
sublime, The, 148, 149

Escurial, The, 60, 130

Ethos, 108

Evil, life without it æsthetic, 19-20
in the second term of expression,
136 *et seq.*
conventional use of the word, 137
an occasion of the sublime, 144
et seq.
excluded from the beautiful, 159

Evolution, its possible tendency to
eliminate imagination, 18

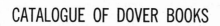

CATALOGUE OF DOVER BOOKS

Philosophy, Religion

GUIDE TO PHILOSOPHY, C. E. M. Joad. A modern classic which examines many crucial problems which man has pondered through the ages: Does free will exist? Is there plan in the universe? How do we know and validate our knowledge? Such opposed solutions as subjective idealism and realism, chance and teleology, vitalism and logical positivism, are evaluated and the contributions of the great philosophers from the Greeks to moderns like Russell, Whitehead, and others, are considered in the context of each problem. "The finest introduction," BOSTON TRANSCRIPT. Index. Classified bibliography. 592pp. 5⅜ x 8.
T297 Paperbound **$2.00**

HISTORY OF ANCIENT PHILOSOPHY, W. Windelband. One of the clearest, most accurate comprehensive surveys of Greek and Roman philosophy. Discusses ancient philosophy in general, intellectual life in Greece in the 7th and 6th centuries B.C., Thales, Anaximander, Anaximenes, Heraclitus, the Eleatics, Empedocles, Anaxagoras, Leucippus, the Pythagoreans, the Sophists, Socrates, Democritus (20 pages), Plato (50 pages), Aristotle (70 pages), the Peripatetics, Stoics, Epicureans, Sceptics, Neo-platonists, Christian Apologists, etc. 2nd German edition translated by H. E. Cushman. xv + 393pp. 5⅜ x 8.
T357 Paperbound **$1.85**

ILLUSTRATIONS OF THE HISTORY OF MEDIEVAL THOUGHT AND LEARNING, R. L. Poole. Basic analysis of the thought and lives of the leading philosophers and ecclesiastics from the 8th to the 14th century—Abailard, Ockham, Wycliffe, Marsiglio of Padua, and many other great thinkers who carried the torch of Western culture and learning through the "Dark Ages": political, religious, and metaphysical views. Long a standard work for scholars and one of the best introductions to medieval thought for beginners. Index. 10 Appendices. xiii + 327pp. 5⅜ x 8.
T674 Paperbound **$1.85**

PHILOSOPHY AND CIVILIZATION IN THE MIDDLE AGES, M. de Wulf. This semi-popular survey covers aspects of medieval intellectual life such as religion, philosophy, science, the arts, etc. It also covers feudalism vs. Catholicism, rise of the universities, mendicant orders, monastic centers, and similar topics. Unabridged. Bibliography. Index. viii + 320pp. 5⅜ x 8.
T284 Paperbound **$1.85**

AN INTRODUCTION TO SCHOLASTIC PHILOSOPHY, Prof. M. de Wulf. Formerly entitled SCHOLASTICISM OLD AND NEW, this volume examines the central scholastic tradition from St. Anselm, Albertus Magnus, Thomas Aquinas, up to Suarez in the 17th century. The relation of scholasticism to ancient and medieval philosophy and science in general is clear and easily followed. The second part of the book considers the modern revival of scholasticism, the Louvain position, relations with Kantianism and Positivism. Unabridged. xvi + 271pp. 5⅜ x 8.
T296 Clothbound **$3.50**
T283 Paperbound **$1.75**

A HISTORY OF MODERN PHILOSOPHY, H. Höffding. An exceptionally clear and detailed coverage of western philosophy from the Renaissance to the end of the 19th century. Major and minor men such as Pomponazzi, Bodin, Boehme, Telesius, Bruno, Copernicus, da Vinci, Kepler, Galileo, Bacon, Descartes, Hobbes, Spinoza, Leibniz, Wolff, Locke, Newton, Berkeley, Hume, Erasmus, Montesquieu, Voltaire, Diderot, Rousseau, Lessing, Kant, Herder, Fichte, Schelling, Hegel, Schopenhauer, Comte, Mill, Darwin, Spencer, Hartmann, Lange, and many others, are discussed in terms of theory of knowledge, logic, cosmology, and psychology. Index. 2 volumes, total of 1159pp. 5⅜ x 8.
T117 Vol. 1, Paperbound **$2.25**
T118 Vol. 2, Paperbound **$2.25**

ARISTOTLE, A. E. Taylor. A brilliant, searching non-technical account of Aristotle and his thought written by a foremost Platonist. It covers the life and works of Aristotle; classification of the sciences; logic; first philosophy; matter and form; causes; motion and eternity; God; physics; metaphysics; and similar topics. Bibliography. New Index compiled for this edition. 128pp. 5⅜ x 8.
T280 Paperbound **$1.00**

THE SYSTEM OF THOMAS AQUINAS, M. de Wulf. Leading Neo-Thomist, one of founders of University of Louvain, gives concise exposition to central doctrines of Aquinas, as a means toward determining his value to modern philosophy, religion. Formerly "Medieval Philosophy Illustrated from the System of Thomas Aquinas." Trans. by E. Messenger. Introduction. 151pp. 5⅜ x 8.
T568 Paperbound **$1.25**

LEIBNIZ, H. W. Carr. Most stimulating middle-level coverage of basic philosophical thought of Leibniz. Easily understood discussion, analysis of major works: "Theodicy," "Principles of Nature and Grace," "Monadology"; Leibniz's influence; intellectual growth; correspondence; disputes with Bayle, Malebranche, Newton; importance of his thought today, with reinterpretation in modern terminology. "Power and mastery," London Times. Bibliography. Index. 226pp. 5⅜ x 8.
T624 Paperbound **$1.35**

CATALOGUE OF DOVER BOOKS

THE SENSE OF BEAUTY, G. Santayana. A revelation of the beauty of language as well as an important philosophic treatise, this work studies the "why, when, and how beauty appears, what conditions an object must fulfill to be beautiful, what elements of our nature make us sensible of beauty, and what the relation is between the constitution of the object and the excitement of our susceptibility." "It is doubtful if a better treatment of the subject has since been published," PEABODY JOURNAL. Index. ix + 275pp. 5⅜ x 8.
T238 Paperbound **$1.00**

PROBLEMS OF ETHICS, Moritz Schlick. The renowned leader of the "Vienna Circle" applies the logical positivist approach to a wide variety of ethical problems: the source and means of attaining knowledge, the formal and material characteristics of the good, moral norms and principles, absolute vs. relative values, free will and responsibility, comparative importance of pleasure and suffering as ethical values, etc. Disarmingly simple and straightforward despite complexity of subject. First English translation, authorized by author before his death, of a thirty-year old classic. Translated and with an introduction by David Rynin. Index. Foreword by Prof. George P. Adams. xxi + 209pp. 5⅜ x 8.
T946 Paperbound **$1.45**

AN INTRODUCTION TO EXISTENTIALISM, Robert G. Olson. A new and indispensable guide to one of the major thought systems of our century, the movement that is central to the thinking of some of the most creative figures of the past hundred years. Stresses Heidegger and Sartre, with careful and objective examination of the existentialist position, values—freedom of choice, individual dignity, personal love, creative effort—and answers to the eternal questions of the human condition. Scholarly, unbiased, analytic, unlike most studies of this difficult subject, Prof. Olson's book is aimed at the student of philosophy as well as at the reader with no formal training who is looking for an absorbing, accessible, and thorough introduction to the basic texts. Index. xv + 221pp. 5⅜ x 8½.
T55 Paperbound **$1.50**

SYMBOLIC LOGIC, C. I. Lewis and C. H. Langford. Since first publication in 1932, this has been among most frequently cited works on symbolic logic. Still one of the best introductions both for beginners and for mathematicians, philosophers. First part covers basic topics which easily lend themselves to beginning study. Second part is rigorous, thorough development of logistic method, examination of some of most difficult and abstract aspects of symbolic logic, including modal logic, logical paradoxes, many-valued logic, with Prof. Lewis' own contributions. 2nd revised (corrected) edition. 3 appendixes, one new to this edition. 524pp. 5⅜ x 8.
S170 Paperbound **$2.00**

WHITEHEAD'S PHILOSOPHY OF CIVILIZATION, A. H. Johnson. A leading authority on Alfred North Whitehead synthesizes the great philosopher's thought on civilization, scattered throughout various writings, into unified whole. Analysis of Whitehead's general definition of civilization, his reflections on history and influences on its development, his religion, including his analysis of Christianity, concept of solitariness as first requirement of personal religion, and so on. Other chapters cover views on minority groups, society, civil liberties, education. Also critical comments on Whitehead's philosophy. Written with general reader in mind. A perceptive introduction to important area of the thought of a leading philosopher of our century. Revised index and bibliography. xii + 211pp. 5⅜ x 8½.
T996 Paperbound **$1.50**

WHITEHEAD'S THEORY OF REALITY, A. H. Johnson. Introductory outline of Whitehead's theory of actual entities, the heart of his philosophy of reality, followed by his views on nature of God, philosophy of mind, theory of value (truth, beauty, goodness and their opposites), analyses of other philosophers, attitude toward science. A perspicacious lucid introduction by author of dissertation on Whitehead, written under the subject's supervision at Harvard. Good basic view for beginning students of philosophy and for those who are simply interested in important contemporary ideas. Revised index and bibliography. xiii + 267pp. 5⅜ x 8½.
T989 Paperbound **$1.50**

MIND AND THE WORLD-ORDER, C. I. Lewis. Building upon the work of Peirce, James, and Dewey, Professor Lewis outlines a theory of knowledge in terms of "conceptual pragmatism." Dividing truth into abstract mathematical certainty and empirical truth, the author demonstrates that the traditional understanding of the a priori must be abandoned. Detailed analyses of philosophy, metaphysics, method, the "given" in experience, knowledge of objects, nature of the a priori, experience and order, and many others. Appendices. xiv + 446pp. 5⅜ x 8.
T359 Paperbound **$2.25**

SCEPTICISM AND ANIMAL FAITH, G. Santayana. To eliminate difficulties in the traditional theory of knowledge, Santayana distinguishes between the independent existence of objects and the essence our mind attributes to them. Scepticism is thereby established as a form of belief, and animal faith is shown to be a necessary condition of knowledge. Belief, classical idealism, intuition, memory, symbols, literary psychology, and much more, discussed with unusual clarity and depth. Index. xii + 314pp. 5⅜ x 8.
T235 Clothbound **$3.50**
T236 Paperbound **$1.50**

LANGUAGE AND MYTH, E. Cassirer. Analyzing the non-rational thought processes which go to make up culture, Cassirer demonstrates that beneath both language and myth there lies a dominant unconscious "grammar" of experience whose categories and canons are not those of logical thought. His analyses of seemingly diverse phenomena such as Indian metaphysics, the Melanesian "mana," the Naturphilosophie of Schelling, modern poetry, etc., are profound without being pedantic. Introduction and translation by Susanne Langer. Index. x + 103pp. 5⅜ x 8.
T51 Paperbound **$1.25**

CATALOGUE OF DOVER BOOKS

THE ANALYSIS OF MATTER, Bertrand Russell. A classic which has retained its importance in understanding the relation between modern physical theory and human perception. Logical analysis of physics, prerelativity physics, causality, scientific inference, Weyl's theory, tensors, invariants and physical interpretations, periodicity, and much more is treated with Russell's usual brilliance. "Masterly piece of clear thinking and clear writing," NATION AND ATHENAEUM. "Most thorough treatment of the subject," THE NATION. Introduction. Index. 8 figures. viii + 408pp. 5⅜ x 8. S231 Paperbound **$1.95**

CONCEPTUAL THINKING (A LOGICAL INQUIRY), S. Körner. Discusses origin, use of general concepts on which language is based, and the light they shed on basic philosophical questions. Rigorously examines how different concepts are related; how they are linked to experience; problems in the field of contact between exact logical, mathematical, and scientific concepts, and the inexactness of everyday experience (studied at length). This work elaborates many new approaches to the traditional problems of philosophy—epistemology, value theories, metaphysics, aesthetics, morality. "Rare originality . . . brings a new rigour into philosophical argument," Philosophical Quarterly. New corrected second edition. Index. vii + 301pp. 5⅜ x 8. T516 Paperbound **$1.75**

INTRODUCTION TO SYMBOLIC LOGIC, S. Langer. No special knowledge of math required — probably the clearest book ever written on symbolic logic, suitable for the layman, general scientist, and philosopher. You start with simple symbols and advance to a knowledge of the Boole-Schroeder and Russell-Whitehead systems. Forms, logical structure, classes, the calculus of propositions, logic of the syllogism, etc., are all covered. "One of the clearest and simplest introductions," MATHEMATICS GAZETTE. Second enlarged, revised edition. 368pp. 5⅜ x 8. S164 Paperbound **$1.75**

LANGUAGE, TRUTH AND LOGIC, A. J. Ayer. A clear, careful analysis of the basic ideas of Logical Positivism. Building on the work of Schlick, Russell, Carnap, and the Viennese School, Mr. Ayer develops a detailed exposition of the nature of philosophy, science, and metaphysics; the Self and the World; logic and common sense, and other philosophic concepts. An aid to clarity of thought as well as the first full-length development of Logical Positivism in English. Introduction by Bertrand Russell. Index. 160pp. 5⅜ x 8. T10 Paperbound **$1.25**

ESSAYS IN EXPERIMENTAL LOGIC, J. Dewey. Based upon the theory that knowledge implies a judgment which in turn implies an inquiry, these papers consider the inquiry stage in terms of: the relationship of thought and subject matter, antecedents of thought, data and meanings. 3 papers examine Bertrand Russell's thought, while 2 others discuss pragmatism and a final essay presents a new theory of the logic of values. Index. viii + 444pp. 5⅜ x 8. T73 Paperbound **$1.95**

TRAGIC SENSE OF LIFE, M. de Unamuno. The acknowledged masterpiece of one of Spain's most influential thinkers. Between the despair at the inevitable death of man and all his works and the desire for something better, Unamuno finds that "saving incertitude" that alone can console us. This dynamic appraisal of man's faith in God and in himself has been called "a masterpiece" by the ENCYCLOPAEDIA BRITANNICA. xxx + 332pp. 5⅜ x 8. T257 Paperbound **$2.00**

HISTORY OF DOGMA, A. Harnack. Adolph Harnack, who died in 1930, was perhaps the greatest Church historian of all time. In this epoch-making history, which has never been surpassed in comprehensiveness and wealth of learning, he traces the development of the authoritative Christian doctrinal system from its first crystallization in the 4th century down through the Reformation, including also a brief survey of the later developments through the Infallibility decree of 1870. He reveals the enormous influence of Greek thought on the early Fathers, and discusses such topics as the Apologists, the great councils, Manichaeism, the historical position of Augustine, the medieval opposition to indulgences, the rise of Protestantism, the relations of Luther's doctrines with modern tendencies of thought, and much more. "Monumental work; still the most valuable history of dogma . . . luminous analysis of the problems . . . abounds in suggestion and stimulus and can be neglected by no one who desires to understand the history of thought in this most important field," Dutcher's Guide to Historical Literature. Translated by Neil Buchanan. Index. Unabridged reprint in 4 volumes. Vol I: Beginnings to the Gnostics and Marcion. Vol II & III: 2nd century to the 4th century Fathers. Vol IV & V: 4th century Councils to the Carlovingian Renaissance. Vol VI & VII: Period of Clugny (c. 1000) to the Reformation, and after. Total of cii + 2407pp. 5⅜ x 8.

T904 Vol I	Paperbound	**$2.50**
T905 Vol II & III	Paperbound	**$2.50**
T906 Vol IV & V	Paperbound	**$2.50**
T907 Vol VI & VII	Paperbound	**$2.50**
	The set	**$10.00**

THE GUIDE FOR THE PERPLEXED, Maimonides. One of the great philosophical works of all time and a necessity for everyone interested in the philosophy of the Middle Ages in the Jewish, Christian, and Moslem traditions. Maimonides develops a common meeting-point for the Old Testament and the Aristotelian thought which pervaded the medieval world. His ideas and methods predate such scholastics as Aquinas and Scotus and throw light on the entire problem of philosophy or science vs. religion. 2nd revised edition. Complete unabridged Friedländer translation. 55 page introduction to Maimonides's life, period, etc., with an important summary of the GUIDE. Index. lix + 414pp. 5⅜ x 8. T351 Paperbound **$2.00**

Americana

THE EYES OF DISCOVERY, J. Bakeless. A vivid reconstruction of how unspoiled America appeared to the first white men. Authentic and enlightening accounts of Hudson's landing in New York, Coronado's trek through the Southwest; scores of explorers, settlers, trappers, soldiers. America's pristine flora, fauna, and Indians in every region and state in fresh and unusual new aspects. "A fascinating view of what the land was like before the first highway went through," Time. 68 contemporary illustrations, 39 newly added in this edition. Index. Bibliography. x + 500pp. 5⅜ x 8.   T761 Paperbound **$2.00**

AUDUBON AND HIS JOURNALS, J. J. Audubon. A collection of fascinating accounts of Europe and America in the early 1800's through Audubon's own eyes. Includes the Missouri River Journals —an eventful trip through America's untouched heartland, the Labrador Journals, the European Journals, the famous "Episodes", and other rare Audubon material, including the descriptive chapters from the original letterpress edition of the "Ornithological Studies", omitted in all later editions. Indispensable for ornithologists, naturalists, and all lovers of Americana and adventure. 70-page biography by Audubon's granddaughter. 38 illustrations. Total of 1106pp. 5⅜ x 8.   T675 Vol I Paperbound **$2.25**
T676 Vol II Paperbound **$2.25**
The set **$4.50**

TRAVELS OF WILLIAM BARTRAM, edited by Mark Van Doren. The first inexpensive illustrated edition of one of the 18th century's most delightful books is an excellent source of first-hand material on American geography, anthropology, and natural history. Many descriptions of early Indian tribes are our only source of information on them prior to the infiltration of the white man. "The mind of a scientist with the soul of a poet," John Livingston Lowes. 13 original illustrations and maps. Edited with an introduction by Mark Van Doren. 448pp. 5⅜ x 8.
T13 Paperbound **$2.00**

GARRETS AND PRETENDERS: A HISTORY OF BOHEMIANISM IN AMERICA, A. Parry. The colorful and fantastic history of American Bohemianism from Poe to Kerouac. This is the only complete record of hoboes, cranks, starving poets, and suicides. Here are Pfaff, Whitman, Crane, Bierce, Pound, and many others. New chapters by the author and by H. T. Moore bring this thorough and well-documented history down to the Beatniks. "An excellent account," N. Y. Times. Scores of cartoons, drawings, and caricatures. Bibliography. Index. xxviii + 421pp. 5⅝ x 8⅜.   T708 Paperbound **$1.95**

THE EXPLORATION OF THE COLORADO RIVER AND ITS CANYONS, J. W. Powell. The thrilling first-hand account of the expedition that filled in the last white space on the map of the United States. Rapids, famine, hostile Indians, and mutiny are among the perils encountered as the unknown Colorado Valley reveals its secrets. This is the only uncut version of Major Powell's classic of exploration that has been printed in the last 60 years. Includes later reflections and subsequent expedition. 250 illustrations, new map. 400pp. 5⅝ x 8⅜.
T94 Paperbound **$2.00**

THE JOURNAL OF HENRY D. THOREAU, Edited by Bradford Torrey and Francis H. Allen. Henry Thoreau is not only one of the most important figures in American literature and social thought; his voluminous journals (from which his books emerged as selections and crystallizations) constitute both the longest, most sensitive record of personal internal development and a most penetrating description of a historical moment in American culture. This present set, which was first issued in fourteen volumes, contains Thoreau's entire journals from 1837 to 1862, with the exception of the lost years which were found only recently. We are reissuing it, complete and unabridged, with a new introduction by Walter Harding, Secretary of the Thoreau Society. Fourteen volumes reissued in two volumes. Foreword by Henry Seidel Canby. Total of 1888pp. 8⅜ x 12¼.   T312-3 Two volume set, Clothbound **$20.00**

GAMES AND SONGS OF AMERICAN CHILDREN, collected by William Wells Newell. A remarkable collection of 190 games with songs that accompany many of them; cross references to show similarities, differences among them; variations; musical notation for 38 songs. Textual discussions show relations with folk-drama and other aspects of folk tradition. Grouped into categories for ready comparative study: Love-games, histories, playing at work, human life, bird and beast, mythology, guessing-games, etc. New introduction covers relations of songs and dances to timeless heritage of folklore, biographical sketch of Newell, other pertinent data. A good source of inspiration for those in charge of groups of children and a valuable reference for anthropologists, sociologists, psychiatrists. Introduction by Carl Withers. New indexes of first lines, games. 5⅜ x 8½. xii + 242pp.   T354 Paperbound **$1.75**

GARDNER'S PHOTOGRAPHIC SKETCH BOOK OF THE CIVIL WAR, Alexander Gardner. The first published collection of Civil War photographs, by one of the two or three most famous photographers of the era, outstandingly reproduced from the original positives. Scenes of crucial battles: Appomattox, Manassas, Mechanicsville, Bull Run, Yorktown, Fredericksburg, etc. Gettysburg immediately after retirement of forces. Battle ruins at Richmond, Petersburg, Gaines'Mill. Prisons, arsenals, a slave pen, fortifications, headquarters, pontoon bridges, soldiers, a field hospital. A unique glimpse into the realities of one of the bloodiest wars in history, with an introductory text to each picture by Gardner himself. Until this edition, there were only five known copies in libraries, and fewer in private hands, one of which sold at auction in 1952 for $425. Introduction by E. F. Bleiler. 100 full page 7 x 10 photographs (original size). 224pp. 8½ x 10¾. T476 Clothbound **$6.00**

A BIBLIOGRAPHY OF NORTH AMERICAN FOLKLORE AND FOLKSONG, Charles Haywood, Ph.D. The only book that brings together bibliographic information on so wide a range of folklore material. Lists practically everything published about American folksongs, ballads, dances, folk beliefs and practices, popular music, tales, similar material—more than 35,000 titles of books, articles, periodicals, monographs, music publications, phonograph records. Each entry complete with author, title, date and place of publication, arranger and performer of particular examples of folk music, many with Dr. Haywood's valuable criticism, evaluation. Volume I, "The American People," is complete listing of general and regional studies, titles of tales and songs of Negro and non-English speaking groups and where to find them, Occupational Bibliography including sections listing sources of information, folk material on cowboys, riverboat men, 49ers, American characters like Mike Fink, Frankie and Johnnie, John Henry, many more. Volume II, "The American Indian," tells where to find information on dances, myths, songs, ritual of more than 250 tribes in U.S., Canada. A monumental product of 10 years' labor, carefully classified for easy use. "All students of this subject . . . will find themselves in debt to Professor Haywood," Stith Thompson, in American Anthropologist. ". . . a most useful and excellent work," Duncan Emrich, Chief Folklore Section, Library of Congress, in "Notes." Corrected, enlarged republication of 1951 edition. New Preface. New index of composers, arrangers, performers. General index of more than 15,000 items. Two volumes. Total of 1301pp. 6⅛ x 9¼. T797-798 Clothbound **$12.50**

INCIDENTS OF TRAVEL IN YUCATAN, John L. Stephens. One of first white men to penetrate interior of Yucatan tells the thrilling story of his discoveries of 44 cities, remains of once-powerful Maya civilization. Compelling text combines narrative power with historical significance as it takes you through heat, dust, storms of Yucatan; native festivals with brutal bull fights; great ruined temples atop man-made mounds. Countless idols, sculptures, tombs, examples of Mayan taste for rich ornamentation, from gateways to personal trinkets, accurately illustrated, discussed in text. Will appeal to those interested in ancient civilizations, and those who like stories of exploration, discovery, adventure. Republication of last (1843) edition. 124 illustrations by English artist, F. Catherwood. Appendix on Mayan architecture, chronology. Two volume set. Total of xxviii + 927pp.
Vol I T926 Paperbound **$2.00**
Vol II T927 Paperbound **$2.00**
The set **$4.00**

A GENIUS IN THE FAMILY, Hiram Percy Maxim. Sir Hiram Stevens Maxim was known to the public as the inventive genius who created the Maxim gun, automatic sprinkler, and a heavier-than-air plane that got off the ground in 1894. Here, his son reminisces—this is by no means a formal biography—about the exciting and often downright scandalous private life of his brilliant, eccentric father. A warm and winning portrait of a prankish, mischievous, impious personality, a genuine character. The style is fresh and direct, the effect is unadulterated pleasure. "A book of charm and lasting humor . . . belongs on the 'must read' list of all fathers," New York Times. "A truly gorgeous affair," New Statesman and Nation. 17 illustrations, 16 specially for this edition. viii + 108pp. 5⅜ x 8½.
T948 Paperbound **$1.00**

HORSELESS CARRIAGE DAYS, Hiram P. Maxim. The best account of an important technological revolution by one of its leading figures. The delightful and rewarding story of the author's experiments with the exact combustibility of gasoline, stopping and starting mechanisms, carriage design, and engines. Captures remarkably well the flavor of an age of scoffers and rival inventors not above sabotage; of noisy, uncontrollable gasoline vehicles and incredible mobile steam kettles. ". . . historic information and light humor are combined to furnish highly entertaining reading," New York Times. 56 photographs, 12 specially for this edition. xi + 175pp. 5⅜ x 8½. T964 Paperbound **$1.35**

BODY, BOOTS AND BRITCHES: FOLKTALES, BALLADS AND SPEECH FROM COUNTRY NEW YORK, Harold W. Thompson. A unique collection, discussion of songs, stories, anecdotes, proverbs handed down orally from Scotch-Irish grandfathers, German nurse-maids, Negro workmen, gathered from all over Upper New York State. Tall tales by and about lumbermen and pirates, canalers and injun-fighters, tragic and comic ballads, scores of sayings and proverbs all tied together by an informative, delightful narrative by former president of New York Historical Society. ". . . a sparkling homespun tapestry that every lover of Americana will want to have around the house," Carl Carmer, New York Times. Republication of 1939 edition. 20 line-drawings. Index. Appendix (Sources of material, bibliography). 530pp. 5⅜ x 8½. T411 Paperbound **$2.00**

Dover Classical Records

Now available directly to the public exclusively from Dover: top-quality recordings of fine classical music for only $2 per record! Almost all were released by major record companies to sell for $5 and $6. These recordings were issued under our imprint only after they had passed a severe critical test. We insisted upon:

First-rate music that is enjoyable, musically important and culturally significant.

First-rate performances, where the artists have carried out the composer's intentions, in which the music is alive, vigorous, played with understanding and sensitivity.

First-rate sound—clear, sonorous, fully balanced, crackle-free, whir-free.

Have in your home music by major composers, performed by such gifted musicians as Elsner, Gitlis, Wührer, Beveridge Webster, the Barchet Quartet, Gimpel, etc. Enthusiastically received when first released, many of these performances are definitive. The records are not seconds or remainders, but brand new pressings made on pure vinyl from carefully chosen master tapes. "All purpose" 12″ monaural 33⅓ rpm records, they play equally well on hi-fi and stereo equipment. Fine music for discriminating music lovers, superlatively played, flawlessly recorded: there is no better way to build your library of recorded classical music at remarkable savings. There are no strings; this is not a come-on, not a club, forcing you to buy records you may not want in order to get a few at a lower price. Buy whatever records you want in any quantity, and never pay more than $2 each. Your obligation ends with your first purchase. And that's when ours begins. Dover's money-back guarantee allows you to return any record for any reason, even if you don't like the music, for a full, immediate refund—no questions asked.

MOZART: STRING QUARTETS: IN A (K. 464) AND C ("DISSONANT") (K. 465), Barchet Quartet. The final two of the famous Haydn Quartets, high-points in the history of music. The A Major was accepted with delight by Mozart's contemporaries, but the C Major, with its dissonant opening, aroused strong protest. Today, of course, the remarkable resolutions of the dissonances are recognized as major musical achievements. "Beautiful warm playing," MUSICAL AMERICA. "Two of Mozart's loveliest quartets in a distinguished performance," REV. OF RECORDED MUSIC. (Playing time 58 mins.)   HCR 5200 **$2.00**

MOZART: STRING QUARTETS: IN G (K. 80), D (K. 156), and C (K. 157), Barchet Quartet. The early chamber music of Mozart receives unfortunately little attention. First-rate music of the Italian school, it contains all the lightness and charm that belongs only to the youthful Mozart. This is currently the only separate source for the composer's work of this period. "Excellent," HIGH FIDELITY. "Filled with sunshine and youthful joy; played with verve, recorded sound live and brilliant," CHRISTIAN SCI. MONITOR. (playing time 51 mins.)   HCR 5201 **$2.00**

MOZART: SERENADES: #9 IN D ("POSTHORN") (K. 320), #6 IN D ("SERENATA NOTTURNA") (K. 239), Pro Musica Orch. of Stuttgart, under Edouard van Remoortel. For Mozart, the serenade was a highly effective form, since he could bring to it the immediacy and intimacy of chamber music as well as the free fantasy of larger group music. Both these serenades are distinguished by a playful, mischievous quality, a spirit perfectly captured in this fine performance. "A triumph, polished playing from the orchestra," HI FI MUSIC AT HOME. "Sound is rich and resonant, fidelity is wonderful," REV. OF RECORDED MUSIC. (Playing time 51 mins.)   HCR 5202 **$2.00**

MOZART: DIVERTIMENTO FOR VIOLIN, VIOLA AND CELLO IN E FLAT (K. 563); ADAGIO AND FUGUE IN F MINOR (K. 404a), Kehr Trio. The divertimento is one of Mozart's most beloved pieces, called by Einstein "the finest and most perfect trio ever heard." It is difficult to imagine a music lover who will not be delighted by it. This is the only recording of the lesser known Adagio and Fugue, written in 1782 and influenced by Bach's Well-Tempered Clavichord. "Extremely beautiful recording, strongly recommended," THE OBSERVER. "Superior to rival editions," HIGH FIDELITY. (Playing time 51 mins.)   HCR 5203 **$2.00**

SCHUMANN: KREISLERIANA (OPUS 16) AND FANTASIA IN C (OPUS 17), Vlado Perlemuter, Piano. The vigorous Romantic imagination and the remarkable emotional qualities of Schumann's piano music raise it to a special eminence in 19th-century creativity. Both these pieces are rooted to the composer's tortuous romance with his future wife, Clara, and both receive brilliant treatment at the hands of Vlado Perlemuter, Paris Conservatory, proclaimed by Alfred Cortot "not only a great virtuoso but also a great musician." "The best Kreisleriana to date," BILLBOARD. (Playing time 55 mins.)   HCR 5204 **$2.00**

CATALOGUE OF DOVER BOOKS

SCHUMANN: TRIOS #1 IN D MINOR (OPUS 63) AND #3 IN G MINOR (OPUS 110), Trio di Bolzano. The fiery, romantic, melodic Trio #1 and the dramatic, seldom heard Trio #3 are both movingly played by a fine chamber ensemble. No one personified Romanticism to the general public of the 1840's more than did Robert Schumann, and among his most romantic works are these trios for cello, violin and piano. "Ensemble and overall interpretation leave little to be desired," HIGH FIDELITY. "An especially understanding performance," REV. OF RECORDED MUSIC. (Playing time 54 mins.)   HCR 5205 **$2.00**

SCHUBERT: QUINTET IN A ("TROUT") (OPUS 114), AND NOCTURNE IN E FLAT (OPUS 148), Friedrich Wührer, Piano and Barchet Quartet. If there is a single piece of chamber music that is a universal favorite, it is probably Schubert's "Trout" Quintet. Delightful melody, harmonic resources, musical exuberance are its characteristics. The Nocturne (played by Wührer, Barchet, and Reimann) is an exquisite piece with a deceptively simple theme and harmony. "The best Trout on the market—Wührer is a fine Viennese-style Schubertian, and his spirit infects the Barchets," ATLANTIC MONTHLY. "Exquisitely recorded," ETUDE. (Playing time 44 mins.)   HCR 5206 **$2.00**

SCHUBERT: PIANO SONATAS IN C MINOR AND B (OPUS 147), Friedrich Wührer. Schubert's sonatas retain the structure of the classical form, but delight listeners with romantic freedom and a special melodic richness. The C Minor, one of the Three Grand Sonatas, is a product of the composer's maturity. The B Major was not published until 15 years after his death. "Remarkable interpretation, reproduction of the first rank," DISQUES. "A superb pianist for music like this, musicianship, sweep, power, and an ability to integrate Schubert's measures such as few pianists have had since Schnabel," Harold Schonberg. (Playing time 49 mins.)   HCR 5207 **$2.00**

STRAVINSKY: VIOLIN CONCERTO IN D, Ivry Gitlis, Cologne Orchestra; DUO CONCERTANTE, Ivry Gitlis, Violin, Charlotte Zelka, Piano, Cologne Orchestra; JEU DE CARTES, Bamberg Symphony, under Hollreiser. Igor Stravinsky is probably the most important composer of this century, and these three works are among the most significant of his neoclassical period of the 30's. The Violin Concerto is one of the few modern classics. Jeu de Cartes, a ballet score, bubbles with gaiety, color and melodiousness. "Imaginatively played and beautifully recorded," E. T. Canby, HARPERS MAGAZINE. "Gitlis is excellent, Hollreiser beautifully worked out," HIGH FIDELITY. (Playing time 55 mins.)   HCR 5208 **$2.00**

GEMINIANI: SIX CONCERTI GROSSI, OPUS 3, Helma Elsner, Harpsichord, Barchet Quartet, Pro Musica Orch. of Stuttgart, under Reinhardt. Francesco Geminiani (1687-1762) has been rediscovered in the same musical exploration that revealed Scarlatti, Vivaldi, and Corelli. In form he is more sophisticated than the earlier Italians, but his music delights modern listeners with its combination of contrapuntal techniques and the full harmonies and rich melodies charcteristic of Italian music. This is the only recording of the six 1733 concerti: D Major, B Flat Minor, E Minor, G Minor, E Minor (bis), and D Minor. "I warmly recommend it, spacious, magnificent, I enjoyed every bar," C. Cudworth, RECORD NEWS. "Works of real charm, recorded with understanding and style," ETUDE. (Playing time 52 mins.)   HCR 5209 **$2.00**

MODERN PIANO SONATAS: BARTOK: SONATA FOR PIANO; BLOCH: SONATA FOR PIANO (1935); PROKOFIEV, PIANO SONATA #7 IN B FLAT ("STALINGRAD"); STRAVINSKY: PIANO SONATA (1924), István Nádas, Piano. Shows some of the major forces and directions in modern piano music: Stravinsky's crisp austerity; Bartok's fusion of Hungarian folk motives; incisive diverse rhythms, and driving power; Bloch's distinctive emotional vigor; Prokofiev's brilliance and melodic beauty couched in pre-Romantic forms. "A most interesting documentation of the contemporary piano sonata. Nadas is a very good pianist." HIGH FIDELITY. (Playing time 59 mins.)   HCR 5215 **$2.00**

VIVALDI: CONCERTI FOR FLUTE, VIOLIN, BASSOON, AND HARPSICHORD: #8 IN G MINOR, #21 IN F, #27 IN D, #7 IN D; SONATA #1 IN A MINOR, Gastone Tassinari, Renato Giangrandi, Giorgio Semprini, Arlette Eggmann. More than any other Baroque composer, Vivaldi moved the concerto grosso closer to the solo concert we deem standard today. In these concerti he wrote virtuosi music for the solo instruments, allowing each to introduce new material or expand on musical ideas, creating tone colors unusual even for Vivaldi. As a result, this record displays a new area of his genius, offering some of his most brilliant music. Performed by a top-rank European group. (Playing time 45 mins.)   HCR 5216 **$2.00**

LÜBECK: CANTATAS: HILF DEINEM VOLK; GOTT, WIE DEIN NAME, Stuttgart Choral Society, Swabian Symphony Orch.; PRELUDES AND FUGUES IN C MINOR AND IN E, Eva Hölderlin, Organ. Vincent Lübeck (1654-1740), contemporary of Bach and Buxtehude, was one of the great figures of the 18th-century North German school. These examples of Lübeck's few surviving works indicate his power and brilliance. Voice and instrument lines in the cantatas are strongly reminiscent of the organ: the preludes and fugues show the influence of Bach and Buxtehude. This is the only recording of the superb cantatas. Text and translation included. "Outstanding record," E. T. Canby, SAT. REVIEW. "Hölderlin's playing is exceptional," AM. RECORD REVIEW. "Will make [Lübeck] many new friends," Philip Miller. (Playing time 37 mins.)   HCR 5217 **$2.00**

CATALOGUE OF DOVER BOOKS

DONIZETTI, BETLY (LA CAPANNA SVIZZERA), Soloists of Compagnia del Teatro dell'Opera Comica di Roma, Societa del Quartetto, Rome, Chorus and Orch. Betly, a delightful one-act opera written in 1836, is similar in style and story to one of Donizetti's better-known operas, L'Elisir. Betly is lighthearted and farcical, with bright melodies and a freshness character- istic of the best of Donizetti. Libretto (English and Italian) included. "The chief honors go to Angela Tuccari who sings the title role, and the record is worth having for her alone," M. Rayment, GRAMOPHONE REC. REVIEW. "The interpretation . . . is excellent . . . This is a charming record which we recommend to lovers of little-known works," DISQUES.
HCR 5218 **$2.00**

ROSSINI: L'OCCASIONE FA IL LADRO (IL CAMBIO DELLA VALIGIA), Soloists of Compagnia del Teatro dell'Opera Comica di Roma, Societa del Quartetto, Rome, Chorus and Orch. A charm- ing one-act opera buffa, this is one of the first works of Rossini's maturity, and it is filled with the wit, gaiety and sparkle that make his comic operas second only to Mozart's. Like other Rossini works, L'Occasione makes use of the theme of impersonation and attendant amusing confusions. This is the only recording of this important buffa. Full libretto (English and Italian) included. "A major rebirth, a stylish performance . . . the Roman recording engineers have outdone themselves," H. Weinstock, SAT. REVIEW. (Playing time 53 mins.)
HCR 5219 **$2.00**

DOWLAND: "FIRST BOOKE OF AYRES," Pro Musica Antiqua of Brussels, Safford Cape, Director. This is the first recording to include all 22 of the songs of this great collection, written by John Dowland, one of the most important writers of songs of 16th and 17th century Eng- land. The participation of the Brussels Pro Musica under Safford Cape insures scholarly ac- curacy and musical artistry. "Powerfully expressive and very beautiful," B. Haggin. "The musicianly singers . . . never fall below an impressive standard," Philip Miller. Text included. (Playing time 51 mins.)
HCR 5220 **$2.00**

FRENCH CHANSONS AND DANCES OF THE 16TH CENTURY, Pro Musica Antiqua of Brussels, Safford Cape, Director. A remarkable selection of 26 three- or four-part chansons and de- lightful dances from the French Golden Age—by such composers as Orlando Lasso, Crecquil- lon, Claude Gervaise, etc. Text and translation included. "Delightful, well-varied with respect to mood and to vocal and instrumental color," HIGH FIDELITY. "Performed with . . . dis- crimination and musical taste, full of melodic distinction and harmonic resource," Irving Kolodin. (Playing time 39 mins.)
HCR 5221 **$2.00**

GALUPPI: CONCERTI A QUATRO: #1 IN G MINOR, #2 IN G, #3 IN D, #4 IN C MINOR, #5 IN E FLAT, AND #6 IN B FLAT, Biffoli Quartet. During Baldassare Galuppi's lifetime, his instru- mental music was widely renowned, and his contemporaries Mozart and Haydn thought highly of his work. These 6 concerti reflect his great ability; and they are among the most interesting compositions of the period. They are remarkable for their unusual combinations of timbres and for emotional elements that were only then beginning to be introduced into music. Performed by the well-known Biffoli Quartet, this is the only record devoted exclu- sively to Galuppi. (Playing time 47 mins.)
HCR 5222 **$2.00**

HAYDN: DIVERTIMENTI FOR WIND BAND, IN C; IN F; DIVERTIMENTO A NOVE STROMENTI IN C FOR STRINGS AND WIND INSTRUMENTS, reconstructed by H. C. Robbins Landon, performed by members of Vienna State Opera Orch.; MOZART DIVERTIMENTI IN C, III (K. 187) AND IV (K. 188), Salzburg Wind Ensemble. Robbins Landon discovered Haydn manuscripts in a Bene- dictine monastery in Lower Austria, edited them and restored their original instrumentation The result is this magnificent record. Two little-known divertimenti by Mozart—of great charm and appeal—are also included. None of this music is available elsewhere (Playing time 58 mins.)
HCR 5223 **$2.00**

PURCELL: TRIO SONATAS FROM "SONATAS OF FOUR PARTS" (1697): #9 IN F ("GOLDEN"), #7 IN C, #1 IN B MINOR, #10 IN D, #4 IN D MINOR, #2 IN E FLAT, AND #8 IN G MINOR, Giorgio Ciompi, and Werner Torkanowsky, Violins, Geo. Koutzen, Cello, and Herman Chessid, Harpsichord. These posthumously-published sonatas show Purcell at his most advanced and mature. They are certainly among the finest musical examples of pre-modern chamber music. Those not familiar with his instrumental music are well-advised to hear these outstanding pieces. "Performance sounds excellent," Harold Schonberg. "Some of the most noble and touching music known to anyone," AMERICAN RECORD GUIDE. (Playing time 58 mins.)
HCR 5224 **$2.00**

BARTOK: VIOLIN CONCERTO; SONATA FOR UNACCOMPANIED VIOLIN, Ivry Gitlis, Pro Musica of Vienna, under Hornstein. Both these works are outstanding examples of Bartok's final period, and they show his powers at their fullest. The Violin Concerto is, in the opinion of many authorities, Bartok's finest work, and the Sonata, his last work, is "a masterpiece" (F. Sackville West). "Wonderful, finest performance of both Bartok works I have ever heard," GRAMOPHONE. "Gitlis makes such potent and musical sense out of these works that I suspect many general music lovers (not otherwise in sympathy with modern music) will discover to their amazement that they like it. Exceptionally good sound," AUDITOR. (Playing time 54 mins.)
HCR 5211 **$2.00**

New Books

101 PATCHWORK PATTERNS, Ruby Short McKim. With no more ability than the fundamentals of ordinary sewing, you will learn to make over 100 beautiful quilts: flowers, rainbows, Irish chains, fish and bird designs, leaf designs, unusual geometric patterns, many others. Cutting designs carefully diagrammed and described, suggestions for materials, yardage estimates, step-by-step instructions, plus entertaining stories of origins of quilt names, other folklore. Revised 1962. 101 full-sized patterns. 140 illustrations. Index. 128pp. 7⅞ x 10¾.
T773 Paperbound **$1.85**

ESSENTIAL GRAMMAR SERIES
By concentrating on the essential core of material that constitutes the semantically most important forms and areas of a language and by stressing explanation (often bringing parallel English forms into the discussion) rather than rote memory, this new series of grammar books is among the handiest language aids ever devised. Designed by linguists and teachers for adults with limited learning objectives and learning time, these books omit nothing important, yet they teach more usable language material and do it more quickly and permanently than any other self-study material. Clear and rigidly economical, they concentrate upon immediately usable language material, logically organized so that related material is always presented together. Any reader of typical capability can use them to refresh his grasp of language, to supplement self-study language records or conventional grammars used in schools, or to begin language study on his own. Now available:

ESSENTIAL GERMAN GRAMMAR, Dr. Guy Stern & E. F. Bleiler. Index. Glossary of terms. 128pp. 5⅜ x 8.
T422 Paperbound **$1.00**

ESSENTIAL FRENCH GRAMMAR, Dr. Seymour Resnick. Index. Cognate list. Glossary. 159pp. 5⅜ x 8.
T419 Paperbound **$1.00**

ESSENTIAL ITALIAN GRAMMAR, Dr. Olga Ragusa. Index. Glossary. 111pp. 5⅜ x 8.
T779 Paperbound **$1.00**

ESSENTIAL SPANISH GRAMMAR, Dr. Seymour Resnick. Index. 50-page cognate list. Glossary. 138pp. 5⅜ x 8.
T780 Paperbound **$1.00**

PHILOSOPHIES OF MUSIC HISTORY: A Study of General Histories of Music, 1600-1960, Warren D. Allen. Unquestionably one of the most significant documents yet to appear in musicology, this thorough survey covers the entire field of historical research in music. An influential masterpiece of scholarship, it includes early music histories; theories on the ethos of music; lexicons, dictionaries and encyclopedias of music; musical historiography through the centuries; philosophies of music history; scores of related topics. Copiously documented. New preface brings work up to 1960. Index. 317-item bibliography. 9 illustrations; 3 full-page plates. 5⅜ x 8½. xxxiv + 382pp.
T282 Paperbound **$2.00**

MR. DOOLEY ON IVRYTHING AND IVRYBODY, Finley Peter Dunne. The largest collection in print of hilarious utterances by the irrepressible Irishman of Archey Street, one of the most vital characters in American fiction. Gathered from the half dozen books that appeared during the height of Mr. Dooley's popularity, these 102 pieces are all unaltered and uncut, and they are all remarkably fresh and pertinent even today. Selected and edited by Robert Hutchinson. 5⅜ x 8½. xii + 244p.
T626 Paperbound **$1.00**

TREATISE ON PHYSIOLOGICAL OPTICS, Hermann von Helmholtz. Despite new investigations, this important work will probably remain preeminent. Contains everything known about physiological optics up to 1925, covering scores of topics under the general headings of dioptrics of the eye, sensations of vision, and pereceptions of vision. Von Helmholtz's voluminous data are all included, as are extensive supplementary matter incorporated into the third German edition, new material prepared for 1925 English edition, and copious textual annotations by J. P. C. Southall. The most exhaustive treatise ever prepared on the subject, it has behind it a list of contributors that will never again be duplicated. Translated and edited by J. P. C. Southall. Bibliography. Indexes. 312 illustrations. 3 volumes bound as 2. Total of 1749pp. 5⅜ x 8.
S15-16 Two volume set, Clothbound **$15.00**

THE ARTISTIC ANATOMY OF TREES, Rex Vicat Cole. Even the novice with but an elementary knowledge of drawing and none of the structure of trees can learn to draw, paint trees from this systematic, lucid instruction book. Copiously illustrated with the author's own sketches, diagrams, and 50 paintings from the early Renaissance to today, it covers composition; structure of twigs, boughs, buds, branch systems; outline forms of major species; how leaf is set on twig; flowers and fruit and their arrangement; etc. 500 illustrations. Bibliography. Indexes. 347pp. 5⅜ x 8.
T1016 Clothbound **$4.50**

CATALOGUE OF DOVER BOOKS

GEOMETRY OF FOUR DIMENSIONS, H. P. Manning. Unique in English as a clear, concise intro-duction to this fascinating subject. Treatment is primarily synthetic and Euclidean, although hyperplanes and hyperspheres at infinity are considered by non-Euclidean forms. Historical introduction and foundations of 4-dimensional geometry; perpendicularity; simple angles; angles of planes; higher order; symmetry; order, motion; hyperpyramids, hypercones, hyper-spheres; figures with parallel elements; volume, hypervolume in space; regular polyhedroids. Glossary of terms. 74 illustrations. ix + 348pp. 5⅜ x 8. S182 Paperbound **$2.00**

PAPER FOLDING FOR BEGINNERS, W. D. Murray and F. J. Rigney. A delightful introduction to the varied and entertaining Japanese art of origami (paper folding), with a full, crystal-clear text that anticipates every difficulty; over 275 clearly labeled diagrams of all important stages in creation. You get results at each stage, since complex figures are logically developed from simpler ones. 43 different pieces are explained: sailboats, frogs, roosters, etc. 6 photographic plates. 279 diagrams. 95pp. 5⅝ x 8⅜. T713 Paperbound **$1.00**

SATELLITES AND SCIENTIFIC RESEARCH, D. King-Hele. An up-to-the-minute non-technical ac-count of the man-made satellites and the discoveries they have yielded up to September of 1961. Brings together information hitherto published only in hard-to-get scientific journals. In-cludes the life history of a typical satellite, methods of tracking, new information on the shape of the earth, zones of radiation, etc. Over 60 diagrams and 6 photographs. Mathemati-cal appendix. Bibliography of over 100 items. Index. xii + 180pp. 5⅜ x 8½.
T703 Paperbound **$2.00**

LOUIS PASTEUR, S. J. Holmes. A brief, very clear, and warmly understanding biography of the great French scientist by a former Professor of Zoology in the University of California. Traces his home life, the fortunate effects of his education, his early researches and first theses, and his constant struggle with superstition and institutionalism in his work on microorganisms, fermentation, anthrax, rabies, etc. New preface by the author. 159pp. 5⅜ x 8.
T197 Paperbound **$1.00**

THE ENJOYMENT OF CHESS PROBLEMS, K. S. Howard. A classic treatise on this minor art by an internationally recognized authority that gives a basic knowledge of terms and themes for the everyday chess player as well as the problem fan: 7 chapters on the two-mover; 7 more on 3- and 4-move problems; a chapter on selfmates; and much more. "The most important one-volume contribution originating solely in the U.S.A.," Alain White. 200 diagrams. Index. Solutions, viii + 212pp. 5⅜ x 8. T742 Paperbound **$1.25**

SAM LOYD AND HIS CHESS PROBLEMS, Alain C. White. Loyd was (for all practical purposes) the father of the American chess problem and his protégé and successor presents here the diamonds of his production, chess problems embodying a whimsy and bizarre fancy entirely unique. More than 725 in all, ranging from two-move to extremely elaborate five-movers, including Loyd's contributions to chess oddities—problems in which pieces are arranged to form initials, figures, other by-paths of chess problem found nowhere else. Classified accord-ing to major concept, with full text analyzing problems, containing selections from Loyd's own writings. A classic to challenge your ingenuity, increase your skill. Corrected republica-tion of 1913 edition. Over 750 diagrams and illustrations. 744 problems with solutions. 471pp. 5⅜ x 8½. T928 Paperbound **$2.25**

FABLES IN SLANG & MORE FABLES IN SLANG, George Ade. 2 complete books of major American humorist in pungent colloquial tradition of Twain, Billings. 1st reprinting in over 30 years includes "The Two Mandolin Players and the Willing Performer," "The Base Ball Fan Who Took the Only Known Cure," "The Slim Girl Who Tried to Keep a Date that was Never Made," 42 other tales of eccentric, perverse, but always funny characters. "Touch of genius," H. L. Mencken. New introduction by E. F. Bleiler. 86 illus. 208pp. 5⅜ x 8.
T533 Paperbound **$1.00**

Prices subject to change without notice.

Dover publishes books on art, music, philosophy, literature, languages, history, social sciences, psychology, handcrafts, orientalia, puzzles and entertainments, chess, pets and gardens, books explaining science, intermediate and higher mathematics, math-ematical physics, engineering, biological sciences, earth sciences; classics of science, etc. Write to:

Dept. catrr.
Dover Publications, Inc.
180 Varick Street, N.Y. 14, N.Y.

A Manual of Textual Analysis

A Manual
of Textual
Analysis

BY VINTON A. DEARING

UNIVERSITY OF CALIFORNIA PRESS

Berkeley and Los Angeles / 1959

University of California Press
Berkeley and Los Angeles, California

Cambridge University Press
London, England

© 1959, by
The Regents of the University of California
Library of Congress Catalog Card Number: 58–10287
Printed in the United States of America

Designed by A. R. Tommasini

TO MY WIFE

Preface

The method of analysis described in the following pages may be applied to the transmission and embodiment in any form of any idea or complex of ideas, but it was developed specifically to deal with the complicated interrelations of the manuscripts of the Bible, especially of the Greek New Testament. Resting upon wholly different principles from any earlier method, it is, however, indebted in various ways to them all. A brief survey of these earlier methods will therefore not be amiss here.

The method that commonly bears the name of Karl Lachmann, but is also known as the genealogical method, is the oldest and has attained the widest popularity. The principle of this method is that states of a text having common errors have a common ancestor; and that when there are no common errors, states agreeing in striking readings have a common ancestor; and that when there are no striking readings, states commonly agreeing have a common ancestor. Although this principle may seem self-evident, it will serve in the analysis of only the simplest textual relationships. When there are difficulties—as there usually are—the scholar picks his own way among the logical pitfalls that beset him—often with indifferent success. Yet practitioners of the Lachmannian method are principally responsible for identifying and refining upon the evidence that one reading is earlier than another, and I have gratefully availed myself of this body of information.

Three more recently developed methods of analysis demand attention.

That of Dom Henri Quentin has been shown by J. Burke Severs to be defective in its handling of conflation. Its central principle, however, has generally been accepted as valid: if one state of a text agrees now with a second, now with a third, and now with both, but they never or almost never agree against it (they yield "zero" or "quasi-zero"), it is either the ancestor of both, neither being the ancestor of the other, or it is the descendant of one and the ancestor of the other. This statement is not universally true, but I am indebted to it for the universally valid principle of exclusion, which I discovered when trying to fit Quentin's rule to triads yielding two or no zeros.

About the same time Sir Walter Greg developed his calculus of variants. Greg provides a method for assuring the recognition in certain textual relationships of the fact that states agreeing against other states have a common ancestor, and of the fact that the exact pattern of these ancestors is not indicated by the nature of the agreements. The method is as important for its explicit limitations as for its operation within them, but its special assumptions and special conditions leave the scholar on his own when faced, for example, by conflation. I have therefore drawn upon it principally for terminology and for methods of notation. Nevertheless, constant reference to Greg's volume has corrected many an error in the part of my own method that includes the problems he discusses.

More recently Archibald Hill has proposed a method of simplifying the solution of textual problems by weighing the assumptions implied in the alternate trees when there is more than one possible way of relating the states to one another. Very little of Hill's discussion of textual analysis now seems to me valid, though at one time I accepted it all, even where it conflicted with Greg's. Hill did, however, introduce the principle of simplicity—Morgan's Canon, the animal psychologists call it—into textual analysis; for this important advance I am indebted to him in my own method.

I trust that none of the foregoing remarks spring from failure to understand the work of my predecessors, as Hill misunderstood parts of Greg's method, and as E. K. Rand, a Lachmannian, misunderstood almost all of Quentin's. Friend as well as foe may misunderstand, approval as well as disapproval may be mistaken, and disapproval of false conclusions may rest on an incorrect countertheory.

My method will not appeal at once to those who feel that "common sense" is a sufficient guide in textual matters, or to those who are familiar with other methods. It is difficult to accept a new method for doing what is obvious or what an older method will do just as well. But any method is necessarily homogeneous. Because the older methods defy extension or development, a more comprehensive method necessarily presents alternate solutions to familiar problems. My method for the first time distinguishes the text conveyed by the manuscript—a mental phenomenon —from the manuscript conveying the text—a physical phenomenon. It concerns only mental phenomena, which once they have come into existence either continue to be recoverable from the physical records or else vanish forever. Therefore it operates with only two assumptions, both necessary in dating the states of the text. And it follows that its results, except where they depend upon the assumptions, are independent of opinion. When the evidence will allow alternate conclusions, the analyst will be aware of it. The principle of exclusion mentioned above allows easy analysis of variations of any complexity and easy adjustment of the textual tree to account for the relative dates of the different textual states. Finally, I have set forth what seems to me a logical way of handling conflation. Because this work is a handbook, I have included much general textual methodology, ranging from how to record variants to the possibilities of using computing machines; but this has nothing to do with the method of analysis, and ought to be evaluated separately from it.

With the exceptions noted, I am solely responsible for the theory and method of textual analysis here advanced. Most valuable suggestions for improvement of its elucidation have come from my colleagues Hugh G. Dick, John J. Espey, Earl R. Miner, and H. T. Swedenberg. I have drawn on the specialized knowledge of Donald A. Bird and William Matthews in preparing the examples in Chapter iv. In preparing the discussion of sorting methods in Chapter iii, I received help from Donald F. Criley of International Business Machines Corporation, Everett S. Calhoun of the Stanford Research Institute, and Thomas H. Southard of the University of California, Los Angeles. Sir Walter Greg and Mrs. Silva Lake were kind enough to read parts of the manuscript in its earlier stages and to offer salutary criticisms and encouragement, but I have not sought their endorsement of my work as it now stands.

V.A.D.

Contents

I

Preliminary Distinctions

Laws of science and events of history, using these terms in a general
sense, are alike in one respect: they communicate themselves only to their
observers. If an observer wishes to communicate these laws or events in
turn to others who cannot observe for themselves, he must transmute his
experience into a series of mental images, and these in turn into units of
meaning (language, in a general sense) that have standard physical representations (letters, sounds, pictures, and so on) and so cause similar
series of images to form in the minds of his audience. The same process
must be followed by the writer of imaginative literature, the abstract
reasoner in mathematics or logic, and others who wish to communicate
mental images or ideas that have no direct source in the phenomena of
either science or history. In the process of communication from one person to another, a series of mental images is subject to alteration of various
kinds springing from various causes. When it is possible for one mind to
grasp differing forms of what may be called the same pattern of ideas,
analysis is usually desirable to determine as nearly as possible the original
form and the circumstances under which the other forms came into existence and had currency. I shall confine my discussion to examples in which
the patterns of ideas, or *texts*, are works of literature, and in which the
means of communication, or *records*, are manuscripts (or printed books).
The principles involved, however, are the same for any sort of ideas and
for any means of communication.

1

Suppose that Jonathan Swift wrote his maxim "No wise man ever wished to be younger" just as it sprang to his mind; that he made a copy of his first manuscript, in which he changed the text to read "No wise man has ever desired to be younger"; and that he made a copy of his second manuscript, in which he gave up one of his former changes, writing "No wise man ever desired to be younger."

Three things have happened:

(1) The author has written an *original* manuscript, a copy or *descendant* of this original or *ancestor*, and a copy of this descendant. The relationship of the three manuscripts may be expressed in the conventional form of a *tree* or *scheme:*

M1

M2

M3

This particular pattern is called *direct descent*. The second manuscript is the *latest ancestor* of the third; the first is the *common ancestor* of the two others; the second manuscript may be called an *intermediary* between the other two; the third may be described as *terminal;* all are *extant*.

(2) These three manuscripts record and transmit three different forms or *states* of the maxim: the first giving the author's *original* thought, the second giving a modification or *descendant* of the original, the third giving a modification that is closer to the original than the second. The third state is therefore a descendant of a *hypothetical intermediary* between the original and the first descendant, and a *collateral* of the latter. The tree or scheme will then be:

S1

S2   S3

It might be argued that the third state is intermediary between the first and second, but this is to disregard the element of time. It is impossible to place the third state between the other two, because it did not come into existence until after the second state. If the element of time is disregarded, it cannot be said that any of the states is the ancestor or descendant of the others. The particular pattern of this tree is called *radiation*. The relationship between the second and third states is called *independent descent*. By convention the later collaterals are written to the right of the earlier. All three extant states are *terminal* (it will be observed that an original manuscript is not regarded as terminal; the reasons for the distinction will appear later).

(3) In copying the third manuscript from the second, the author mentally consulted his original pattern of ideas, and produced a *convergence* of his first two patterns into a third. The tree illustrative of this is:

A copyist other than the author may similarly consult a mental record when copying a physical. Mrs. Silva Lake says that when collating Biblical manuscripts aloud in Greek monastic libraries she was almost always interrupted by the librarians when they heard unfamiliar readings.[1] When the copyist is not the author, convergence is called *contamination* or *conflation* (sometimes "contamination" is used when the descendant omits elements from one ancestor in favor of varying elements in another, and "conflation" is used when the descendant combines all the varying elements in the ancestors).

The descent of the manuscripts may be called *bibliographical*; the descent of the states, *textual*. The determination of the descent of manuscripts is *bibliographical analysis;* the determination of the descent of texts, *textual analysis*. The combination of the results of these two kinds of analysis is a function of literary history.

In the following pages, the methods for establishing the genetic relationships of states of a text will be worked out in detail. The special methods of establishing the genetic relationships of manuscripts will be referred to only in summary. No special discussion is necessary here of the techniques by which the literary historian combines the results of textual and bibliographical analysis. It is worth emphasizing, however, that he does combine them; he does not simply restate in another way the results of bibliographical analysis alone.

Since bibliographical and textual analyses concern themselves with distinct phenomena, the terms that they share have on occasion distinct meanings, as we have already seen in part. To repeat, the genetic relationships of manuscripts result solely from a copying process, whereas the genetic relationships of states of a text result from the continuity of the likenesses and differences among the units of meaning comprising the states as they come into existence. Since the copying process produces continuity also, it is not always easy to see the difference, but an example will make it clear.

Three manuscripts, A, B, and C, are datable in that order. The first and last correspond page for page, and share certain peculiarities of spelling, facts that indicate a close connection between them. Either C was copied directly from A, or it stands at the end of a lost series of close and careful copies. As for B, its colophon states that it was copied from A. The tree indicative of the descent of the three manuscripts is therefore:

But the units of meaning recorded in C, when they differ from those in A, tend to agree with those in B; the units of meaning in B, when they differ from those in A, always find agreements in C. In other words, B is more like A and C than they are like each other, as far as the text is concerned. This state of affairs indicates a textual continuity passing from A to B with some changes, and from B to C with some additional changes. The textual tree showing this is:

How the textual continuity came to differ from the bibliographical may not be determinable, and does not matter; the textual continuity, as opposed to the bibliographical, is not determined solely by the physical causes for the changes from one state to another. Once this distinction is grasped, what follows will not be confusing.

The nature of textual continuity requires that an original in the textual sense be considered an intermediary when it has two or more independent descendants, because they owe to it their likenesses to each other. In bibliographical analysis, on the contrary, the causal relationship requires that the descendants be considered independent, and the original never an intermediary.

The concept of the original differs in another way also between the two methods. If Swift had written out his second manuscript without reference to the original, he would have produced two originals in the biblio-

graphical sense. On the other hand, if he had copied the second manuscript from the original but had changed the text to read "No man ever
wished to be younger," he would have produced a second original in the
textual sense, because he would have completely changed the meaning.
The original in the bibliographical sense is a physical phenomenon, and a
new original results if the method of transmission is altered or interrupted; a period of oral transmission, for example, produces a second
original manuscript when the text is written again. The original in the
textual sense is a mental phenomenon; if the first manuscript is preceded
by much cogitation, the only record of the original state of the text may
be in the author's memory.

The special problems introduced by the textual definition of an original
have long been felt, but they have not always been identified as such. The
question of when a new original has sprung out of an old, so that the old
may be described as a source for the new, can usually be resolved by some
common-sense application of the principle that when two patterns of
ideas agree more than they differ they are two states of the same text and
that when they differ more than they agree they are states of different
texts. Thus historians of Restoration drama distinguish between Shakespeare's *Hamlet* or *Macbeth* as altered by Davenant, which are still
Shakespeare's, and the Davenant-Dryden *Tempest*, which is no longer
Shakespeare's. The relationships among a series of sources are of course
resolved by deciding upon the significant elements of likeness and difference and by abstracting them from their peculiar contexts. Folklorists
call these abstractions *motifs*, a convenient terminology. Motifs, then,
are the units of meaning upon which to base the analysis of texts that
have no word-for-word correspondences.

When word-for-word correspondences do occur between works commonly regarded as distinct, it is not satisfactory to limit the analysis to
motifs. For example, since the Synoptic Gospels report some of Jesus'
sayings and activities in the same or almost the same words, it is not
satisfactory to base an analysis of their relationship merely on the order
in which the different authors place these sayings and activities. Such
works must first be divided into sections. Then the sections in which the
correspondences are sufficient to allow analysis of the differences in individual words or groups of words must be considered before proceeding
to those in which analysis is possible only of motifs and in turn to those
in which the agreements are confined to still more general characteristics.
If the relationships apparent at each successive level of abstraction differ
from each other, they must be integrated finally into a relationship in

which all the correspondences are adequately represented, because all the correspondences do exist. This is not to say that the analysis must be pushed to its highest possible level of abstraction. It will be quite satisfactory, for example, to examine the Biblical records of Jesus' life without concern for the fact that some information occurs in the Gospels, some in Paul's letters, and so on. But analysis must always begin at the lowest possible level, since it contains the most obvious correspondences. The method of delimiting sections of word-for-word correspondences from sections that must be analyzed for their motifs alone is not a problem to be solved by abstract reasoning, but it seems likely that often the division between the sections will be marked already by some break in the sense commonly recognized or likely to be commonly recognized.

The nature of textual continuity does not require that lost states stand at junctures in the pattern of descent. These junctures are called hypothetical intermediaries only because states occasionally turn up that do stand at these points; otherwise, they could be called conceptual intermediaries. The nature of bibliographical continuity, however, demands that a manuscript shall stand at each such point to preserve the chain of copies. Therefore, if the manuscripts are not extant, they are *inferential*. In a bibliographical pattern of direct descent, also, a descendant may differ from its extant ancestor in a way not explicable from the nature of that ancestor—for example, when omissions in the descendant tend to run to standard lengths and apparently therefore represent the omission of whole lines or groups of lines in an ancestor, and when the standard is shorter or longer than the average line in the extant ancestor. Lost intermediaries apprehensible in this way are called *potential*.

The nature of textual continuity does not provide evidence for potential intermediaries, and of course manuscripts in patterns of direct descent usually leave no traces when they vanish. In both textual and bibliographical analysis, therefore, it is dangerous to assert that the original has been identified, because, unless there is definite external evidence to the contrary, there may always have been a manuscript or state before the one that stands at the top of the tree.

The recovery or creation of additional manuscripts will only fill in or extend a bibliographical scheme; however, if conflation is present, the recovery or creation of additional states may require the alteration of a textual scheme. Since textual continuity results from the regular shift of likenesses and differences from one state to the next, conflicting chains of likeness and difference brought about by conflation force the choice of the simplest of several possibilities. Then the appearance of additional states may shift the balance in favor of a possibility previously rejected. This is a peculiarity of conceptual schemes of all kinds and does not affect their validity.

The term "conflation" and its companion "contamination" have different implications in textual and bibliographical analysis. In the latter the terms imply that the readings are deliberate; there is no standard term for readings that resemble conflations but that are (presumably) not deliberate. In textual study, the element of will is not implied, for the textual continuities that result from deliberate comparison of records and from chance coincidence are the same.

Finally, a single manuscript may record more than one state of a text, either successively, if the manuscript is mutilated, or at the same time, if it has undergone correction without or with only imperfect erasure; on the other hand, a series of manuscripts may record the same state of the text, if they convey to the reader the same units of meaning in the same order. In literary manuscripts in which the illustrations and so on are not an integral part of the text, the units of meaning are called *readings*. The term may be extended to cover all sorts of meaningful phenomena.

It is perhaps helpful to speak of differences between states as *variations*, and to reserve *variants* for the readings that by their diversity make the variations. Greg's classification of the differences into types is most useful. *Simple* types are type–1, in which one state stands alone against all the others (A:BC . . .), and type–2, in which the states are divided into two groups each of at least two members (AB:CD . . ., ABC:DE . . ., and so on). *Complex* types are type–3 and so on to type–n, in which there are from three variants to as many variants as there are states. Variations may result from additions or omissions of readings ($x:xy$, or the reverse); from substitutions, which are essentially both omissions and additions ($xy:xz$); and from transpositions, which are essentially double substitutions ($xy:yx$). The substitution of, say, a description for a picture, or the reverse, is a bibliographical, not a textual, variation; this variation results simply from the substitution of one form of transmission for another. No one would suppose that the text had been altered if he saw the following:

The quick brown 🦊 jumped over the lazy 🐕.

Substitutions and *add-omissions* (the term proposed by Hill as not implying any particular interpretation of the variation) occur at a single point in the context—that is, the context on either side is undisturbed. Therefore a substitution and an add-omission may be expressed together as a complex variation: $wxz:wyz:wz$ = A:B:C. Transpositions, however, being double substitutions, occur, so to speak, at two points in the context. Therefore add-omissions cannot simply be combined with them: $yz:zy:z$ ≠ A:B:C. A and B have y, even though in different places; although they differ, they still agree against C. Two contiguous add-omissions also may have a specious resemblance to a substitution and an add-omission, but $xz:xyz:yz$ ≠ A:B:C. A and B agree in having x; B and C agree in having y. These apparently complex variations may be called *compound*, because it is usually convenient to write them in their compound form; but it is almost always better to resolve them into their components for purposes of calculation. The last example, then, is a compound of AB:C and A:BC; the earlier one, of AB:C and A:B (C being out of the question). More convenient methods of writing the variations will be given below. It should be observed in this connection that when the variation is $xyz:yz:z$, A and B agree against C in the matter of y; but B and C do not agree against A in the matter of x, because C has the nonreading $-xy$, not two nonreadings, $-x$ (agreeing with B) and $-y$. The variation $xyz:yz:z$ is therefore a compound of AB:C and A:B:C.

These introductory distinctions would not be complete without some discussion of the function of judgment in textual and bibliographical analysis. Not all the possible evidence for bibliographical descent has the same weight. When some evidence points to one conclusion, some to another, the relative weight of the evidence needs to be considered. In other words, the perennial question is, what is the most likely pattern of descent for a set of manuscripts? In textual analysis, on the contrary, all the evidence is of equal weight. In the event that two or more solutions to a problem are equally satisfactory, a choice may be made between them, but that is all. This distinction arises again from the disparate natures of the two kinds of analysis. Bibliographical analysis seeks to reconstruct a process that cannot be repeated in the laboratory. Judgment is necessary to separate the evidence for this process from adventitious phenomena of similar appearance. Textual analysis establishes a relationship among varying contextures of ideas that can be reexamined at will. Judgment is not necessary, and indeed is forbidden, during the analysis proper. In short, a bibliographer may perhaps foresee his conclusions to some extent before verifying them, and not feel that he is tampering with the evidence. A textual analyst, in the sense of the term used in this book, can never do so.

II

Rules of Analysis

Because textual continuity would be interrupted by placing between two states another that disagreed with them where they agreed, the basic rule for textual analysis is to arrange the states of a text as far as possible so that none will be intermediary between two others that agree against it in any respect. When contamination is present, and therefore one or more conflicts exist in the textual continuity, the optimum arrangement of the states is that in which the continuities are interrupted as little as possible. As long as contamination is not present, it may be said that if a state disagrees in some respect with two others that agree in this respect, the first is excluded from being intermediary between the others. These exclusions are independent of the ancestor-descendant relationship, and may therefore be expressed in a *general diagram*, into which the concept of temporality has not been introduced. The absence of a temporal relationship in these diagrams will be indicated in the present book by writing them whenever possible with what seems to be the main axis horizontal and with two or more states equally prominent at the left. Of course the temporal relationships of the states may result in additional exclusions. Therefore a *special diagram*, in which the temporal element is represented, will not always be merely a general diagram upended.

The element of temporality may be introduced either by dating the states themselves or by showing that some of the readings in one are more original than those in another. Here the textual analyst adopts two

9

assumptions as rules. The first is that a state is to be dated by the earliest extant manuscript in which it is recorded. Conceivably it might have been recorded in an earlier manuscript now lost. Human and mechanical inefficiency is such, however, that a copy of any length is almost sure to present a different state than its exemplar. Consequently the textual scholar will never assume that he has before him a perfect copy of a lost manuscript. It has been vigorously argued that the dates of manuscripts are immaterial in textual analysis, but the fact remains that an ancestor must have come into existence before its descendants.

The second assumption the textual scholar elevates to a rule is that one variant reading is more original than another if the second could easily have resulted from the first by a known type of error in transmission, and the first could have resulted from the second only by a correction or through mere chance. Experience seems to show that chance hitting upon a better reading is rarer than deliberate correction, and that correction in turn is rarer than error. Of course, where the general conclusion from experience can be shown not to fit the particular instance, the textual scholar accepts the fact.

The kinds of errors will vary according to the method of transmitting the text—whether oral-aural or manual-visual (manual-tactile—braille— may be ignored)—and according to whether they result from mental or mechanical (including muscular) failures or from damage to the records involved in the transmission. Variations in which a temporal relationship may be established between the variants may be called *directional*, because the variations indicate the direction of transmission of at least a part of the text from one state to another. In this book A→B will indicate a variation in which the reading of A is more original than that of B. The following list is complete (or nearly so) for transmission when the records are manuscripts (including typescripts) or handset printed books, and where the variations occur in contexts otherwise identical in the different states. Other records will provide additions or require subtractions from this list because of the different mechanical processes by which they are produced, and so will variations in contexts only generally parallel in different states or different texts.

Confusion of similar letters. The first examples result from transcription from majuscule to minuscule and the reverse:

ΠΑΡΕΤΗ'ΡΟΥΝ
γὰρ ἐτήρουν   (114 etc.)[1]

ἔκφοβοι
ἜΜΦΟΒΟΙ   (Κ)[2]

The remaining examples result from peculiarities in the hand or type. The first results from the form of open capital P:

CLAVDVNT
PLAVDVNT   (R)[3]

The second results from long s:

savors
favors   (Gregory Smith's ed.)[4]

A knowledge of paleography and typography is therefore necessary for determining between random error, which has no directional value, and confusions of this kind. The decision for the latter will be more convincing also if the surrounding text is untouched. Thus in Dryden's *Mac Flecknoe*, line 33, two states (82 and M) read "Russet," and one (H) "Russell"; thus it might be concluded that the second had resulted from the first—"t," especially when uncrossed, resembles "l" in the Italian hand. But 82 and M read "Drugget Russet" where H reads "Russell drugget." This fact introduces an additional consideration, because other states read "rusty" or "rustick drugget." The reading of H may be a simple corruption of one of these.[5]

Misinterpretation of contractions. The first example results from a common "head-and-tail" contraction:

ις ['Iησοῦs]
εἰς   (346)[6]

The second involves a name and a number:

CL [i.e., Claudius]
centesimo quinquagesimo   (β)[7]

G. B. Harrison has suggested that "O, Glendower" in *1 Henry IV*, II. iv. 373 resulted from a misreading of "O." (i.e., "Owen").[8] It is also possible for a scribe to suppose a contraction where none exists:

constantissimo
consulibus tantissimo   (Vindobonensis)[9]

As before, a knowledge of paleography and typography is necessary to interpret the evidence.

Confusion of words generally resembling each other. Here again it must be clear that a real confusion has arisen, and not just the chance substitution of one word for another. A knowledge of paleography and typography is again required, because confusions possible in one type face or hand may be impossible in another. If it is impossible or unlikely that the confusion could have occurred in the process of transcribing the copy, the possibility of confusion in an intermediate copy needs still to be taken into account. Many confusions of this kind have their source in incorrect division or combination of words (see below), and some are apparently assisted by similar formations in the neighboring context.

Progress	Scream
Process (8vo ed.)	Stream (8vo ed.)[10]

Names may appear, disappear, or replace each other for this reason:

Lucullorum
iucoliorum (R)[11]

Numbers are also subject to errors of confusion with other numbers (∞, 1,000, and X, 10) and with similar words or parts of words (iii seems once to have been mistaken forvir;and OI Λ, where Λ = 30, for OIΔE).[12] Confusion of similar sounding words is called *homophony*. In the following example the standard text is apparently in error; the margin and, in many manuscripts, the text itself give the more correct reading, upon which the Greek is based:

א֥ב   (Qere)
יֽב   (Kethib)[13]

Mistaken combination or separation of words. More specific terms are *fusion* and *fission*. In manuscripts these conditions often result from mistaken interpretation of continuous script:

εἰν ᾽Αρίμοις *Iliad* ii. 783
Inarime   *Aeneid* ix. 716[14]

all together
altogether (8vo ed.)[15]

False punctuation may result in the grouping of words out of their proper context, and sometimes in insertions to patch up the sense:

He grieved the land he freed should be oppressed
He grieved the land, he freed, should be oppressed   (1668)[16]

Transposition. Transposition of letters is called *anagrammatism* or *metathesis*. Once again, familiarity with paleography and typography is essential; in type, ligatures prevent transposition of the individual letters of which they are composed, and it seems likely that they would be thought of by the scribe also as compound letters. McKerrow gives as an impossible transposition in type the words "file" and "life" in which the former will be made up of only three sorts, the latter of four.[17] Of course both compositors and scribes may conceivably misread their copy. Hall records that anagrammatism is especially common in the transcription of proper names. Further, he says that although anagrammatism in a name often results from general resemblance, it probably results also from the scribe's failure to pronounce correctly to himself while writing. In verse, scribes sometimes write in prose order; in prose, they sometimes reverse familiar antitheses. Scribes generally prefer to insert omitted words later in the context if the structure of the language and the sense of the passage will allow. It is common also for scribes, finding omitted passages supplied in the margins of their exemplars, to insert them in the wrong places in the copies:

> ἄγοντες ἥκομεν
> ἥκοντες ἄγομεν (R)[18]

> τἀμά δ'οὐκ
> τὰ δ' ἀμ' οὐκ (C)[19]

> correct Love, and elegant Desires
> corrects Love, and elegant Desire (8vo ed.)[20]

A leaf or a multiple of leaves may also be transposed.

Mistranscriptions from one alphabet to another. In the following example the earliest reading has had to be established by retranscription:

> ἰχθὺν et ἵππον
> ἰχθὺν et ippon
> ἰχθὺν καὶ ἵρον (ς)[21]

The reading "Oncaymeon" (i.e., ὂν καὶ μὴ ὄν) in Marlowe's *Dr. Faustus*, i, 12, resulted in a similar way; here the original reading was recovered only by emendation.

Retention of once meaningful signs in contexts where they have no place. In the first example the original is restored from a parallel passage; here the marginal notation of an omission (τὰ) has been inserted in the wrong place, catchword (περὶ) and all:

> θεάσασθαι τὸν οὐρανὸν καὶ τὰ περὶ αὐτὸν ἄστρα
> θεάσασθαι τὰ περὶ τὸν οὐρανὸν καὶ περὶ αὐτὸν ἄστρα[22]

In the second example a marginal note has (twice) been misunderstood and taken into the text:

ꝗ [= quaere] (F)
quae (H)[23]

The last example is from printed books:

fran-/tick
fran-tick (1592C)[24]

Imperfect corrections.

τῶν γε ζώντων
τῶν τε ζώντων (C)
τῶν πεζῶν τῶν (A, G)[25]

genu esset aut talus
genuisset aut talus (B)
genuisset aut sibi aut aliis (F)
genu esset aut tibia aut talus (u)[26]

The confutation of Citizens obiections against Players
The confutation of Citizens against Players (4th ed.)
The coniuration of Citizens against Players (5th ed.)[27]

It is normally necessary to have a chain of at least three readings to determine direction, but even with two if one occurs in a damaged archetype or in a manuscript that clearly indicates a damaged archetype the necessary conditions will be met. In other words, if the scholar has only a correct and an incorrect reading, he cannot be sure but that the "correct" reading is merely a plausible emendation of the incorrect; but if he has an *imperfect* reading that is not otherwise incorrect, he may conclude that it is earlier than the incorrect reading. Hill refers to the example of the *Dialogues* of Epictetus of which the archetype has a stain on the text; the descendants either leave a blank at this place or run together the context on each side of the stain.[28] Once again, this is an example of bibliographical evidence. Hall's term for imperfect correction is *interpolation*, which in this sense does not necessarily imply insertion.

Failure to repeat. This is called *haplography*, and may involve a letter (often when letters are used for numerals), syllable, word, or phrase. The repetition in the following example is a peculiarity of the author:

Ἀμὴν ἀμὴν λέγω ὑμῖν
Ἀμὴν λέγω ὑμῖν (28)[29]

Omissions resulting from similarities in words or syllables. These are sometimes called *eye skips*, sometimes *homoeoteleuta* (same ending, so that skips caused by similar beginnings of words are sometimes called *homoeoarchy*); they are called ὁμοιότης (abbreviated ὁμ.) by Clark and *homoeographa* by Postgate. The resemblances causing the skip need not be exact. In the first example, the error was noticed and corrected in the margin of the papyrus:

> οἱ ἄνδρες ἐν τῇ νήσῳ ἐπολιορκήθησαν ἀπὸ τῆς
> ναυμαχίας μέχρι τῆς ἐν τῇ νήσῳ μάχης
> οἱ ἄνδρες ἐν τῇ νήσῳ μάχης (Oxyrynchus pap. no. 16)[30]

In the second example the correct text is known only from a quotation in Donatus:

> qui in hortus fuerit, qui unguenta sumpserit
> qui unguenta sumpserit[31]

The following examples are from printed books:

bore arms. / *2. Clo.* Why, he had none. / *1. Clo.* What, art a heathen? How dost thou understand the Scripture? The Scripture says Adam digg'd; could he dig without arms? I'll put
bore arms. I'll put (Q2)[32]

his recoveries. Is this the fine of his fines, and the recovery of his recoveries, to have his recoveries, to have (Q2)[33]

Simple omission. More technical terms are *lipography* and *parablepsia.* Normally these variations are not directional, since it cannot be determined that the fuller reading is not a plausible emendation. But if, as Clark has pointed out, the omission corresponds exactly to a line or group of lines in the manuscript with the fuller state of the text, the fuller state is doubtless earlier; it is unlikely that an emendation or interpolation would exactly fill a line or group of lines in a manuscript, if the lines are written from margin to margin:

> . . . qui hac ratione
> philosophentur ii nihil habeant quod sequantur. Dictum est omnino
> de hac re alio loco . . . (Leid. Voss. 86 [B])
> . . . qui hac ratione de hac re alio loco . . . (Flor. Marc. 257)[34]

> . . . pos-
> sent et ex sese similia sui gignere. Sunt autem qui omnia naturae nomine appel-
> lent ut Epicurus . . . (Leid. Voss. 86 [B])
> . . . possent ut Epicurus . . . (Flor. Marc. 257)[35]

Something similar occurred in *Letters of Mr. Alexander Pope, and Several of his Friends* (1737), of which there are impressions in quarto and folio; when the pages were remade for the quarto, the line belonging at the foot of page 326 was placed at the head.

Omissions of standard lengths. Clark has shown that when the text is written from margin to margin, omissions of the same or nearly the same number of letters, or of multiples of the base number, indicate that whole lines of an ancestor manuscript have been omitted. The shorter state will then be later than the longer, even when neither happens to have been preserved in the specific ancestor and descendant between which the loss occurred. Examples are necessarily too lengthy for reproduction here; Clark provides a great number, mostly from classical Latin texts.[36]

Repetition from neighboring contexts. Repetition from the immediate context (*dittography*) is usually either obviously wrong and easily correctible or not certainly wrong and so not satisfactory directional evidence. It may occasionally happen, however, that a dittography, although not obviously wrong, is sufficiently uncharacteristic of the writer, or is obviously wrong but suggests no easy emendation. The first two examples are of this kind:

> 'Αμὴν λέγω ὑμῖν
> 'Αμὴν ἀμὴν λέγω ὑμῖν (106, 579)[37]

> iussu eius Romam
> iussueiussuromam (Vind. lat. 15)[38]

The next example, although apparently easy of correction, was not in fact corrected until the editions were collated by Bond:

> to bound his Existence
> to bound to his Existence (8vo ed.)[39]

When the repetition occurs after a longer interval, it may displace some other part of the text. Hall notes that when the scribe's eye travels forward, the repetitions are likely to be shorter than when it travels backward. The repetition need not be exact.

> Some were dazzling, like the sun,
> Shining down at summer noon.

> Some were dazzling like the sun,
> Some shining down at summer noon. (*Poet. Wks.*, ed. Shorter)[40]

Insertions from the margin.

> uetus est tutela draconis
> non potuit legi uetus est tutela draconis (Neapolitanus 268)[41]

Insertions of variant readings, glosses, and explanations of the construction are often called *adscripts*; these often replace the original reading. Before a variation can be identified as a gloss, Hall warns, it must be ascertained that one of the alternates invites annotation and that both are in the same construction. Obviously the easier alternative is the gloss. In the first example the original is restored from Harpocration:

> πρὸς τὸν λίθον ἄγοντες καὶ ἐξορκίζοντες
> πρὸς τὸν βωμὸν ἄγοντες καὶ ἐξορκίζοντες[42]

> The swalow mordrer of the foules smale
> The swalow mordrer of the flyes smale (R)[43]

Additions or substitutions from similar writings. In the first example one of the Gospels (Matt. 24:29) has influenced the transcription of another:

> καὶ οἱ ἀστέρες τοῦ οὐρανοῦ ἔσονται ἐκπίπτοντες
> καὶ οἱ ἀστέρες πεσοῦνται ἐκ τοῦ οὐρανοῦ (389, 565, 700)[44]

In the second example the scribe has remembered the passage alluded to (Cowley's *Davideis*, I, 79), and has substituted quotation for allusion:

> Where their vast courts the mother-strumpets keep
> Where their vast courts the mother waters keep (H)[45]

In any of the foregoing errors it is essential not only that the error is not readily correctible but that there is no doubt as to which is the correct reading.

Griesbach has furnished some additional rules:[46] the shorter reading, the harder reading, the harsher reading, the rarer form, the reading at first glance apparently wrong, are probably the earlier; emphatic expressions, pious expressions, the most orthodox expression, are probably the later; the reading repeating a neighboring word or idea, the reading that smells of a gloss, the reading dependent upon the Fathers or the scholiasts, or first found in a lectionary or in a translation are almost certainly later. These rules are based on an expectation of the scribe's actions under certain circumstances.

Finally, the better of two readings may be assumed to be the earlier. A special type of better reading is the reading more characteristic of the author. Presumably the author is more likely to produce a better reading than the copyist. Estimates of these readings differ among individual scholars, but that fact should not prevent the exercise of critical judgment.

When the variations among the states reflect authorial revision, on the other hand, the reading least characteristic of the author may be accepted as the earliest. An authorized edition almost certainly marks the end of the process of revision if it was reprinted without revision in the author's lifetime (and the reprints are not piracies). These indications will not supersede truly directional variations or the relevant Griesbachian types, because the author as reviser is also the author as scribe.

Although directional variations of the type A→B are the most common, they may combine into A→B→C (see also "Imperfect corrections," above) or A←B→C, but never into A→B←C. One reading may be differently corrupted in different descendants, but a single reading cannot be a corruption of two ancestors. At best there will be two readings side by side: one the corruption of one ancestor, the other the corruption of another. The point is of some importance, since what may seem to be conflated readings, with or without additional corruption, are regularly taken as indicative of direction. The fact is that these readings are identifiable as conflated only if the temporal relationship of the manuscripts is known; if the temporal relationship is incompatible with conflation, the same readings are interpreted differently. A scholar, finding ἐκεῖ ἐν τῇ ἐρήμῳ in the Byzantine manuscripts of Mark where ἐκεῖ appears in the Sinaitic Syriac and ἐν τῇ ἐρήμῳ in the Alexandrian or Neutral manuscripts, may argue that the Byzantine reading is therefore later; finding 'Οψίας δὲ γενομένης, ὅτε ἔδυθεν ὁ ἥλιος in Mark, 'Οψίας δὲ γενομένης in Matthew and Δύνοντος δὲ τοῦ ἡλίου in Luke, the same scholar may argue that Mark is therefore earlier. The scholar concerned had other reasons for his datings and these led him to interpret the same type of reading as evidence now for one relationship, now for another.[47]

I shall now proceed to develop the concepts of textual analysis from hypothetical examples, beginning with a text preserved in two states. If the states are identifiable as two, they must vary. Since there are only two, the variations can only be of the type A:B, that is, type–*n*. These variations may be directional or nondirectional. If one or more directional variations A→B occur, then the states belong in an order of direct descent providing that a manuscript in which A is preserved is earlier than any in which B is recorded. If this is not true, then the states belong in an order of independent descent

because B could not have depended for some of its readings upon A if A were not in existence. The textual analyst will not assume that A was also recorded in an earlier manuscript now lost. In these particular instances he will instead ascribe the earlier readings of A to an ancestor from which B has varied but A has not. In the rest of the text there is no way of determining which descendant has varied, or even that the descendants have not both varied independently.

If directional variations conflict with each other instead of with the dates of the manuscripts, the states are again collaterals,

because B could not have depended for some of its reading upon A at the same time that A depended for others of its readings upon B. As before, the earlier readings must be ascribed to a common ancestor, from which now A, now B, has varied—that is, when an earlier reading appears in one or the other, that one has *not* varied from the ancestor.

If there are no directional variations, the states can be arranged in direct descent, since that will be the simplest possible relationship for them, and the one preserved in the earliest extant manuscript can be placed at the head. If no distinction is possible between the dates of the manuscripts, the scholar is at liberty to count as the ancestor the state that for whatever reason appeals to him as the best; he should, however, give the reason, and indicate that more reliable evidence is lacking.

From the foregoing it is apparent that if there is a conflict between relative date of the manuscripts and directional variations or between one directional variation and another, the states involved are collateral.

The possible relationships among three states of a text are naturally more numerous and complicated. If the states are identifiable as three, each must vary in some respect from both the others. The variations may be type–n, A:B:C, or type–1, A:BC, B:AC, or C:AB. With three states, type–1 variations are also type–$n-1$; the evidence provided by type–$n-1$ variations where there are more than three states is somewhat different from that provided by type–1 variations, and will require separate discussion.

When there are three states of a text, one may be intermediary between the others. The conditions that exclude a state from being an intermediary are as follows.

A state will be excluded if it disagrees with the others when they agree against it (type–1 variation). A:BC excludes A; B:AC excludes B; AB:C excludes C.

A state will also be excluded if it does not share in a directional variation (type–n variation). A:B→C or A:B←C excludes A; A→C:B or A←C:B excludes B; A→B:C or A←B:C excludes C. The readings connected by the arrow stand in a cause-and-effect relationship in which the other has no share.

A state will be excluded from being intermediary if it is later in date than both the others. This relative dating may be determined by the dates of the manuscripts recording the states or, when this is not possible, by directional variations.

If there is a conflict between the directional variations and the relative dates of the manuscripts, or between two different directional variations, the states involved are collaterals. Therefore, although each may be intermediary between a descendant and the other, neither may be intermediary between an ancestor and the other.

With three states of a text, it is not always immediately obvious that one possible diagram is simpler than, and therefore to be preferred to, another. In a genetic scheme it is necessary at a minimum that each ancestor have a descendant, and that each descendant have an ancestor. Direct descent is the diagram that fulfills these minimum conditions and no others, and it is therefore the simplest possible diagram. This simplest diagram becomes more complicated when one of the intermediary states is the ancestor—one state has two descendants—and further complicated when the ancestor is a hypothetical intermediary—another state is introduced, and this state has two descendants. In all these diagrams, the textual continuity remains simple, passing from or through one state to another. The textual continuity becomes more complex when more than two states are related through another, for then it branches in passing through the nodal state. If the nodal state is the ancestor of all the others, the diagram is more complicated than if one of the others is the earliest ancestor, for the number of descendants from any one ancestor is then larger. The diagrams become still more complicated as more examples of independent descent appear within them. The textual continuity becomes most complex when it doubles back upon itself in conflation. At first glance the resulting circular diagram appears simpler, but it requires that one descendant have two ancestors, thus exceeding the requirements of simple descent. The possible diagrams for three extant states of a text will therefore fall into the following order of increasing complexity.

Direct descent. The special diagram used here as an illustration can be chosen when the following conditions are not exceeded.

A
|
B
|
C

a. A is excluded from being intermediary by A:BC or A:B→C; C is excluded by AB:C or A→B:C; or both are excluded by A→B→C.

b. A is earlier than B, and B than C, as shown by the dates of the manuscripts, by directional variations A→BC, A→B:C, AB→C, A:B→C, or A→B→C, or by a combination of both kinds of evidence.

Note a. The variations A←B:C and A:B←C, or A←B←C or A←B→C would exclude A and C, but would conflict with the second condition and so would require a more complicated diagram. On the other hand, as long as there is no conflict this diagram will be chosen even if the first condition is only partly fulfilled or not fulfilled—that is, if the variations themselves exclude only A or C or (type-*n* variations alone occurring) neither—because this is the simplest possible diagram.

Note b. Again, since this is the simplest possible diagram, it is sufficient to prove the temporal relationship of only two of the states, or even of none if A is the most characteristic of the author or for some other good reason is to be valued above the others.

Independent descent, with one of the states the common ancestor of the others. The special diagram used as an illustration can be chosen when the following conditions are not exceeded.

B
/ \
A   C

a. A is excluded from being intermediary by A:BC or A:B→C; C is excluded by AB:C or A←B:C; or both are excluded by A←B→C.

b. B is earlier than A and C, as shown by the dates of the manuscripts, by directional variations A←BC or A←B:C and AB→C or A:B→C, or A←B→C alone, or by a combination of both kinds of evidence.

Note a. The variations A:B←C and A→B:C or A→B→C or A←B←C would exclude A and C from being intermediary, but would conflict with the second condition and so require a more complicated diagram.

Note b. If evidence is lacking to show that B is earlier than both the other states, this diagram may still be chosen if B is the most characteristic of the author or for some other good reason is to be valued above the other states.

Partly independent and partly direct descent, the earliest ancestor a hypothetical intermediary between two of the states, one of which has the third state as a descendant. The special diagram used as an illustration can be chosen when the following conditions are not exceeded.

a. A is excluded from being intermediary by A:BC or A:B→C; C is excluded by AB:C or A→B:C or A←B:C; or both are excluded by A→B→C or A←B→C.

b. There is a conflict between A→BC or A→B:C or A→B→C and A←BC or A←B:C or A←B→C; or A→BC or A→B:C or A→B→C occurs, and A is later than B (or B and C) as established by the dates of the manuscripts.

Note a. The variation A:B←C would exclude A, and the variation A←B←C would exclude both A and C; but either would prevent C from being a descendant of B, and would require a more complicated diagram.

Note b. No special evidence is necessary that C is later than B; to assume otherwise would be to exclude B from being intermediary also, and would require a more complicated diagram.

Partly direct and partly independent descent, all the extant states terminal and connected through a single hypothetical intermediary. The special

A
／\
B   C

diagram used as an illustration can be chosen when the following conditions are not exceeded.

a. (1) A is excluded from being intermediary by A:BC or A:B→C or A:B←C, B is excluded by B:AC or B:A→C, and C is excluded by C:AB or C:A→B; or A and B are excluded by A→C→B, A and C are excluded by A→B→C, or B and C are excluded by B←A→C. Or (2) A and B are excluded by the variations, and C is later in date than both A and B; or A and C are excluded by the variations, and B is later in date than both A and C. Or (3) all three states are excluded by a combination of A:B→C and A:B←C when A is the earliest.

b. A is earlier than B and C as shown by the dates of the manuscripts; by directional variations A→BC, AB→C and AC→B, A→B:C and A→C:B, A→B→C, A→C→B, or B←A→C; or by a combination of both kinds of evidence.

Note a. The variations A←C:B, A←B:C, A←B→C, and A←C←B would exclude B and C from being intermediaries, but they would conflict with the second condition and so would require a more complicated diagram. For the same reason A cannot be excluded by conflict of directional variation with relative date, or by conflict of two directional variations in which it is involved.

Note b. Since this is the simplest possible diagram when all extant states are excluded from being intermediary, A may be taken as the ancestor even when it cannot be dated, provided either that directional variations show both the other states to be descendants or that A is the most characteristic of the author or for some other good reason is to be valued above the others.

Independent descent, all the states collateral descendants of a common hypothetical intermediary. In this relationship all the states must be

A   B   C

excluded from being intermediary. The states all being datable, the earliest must have a directional variation pointing to it. Or, only two states being datable, directional variations must point to the earlier and to the undatable state. Or, only one or none being datable, directional variations must point to all the states. Here the earliest state cannot be the ancestor of the others, because it has less original readings, and of course no later state can be the ancestor of an earlier. The directional variations can be type–1 or type–*n*, except that none can be of the sort A→B→C without requiring a more complicated diagram.

Compound independent descent, the earliest ancestor a hypothetical intermediary between one extant state and a second hypothetical intermediary, the common ancestor of the other two extant states. The special diagram

A   B   C

used as an illustration can be chosen when the conditions for the preceding diagram have been met and when there is a directional variation A→B→C, A→C→B, or A→BC. Here a state that cannot be the ancestor has earlier readings than the other states.

Contamination or conflation when one state has both the others as independent descendants, and one of these in turn has both the others as independent ancestors. This diagram will never occur in textual analysis, be-

cause variations of the type A→C←B demanded by the special diagram here given will never occur. Such a diagram may occur in bibliographical analysis if there is evidence for it beyond the mere physical characteristics of the manuscripts, or it may result from the syntheses of literary history.

Contamination or conflation where the earliest ancestor is a hypothetical intermediary between two of the extant states, and the third is an independent intermediary between the other two. The diagrams used as illustrations can

(1)   (2)

be chosen if there are directional variations A→BC, and AB←C or C→A→B, and (1) B is later than A and C than B, as shown by the dates of the manuscripts, or by the variations A→B:C or A→BC and A:B→C, or A→B→C, or by a combination of both kinds of evidence, or (2) B is later than both A and C as shown by the dates of the manuscripts, or by the variations A→B:C or B←A→C, and A:B←C or A←C→B, or A→C→B or C→A→B, or by a combination of both kinds of evidence. B may apparently be excluded from being intermediary by the presence of AC:B, B:A→C, or B:A←C, but these agreements are explicable as resulting from the readings of the earliest ancestor, and do not require an additional hypothetical intermediary. On the other hand, if B's manuscript is earlier than A's, or there are variations B→AC, B→A:C, B→A→C, B→C→A, A←B→C, A←B←C, or (when B's manuscript is later than C's) B→C:A, a more complicated diagram will be necessary.

Conflation or contamination where the earliest ancestor is a hypothetical intermediary from which all the extant states are descended and the two later states are also descended from the earliest either (1) directly or (2) through a second hypothetical intermediary. For the diagrams used as illustrations,

(1)

(2)

A's manuscript must be earlier than B's and B's than C's, and B and C must have a reading or readings earlier than the corresponding readings of each of the others. If A's earlier readings occur only in A→B:C, or A→C:B, or B→A→C, or B←A←C, or B←A→C, or some combination of them, the first diagram is possible; otherwise the second is required.

By themselves the patterns of conflation would be tolerable, and sometimes as part of a larger scheme; but to avoid the possibility of complications that would make a scheme impossible of comprehension, patterns of ordinary descent may be chosen and the evidence of conflation may be recorded separately. If this is done, the earliest state having earlier readings is chosen as the ancestor. When the relative dates cannot be determined, the state having the largest number of earlier readings is chosen, unless a directional variation also points to it alone (A←BC, A←B:C or A←C:B, not AB←C or AC←B), making it a collateral descendant with the other states of a hypothetical ancestor. The annotations are reminders that earlier readings occur not only in the ancestor but also in another state or states, and that the priority of the readings of the ancestor is to be accepted in nondirectional variations only for simplicity's sake.

Greg has developed another aid to ordering the states in type–n variations, which he calls the principle of determinate divergence.[48] According to this principle, two similar readings establish a sufficient continuity to exclude the less similar from being placed between them. By "similarity" Greg does not mean that one reading is dependent upon another, as in a directional variation; nor does he mean that "seven" is more similar to "eight" than to "nine." He has in mind such variations as "to you I tell": "to you I say": "I say to you." These are compound variations, which are usually better resolved into components. If they are not resolved, then A and C being each more like B than like each other, the likeness of A and B excludes C from being intermediary between them, and the likeness of B and C excludes A from being intermediary between them—that is, A:B:C may be expressed as A:BC and AB:C. It does not seem that the principle is capable of rigorous application, because similarity establishes a much lower order of continuity than does identity of reading or dependence of one reading upon another; but when there is no other evidence than the relative dates of the manuscripts, or no other evidence at all, determinate convergence may modify or determine the relationships among the texts.

The same principles govern when there are more than three states. When there is a complete series of type–1 variations, and no other types, every state will be excluded from being the intermediary between any of the others; all will therefore be terminal. The following diagrams will be necessary to indicate the continuity between the states:

The first is indicated when all the states are datable, A is the earliest, and no directional variants point to A, or from any other state in greater number than from A; or, if A is not datable, when either A→BCDE occurs more often than B→ACDE, C→ABDE, D→ABCE, and E→ABCD; or there are B←ACDE, C←ABDE, D←ABCE, and E←ABCD, and only these directional variations. If there are fewer than the full set of the last four variations, and so two or more states as possible ancestors, a choice may be made among them on any reasonable ground. The second diagram is indicated when A→BCDE occurs, A is later than one or more of the other states, and any undatable states have

directional variations pointing to them; or when there are both A→BCDE
and A←BCDE, as long as the former occurs more often than B→ACDE,
C→ABDE, D→ABCE, and E→ABCD. The third diagram is indicated
when directional variations point to the earliest of the datable states and
to any undatable states and when none points away from any of the other
states.

If there are all but one kind of the type–1 variations, one of the texts
is not excluded as an intermediary, and the diagrams are (if ABCD:E
is not found, and there is no conflation):

Two or more sorts will never be wanting, since there would then be no
differences between two or more states; before it can be said that states
exist they must differ.

Type–2 variations, dividing the states into opposing groups, exclude
the members of either group from being intermediary between members
of the other. Therefore, just as type–1 variations show individual states
to be terminal, type–2 variations show groups of states to be terminal.
It is usually convenient to think of the smaller as the terminal group; in
fact both are terminal. Indeed the group of states in a type–1 variation is
terminal. Type–2 variations will not by themselves differentiate all the
states unless contamination has occurred. If the differentiation is accomplished through complex variations, it is possible that the diagram will
not be definable without directional variations or distinguishable dates
among the manuscripts. I shall discuss shortly the problems thus created,
but first I wish to examine the evidence that will occur when the differentiation is accomplished by type–1 variations. If there are only four
states, a diagram can be drawn if there are one type–2 variation and from
two to four type–1 variations. The possible types of diagram are:

$$A—B—C—D \qquad \begin{matrix} C \\ \diagdown \\ D \diagup \end{matrix}\!\!\!>\!—B—A \qquad \begin{matrix} A & & C \\ & >\!\!\!<\!\! & \\ B & & D \end{matrix}$$

The first diagram will result from A:BCD (which makes A terminal),
AB:CD (which makes AB and CD terminal), and ABC:D (which makes

D terminal). Not being individually excluded, B and C stand for the present as intermediaries. The second diagram will result when ABD:C also occurs, making C terminal as well. The third diagram will result when B:ACD occurs in addition, making all the states terminal.

As before, each of these general forms may take a variety of specific forms. The first, for example, may assume the following types:

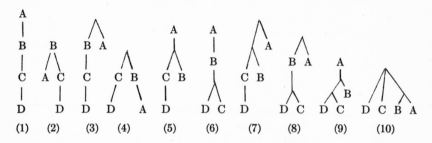

(1)   (2)   (3)   (4)   (5)   (6)   (7)   (8)   (9)   (10)

The first type occurs when there is at least one and no conflicting variation pointing from the direction of A in the direction of D, and when the dates of the manuscripts, if determinable, show that A is earlier than B, and so on; or, if there are no directional variations, when the determinable dates of the manuscripts show A earlier than B, C, or D, B earlier than C or D, or C earlier than D, with no conflicts.

The second type occurs when directional variations point from BCD to A and from AB to CD, and when the manuscript recording B is earlier than those recording A, C, and D, and that recording C is earlier than that recording D. If no directional variations occur, the dates of the manuscripts are sufficient.

The remaining types result from conflicts. The third and fourth occur when directional variations are found pointing in both directions between two states (in the third A→BCD and A←BCD, in the fourth AB→CD and AB←CD). The fifth and sixth can result from conflicts in directional variations only when there are complex variations (as for the fifth A:B←CD, for the sixth AB:C←D). All four occur also when directional variations point from a state preserved in a later manuscript to one preserved in an earlier (in the third A→BCD, when A's manuscript is later than B's; in the fourth AB→CD, when A's manuscript is later than B's and B's than C's; in the fifth AB→CD, when B's manuscript is later than C's; in the sixth ABC→D, when C's manuscript is later than D's). The fifth diagram will also result simply from B's manuscript being later than A's and C's (D's being later than C's or undatable), and the sixth from C's manuscript being later than B's and D's (A's being earlier than B's or undatable).

The seventh diagram results from conflicts involving A and B; the eighth from conflicts involving A and C; the ninth from conflicts involving B and C; and the tenth from conflicts involving A, B, and C. The tenth, with all extant states descendants, may take a variety of other forms, depending on the directional variations.

Of the general diagrams, the first has the greatest number of possible mutations. The second general diagram cannot take the first five special forms possible with the first, and the third cannot take the first eight special forms. In other words, the exclusions required by the nondirectional variations are the primary conditions for the diagram.

I come now to complex variations. The most complex variation, type-*n*, is no different in its indications when there are four or more states than when there are only two or three—that is, directional variations and the dates of the manuscripts determine the relationship among states that are differentiated solely by this type. The others divide the states into at least three groups, of which only one need be a true group of two or more states. The groups composed of two or more states exclude the other states from being intermediary between their members. When one group of states in one variation shares one or more states with another group in another variation, the states not shared are excluded from, and so terminal with respect to the common nucleus.

A successive relationship will be indicated when groups of two or three members each form a chain, each sharing one state with the next (only the intermediary groups may consist of three states and still define the diagram, because in them alone will it be simplest to accept the unshared states as intermediary between the shared; if three states are found in a terminal group, the ultimate and penultimate states cannot be differentiated); or when larger groups form a chain, each sharing $n-1$ states with the next. In the following examples the compounded exclusions will be self-evident:

AB:C:D	AB:C:DE	ABC:D:E
A:BC:D	A:BCD:E	A:BCD:E
A:B:CD		A:B:CDE
A—B—C—D	A—B—C—D—E	A—B—C—D—E

A radiational relationship will be indicated when three or more groups share one state; or when three or more groups are apparently connected in a closed chain; or when all the members of a group of three or more are excluded from being intermediary between any of the others. In the latter event the connection may not be immediately obvious. The following examples illustrate the possibilities:

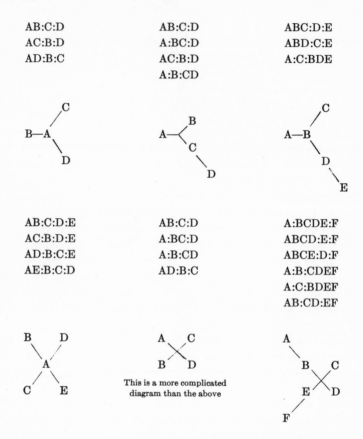

AB:C:D	AB:C:D	ABC:D:E
AC:B:D	A:BC:D	ABD:C:E
AD:B:C	AC:B:D	A:C:BDE
	A:B:CD	

AB:C:D:E	AB:C:D	A:BCDE:F
AC:B:D:E	A:BC:D	ABCD:E:F
AD:B:C:E	A:B:CD	ABCE:D:F
AE:B:C:D	AD:B:C	A:B:CDEF
		A:C:BDEF
		AB:CD:EF

This is a more complicated
diagram than the above

One more peculiarity of complex variations is worth noting: when two groups of states are found in one variation, the intermediary between the members of one group cannot be the intermediary between the members of the other also. The last diagram above could not have resulted if A:BE:CD:F, for example, had occurred among the variations.

When simple and complex variations occur together, they often supplement each other in defining the diagram. The following examples are indicative:

AB:CD	A:BCD	A:BCDE
A:BC:D	AB:CD	B:ACDE
	ABC:D	C:ABDE
A—B—C—D	B:AD:C	D:ABCE
		E:ABCD
		AB:C:DE

A⟍   ⟋C
　 ⟋⟍
B⟋   ⟍D

A⟍
　⟍　　D
B—⟋⟍—⟋
　⟋　⟍E
C⟋

The phenomenon in the second example is worth particular attention. A state paired in a type–2 or more complex variation with a second state known from a type–1 variation to be terminal is itself terminal if it stands alone in a complex variation in which the second state is paired with a third. The rule holds for states found with several terminal states in the one variation as long as they all find new partners in the complex variation (or in the course of several such variations). The rule also holds, of course, for groups of states as well as individuals.

With variations having two or more groups of two or more states each, contamination may be indicated not only by the appearance of directional variations pointing from two terminal states, as with type–1 and type–n variations, but also by evidence from the pattern of exclusions that one of the extant states has drawn its readings from two or more others. This evidence accrues when any two or more states or groups of states agree now the first with a third, the second with a fourth, now the first with the fourth, the second with the third, and so on. The simplest pattern is AB:CD, AC:BD; this may be further complicated by the presence of AD:BC; further complications are possible with more states. Such variations may be said to *conflict*. The parts of the variations that by their alternate agreements cause the conflict may be called *elements*. An element may be one state or a group of states. Variations that do not conflict are then *compatible*. Variations having no or only one group each of two or more states are always compatible. The others may conflict. One of these variations also may be compatible with two conflicting variations; and a set of compatible variations may conflict with another variation or set of variations. In the latter event, the number of elements defining the conflict increases. In complex variations one or more groups of states may not be involved in a conflict involving two or more other groups. In the conflict AB:CDE, AC:BDE, there are four elements—A, B, C, and DE; in the conflict AB:CDE, ABC:DE, AC:BDE, there are four—A, B, C, and DE; in the conflict AB:CDE, ABE:CD, AC:BDE, there are five—A, B, C, D, and E; in the conflict AB:CD:EF, AC:BD: EF, there are four—A, B, C, and D.

As long as it is possible to take one of the conflicting groupings from each conflicting variation and arrange them into a pattern resembling that of direct descent, the general diagram may be described as circular. In the examples below, each state is an element in itself; if two or more states comprise an element their relationship to each other will be established by other variations, and it may be that they will be connected to the ring only through a hypothetical intermediary.

$$
\begin{array}{cc}
\text{AB:CD} & \begin{array}{c} \text{A—B} \\ |\quad| \\ \text{C—D} \end{array} \\
\text{AC:BD} &
\end{array}
$$

Any three or more of: CD:ABE

AB:CDE DE:ABC

BC:ADE EA:BCD

In the special diagrams, the elements remain in a simple ring (1) if any intermediaries between the earliest and latest states are either undatable or are successively later in date as they are farther removed from the earliest; (2) if no element except the latest and next latest on either side stands alone against the rest in type–1 variations; and (3) if there is no evidence of additional conflation from directional variations. Under these circumstances, patterns like the following result:

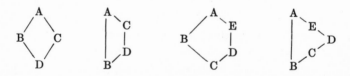

If the first condition is not met, a displaced element will be connected to the ring through a hypothetical intermediary. In the following example, E is the earliest element, C the next, B the next, A the next, and D the latest:

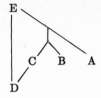

When such connections are made, the elements excluded from the ring may also stand alone against the rest in type–1 variations. In the example, then, all the states may stand alone in turn against the others.

When the first condition is met and the second is not, one or more elements will be excluded from the ring. Thus when there are AB:CD, AC:BD, and A:BCD, and when A is earliest, B next earliest, and D latest, either of the following patterns will express the relationship with equal simplicity:

When the third condition is not met, rings within other rings will appear. And the same sort of diagrams will be called for by greater conflict among the variations. The limit of ready comprehensibility with such diagrams would seem to be reached by those similar to the following, which is demanded by AB:CD, AC:BD, AD:BC. In the example, A is the earliest element, B the next earliest, D the latest.

With more elements, the circular patterns begin to intersect when the conflicts are complicated. The same thing occurs when directional variations indicate a common hypothetical ancestor for two or more elements not all located on the upper planes of the diagram. Some sort of rational simplification is therefore necessary when such conflicting variations occur, and is usually desirable when any conflicts are present.

At least four possibilities present themselves, of which two seem to be generally useful.

It has been proposed that all elements involved in conflation be regarded as terminal—indeed the evidence for conflation has been cited as evidence of radiation—but this cure is worse than the disease. Thus if there are two or all three of AB:CD, AC:BD, and AD:BC, the following diagram is no help:

$$\begin{array}{cc} A & B \\ & \times \\ C & D \end{array}$$

Such a diagram fails to explain the textual continuities indicated in any of the variations. If the intermediary is to agree, for example, with A and B (AB:CD), how did C and D come to agree?

A second possibility is to arrange together the states most alike. Likeness is indicated by infrequency of disagreement rather than by frequency of agreement, because the recovery of additional states that give new type-1 variations and so on will apparently alter the frequency of agreement among the states already analyzed. It is true in direct descent that each terminal state disagrees least with the one contiguous to it, that each intermediary disagrees least with those on each side, and that the disagreements increase progressively between states progressively removed from one another; but if any independent relationships enter the pattern, the rule no longer holds. For example:

5 A:BCD	A/B 6		
1 B:ACD	A/C 8	B/C 4	
2 AB:CD	A/D 12	B/D 8	C/D 6
1 C:ABD			
5 D:ABC			

$$\begin{array}{cc} A & C \\ & \\ B & D \end{array}$$

Here B and C are most alike, but not most closely related. Obviously the same situation will arise when the concern is not with individual states but with groups of states.

The best method seems to be to re-create artificially the alternate possibilities of maximum accumulation of elements without contamination, and to connect the resulting *partial diagrams* into one—the *final diagram.* By such a process the normal principles of construction will be made to extend through the largest possible area within the tree, and the necessary annotation will then make clear where the textual continuities are not indicated by the diagram itself. To do this, a selection is made, from among the elements defining the conflict, of a number of sets that individually include as many elements as possible that do not conflict, together include all the elements, and provide diagrams that can be connected into a larger scheme by overlaying their common parts. The variations ABC:DE, ACD:BE, and ADE:BC furnish an example. Since the first and last conflict with the second, five elements define the conflict. In this very simple example, the elements might be arranged in a ring, A—C—B—E—D—A, but for the purpose of illustration the problem can be assumed to be more complicated. If first B and then E are subtracted from the five, the result will be two sets of variations that do not conflict. One, AC:DE, ACD:E, ADE:C, gives C—A—D—E; the other, ABC:D, ACD:B, AD:BC, gives D—A—C—B. Then the two partial diagrams can be overlaid to obtain the final diagram, B—C—A—D—E. This is simply to break the ring between B and E; ACD:BE is therefore, in effect, read as ACD:B:E.

If, in addition to the three conflicting variations, there is a full set of type–1 variations, the two subtractions will result in:

−B	−E
A:CDE	A:BCD
C:ADE	B:ACD
(from C:ABDE and ADE:BC)	(from B:ACDE and ACD:BE)
AC:DE	C:ABD
D:ACE	D:ABC
E:ACD	(from D:ABCE and ABC:DE)
(from E:ABCD and ACD:BE)	AD:BC

Although at first glance incompatible, the two diagrams fit together:

If a circular diagram had been used, at least two of the elements would have been excluded from the ring; the choice of those to be excluded must have awaited the analysis of the relative dates of the states.

If the desired results are not obtainable by subtracting single elements, more than one may be subtracted at the same time and the resulting diagrams linked into one. When this is necessary, the elements could not have been arranged in a simple ring. For example, with AB:CDEF, ABC:DEF, ACEF:BD, and ACDE:BF, the subtraction of B will give a satisfactory set of variations, but another set is to be obtained only by subtracting both D and F:

$-$B	$-$DF
A:CDEF	AB:CE
AC:DEF	ABC:E
ACEF:D	ACE:B
ACDE:F	ACE:B

$$A\text{—}C\text{—}E\diagup^{D}_{\diagdown F}$$

$$B\text{—}A\text{—}C\text{—}E$$

$$B\text{—}A\text{—}C\text{—}E\diagup^{D}_{\diagdown F}$$

When conflicts arise, it is obviously imperative to be able to recognize which elements will have to be subtracted as a first step toward a solution and what the alternate possibilities of subtraction may be. Any set of three elements will give a partial diagram. The minimum conditions for a partial diagram with more than three elements are fulfilled when any element always agrees either with a second element alone or with a third and fourth together. (It must be carefully determined, also, that one is dealing with elements as a whole, and not with one or more of the states that go to make up elements.) The base four can be expanded by any other element that always either agrees in the usual way with those already grouped together or stands alone against them all. The necessary agreements are more easily discoverable from tables of the agreements in groupings of half the elements or less. In complex variations it is necessary also to mark the groupings by adding colons. Any element in a table that agrees with another single element in the table or with this element and a third, fourth, and so on, but never with the third, say, and not the second (colons mark possible exceptions to the "never"), will, with any elements not shown in the table that do not conflict among themselves, afford a set of variations without conflict in which all these elements are included. Here is a random set of variations that conflict:

AB:CDEFG:HI	A:BCDF:EGHI	ACFI:BDEGH
ABC:DEG:FHI	ADFGHI:BCE	ABCDI:EFGH
ABE:CDFGHI	AF:BCDEGHI	ABCDEFG:HI

The conflicts may be tabulated as follows:

AB:	BA:	CAB:	DEG:	EDG:	FHI:	GDE:	HI:	IH:
ABC:	BAC:	CBDF:	DBCF:	EAB	FBCD:	GEHI:	HFI:	IFH:
ABE	BAE	CBE		EGHI:	FA	GEFH	HEGI:	IEGH:
AF	BCDF:	CAFI		EBC	FACI		HEFG	IACF
ACFI	BCE			EFGH	FEGH		HI	IH

Systematic search of these tables reveals that partial diagrams may be constructed with A, B, D, G, H; A, C, D, G, H; B, C, D, G, H; and so on.

An alternate procedure is to write out the elements defining each conflict as links in a closed chain (their order in the chain does not matter). The conflicts in which the first variation above is involved would appear as follows:

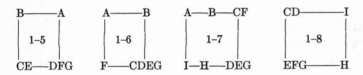

After all the chains have been written out, systematic scrutiny will reveal which states must be subtracted to remove at least one link from each chain with the fewest possible subtractions, and which other states must be subtracted if the former are to be retained. The remaining states in each case will have no conflicts, and partial diagrams may then be constructed from them.

Partial diagrams may be connected only when one extends beyond the extremities of the other (as A—B—C—D and B—C—D—E give A—B—C—D—E), or when one indicates one or more branches between two points which in the other are without an intervening branch:

A⟩–C–D + B–C⟨D/E = A⟩–C⟨D/E (with B)

C/D–C⟨E/F + A–B–C–D = A–B–C⟨D–E–F

A–B–C–D + A⟩–C⟨B/F (E) = A⟩(E/F)–B–C–D

A×C/B D + A⟩–C⟨D/E = A⟩B⟩–C⟨D/E (C)

A⟩–C⟨C/D + A⟩–D–E (C) = A⟩–C⟨C/D–E (B)

No other type of connection is possible.

It may happen that the partial diagrams obtainable may overlie in more than one fashion. Assume that there are a full set of type–1 variations and the following variations as well:

AB:CDEFG	AD:BCEFG	ABCD:EFG
ABC:DEFG	AE:BCDFG	ABCEF:DG

Each of these is in conflict with at least one other, and the conflicts are defined by seven elements. Since there is the full set of type–1 variations, any three elements will give a pattern of radiation, but none of these will overlie each other or the remaining possibilities (—DFG and —EFG not shown):

−AD	−AG	−DE	−ABC	−BCD
B:CEFG	B:CDEF	AB:CFG	:DEFG	A:EFG
BC:EFG	BC:DEF	ABC:FG	:DEFG	A:EFG
:BCEFG	D:BCEF	A:BCFG	D:EFG	A:EFG
E:BCFG	E:BCDF	A:BCFG	E:DFG	AE:FG
BC:EFG	BCD:EF	ABC:FG	D:EFG	A:EFG
BCEF:G	BCEF:D	ABCF:G	EF:DG	AEF:G

(structural diagrams below each column)

Four different overlays are possible with these partial diagrams, the first using the first three, the second using the first and last two, the third using the first, second, and last, the fourth using the first, third, and fourth.

In the first overlay, because it is constructed from partial diagrams each involving more elements, the usual principles of construction are more fully represented, that is, the maximum number of the indicated exclusions is preserved. It is therefore simpler than the others.

If in the foregoing example one or more of the seven elements had not been present, the remaining elements might have had a different relationship. Had B and C been wanting, the last two partial diagrams would have combined as follows:

In the same way, states that have been accepted as related through a single hypothetical intermediary may turn out, as other states are recovered, to be better arranged in a line of successive descent. Assume the following variations:

A:BCDE	AC:BDE	ABCD:E
AB:CDE	ACD:BE	

The diagrams for A, B, and C alone and for all five states are as follows:

With three states, the same evidence will fit either normal radiational descent through a single hypothetical intermediary or contamination. The former is the simpler relationship. With five states, the relationship that best preserves the exclusions indicated by the variations requires that contamination between A and B be posited.

The sets of variations that result from the subtraction of elements from conflicting variations are something like the variations that result when a state is defective. The fact of defectiveness is a variation in itself, and makes the state terminal unless another state is defective in exactly the same respects. In the same way, elements that must be subtracted to give a pair of partial diagrams will always be terminal in the resulting overlay. Again when a state is defective, a second state may appear in a type–1 variation and yet not be terminal: when there is no contamination and the first state is not defective, the second will never agree with a third state against it. Thus with A:BCD, AB:CD, ABC:D, and AB:C (when D is defective), C is not terminal but intermediary in the diagram A—B—C—D. In the same way, as the examples show, states that appear terminal after an element has been subtracted from a conflict may not prove to be when the full diagram is drawn. Finally, if a state that is defective (and so terminal) has an intermediary between it and the other states, according to the evidence of the variations when the defective state is present, the two may constitute a single element in defining a conflict; if so, the imperfect state may not be retained when the other is subtracted. Failure to observe this rule may lead to the supposition that such partial diagrams as A—B—C—D and B—E—C—D have been established, and that they can be connected into A—B—E—C—D.

Should it be possible to construct two or more overlays equally satisfactory, the Gordian knot may be cut by choosing the one that preserves the continuities indicated by the most frequently occurring of the conflicting variations. No other procedure recommends itself when no overlay is possible. With AB:CDE, AC:BDE, AD:BCE, and CE:ABD, three overlays are possible and equally simple:

(1) −A		(2) −BC	(3) −BD	(4) −CD
B:CDE	D:BCE	E:AD	A:CE	AB:E
C:BDE	CE:BD	A:DE	AC:E	A:BE

$$\left.\begin{matrix} B \\ D \end{matrix}\right\rangle\!\!-\!E\!-\!C \qquad A\!-\!D\!-\!E \qquad A\!-\!C\!-\!E \qquad A\!-\!B\!-\!E$$

(1) and (2)   (1) and (3)   (1) and (4)

B   B   A
 \   \   \
  >—E—C   >—E—C—A   B
 /   /   \
D   D   >—E—C
                                            /
/   D
A

(The subtraction of BE, CE, or DE would give patterns of radiation that would not overlie on the first partial diagram.) Under the circumstances the best of the possible overlays will preserve the continuities indicated by the conflicting variations most often occurring. If AB:CDE and CE:ABD occur most often, the last of the three overlays is preferable; if AC:BDE occurs most often, the second is preferable; if AD:BCE and CE:ABD occur most often, the first is preferable. If CE:ABD occurs most often, the choice will lie between the first and the third overlays, according as AB:CDE occurs more often than AD:BCE or the reverse.

No overlay is possible with such a conflict as AB:CDE, ABC:DE, ABD:CE, AE:BCD when all the states also stand alone in type–1 variations. The diagram will then be governed by the conflicting variation (and any variations compatible with it) occurring most often. Do the first, second, and third added together occur more often than the fourth, and, if so, does the second occur more often than the third? The diagrams that will result from the various possibilities are as follows:

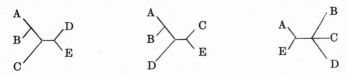

It will sometimes happen that only a part of a diagram can be determined by the process of overlaying partial diagrams, because there are two or more independent conflicts, not all soluble by this method. The following is an example:

ABC:DEFGHIJ   ABCDEF:GHIJ
ACD:BEFGHIJ   ABCDEFG:HIJ
BC:ADEFGHIJ   ABCDEFGH:IJ
A:BCDEFGHIJ   ABCDEFGI:HJ
B:ACDEFGHIJ   ABCDEFJ:GHI
C:ABDEFGHIJ   ABCDEFHIJ:G
D:ABCEFGHIJ   ABCDEFGIJ:H
ABCD:EFGHIJ   ABCDEFGHJ:I
ABCDE:FGHIJ   ABCDEFGHI:J

The elements defining the conflict in the variations in the first column are A, B, C, D, and EFGHIJ. Subtracting first B and then EFGHIJ gives partial diagrams that may be overlaid to make the following:

The elements defining the conflict in the variations in the second column are ABCDEF, G, H, I, and J. No overlay is possible with these variations. But if ABCDEFJ:GHI occurs more often than ABCDEFG:HIJ and ABCDEFGI:HJ or ABCDEFG:HIJ and ABCDEFGH:IJ, the diagram will be:

The last variation in the first column shows that E and F differ; since neither stands alone in type–1 variations, both are intermediary. The final diagram will therefore be:

It is not usually possible, however, to mingle the two methods in the solution of a single conflict. For example:

A:BCDEF	BF:ACDE
AB:CDEF	CF:ABDE
ABC:DEF	DF:ABCE
AE:BCDF	EF:ABCD
AF:BCDE	F:ABCDE

It is apparent that F must be subtracted in any event. Then the alternate subtraction of A and E as well gives partial diagrams that can be overlaid:

No overlay involving F is possible. Now should it happen that any of the conflicting variations in the second column (and any variations compatible with it) occurs more often than AF:BCDE, it will be a simple matter to place F accordingly, for the diagram will only be extended, not altered internally. Thus, if EF:ABCD, AB:CDEF, and ABC:DEF occur more often, the diagram may be extended as follows:

But experience indicates that it will be seldom that one of the elements can be an intermediary; usually all the states will stand alone in type–1 variations, as A and F do in this example.

If AF:BCDE occurs more often, placing F according to this variation will alter the previous diagram internally by introducing F as a nearer collateral to A than is B. Why should B be displaced in this fashion? There is no alternative but to see whether AB:CDEF and its compatible variations do not occur more often than AF:BCDE. This is simply to abandon the method of overlays and to turn entirely to the method of selecting from among the conflicting variations those that most often occur.

The examples have illustrated only the most common kind of compatible variations, in which the groups of states having different readings grow progressively larger or smaller from variation to variation. It must be remembered when counting compatible variations that there are other sorts. Thus AB:CDE is compatible not only with ABC:DE but also with A:BC:DE and even, when A is lacking, with BC:DE.

There is no stronger temptation to abandon strict textual reasoning than when conflation occurs. How convenient it would be always to set aside all the conflicting variations except the one that occurs most often! It would be as reasonable, if AB:CD occurred much less often than the four possible type–1 variations, to ignore it and to simplify the diagram by making the states radiate from a single hypothetical intermediary. Minorities are always troublesome when they run counter to the majority, but they must be heard (there are even some enthusiasts who maintain that they are the more likely to be right). Concern with the relationships of the states as they are must never give way to concern for the copying process by which they came into existence.

Conflicting variations affect the determination of the readings of hypothetical intermediaries. These readings are obtainable, if they are obtainable at all, simply on the basis of majority vote among the immediate extant relatives of the intermediary and the first extant relatives of any hypothetical intermediaries immediately related to the one in question—as long as these are not known to be contaminated. If contamination has occurred between any of these, the readings in the contaminated states can be counted only once each. Assume that the relationship of A, B, C, and D is as follows:

If there is no contamination, agreement between A and B or between any three will establish the reading of the hypothetical state x. But if in addition AD:BC occurs, it is not possible to establish the reading of x in this variation as either that of A and D or B and C. The reading of x can also be established when any two states agree and the others vary independently, except that A:B:CD establishes only the reading of the hypothetical state y; A:B:CD gives three possible readings for x. In such doubtful occurrences some scholars accept the reading of the state that agrees most often with x in the other readings. (Lachmannians employ the same procedure with contamination.) Readings possibly ancestral but excluded by such generalization or passed over because of the intrinsic attractiveness of an alternate are underlined by some editors in the critical apparatus to indicate that mathematically, at any rate, they are as likely as the reading chosen.

In the discussion so far it has been assumed that the dating of manuscripts conditions, and is not conditioned by, the findings of the textual scholar. This is in general correct. It will often happen, however, that the dates assigned to manuscripts, even by laboratory tests, are only approximate and are capable of adjustment by a century or two. Under such circumstances the textual scholar may wish to adjust the traditional dates of the manuscripts if it will simplify his diagram. He should, therefore, unless he is himself an expert bibliographer or paleographer, learn something of the procedure in dating manuscripts and printed books. Even then he will be well advised not to proceed without consulting a specialist.

The laboratory methods of dating are of two kinds. Minute analysis of chemical properties may give direct evidence of age, for certain substances alter with time at known rates. The dating will be approximate, with an approximate range of possible error specified. Cruder chemical or microscopic analysis of ink or paper may identify products whose dates of manufacture and general use are known from other sources.

More often manuscripts are dated by extrapolation. Exemplars are collected that may be dated, either because they bear dates themselves or because their origin or early existence is determinable from other sources (any conflicts in the evidence must be resolvable). According to the theory of consistent evolution, these establish an order of development of the material, design, and script used. Therefore undated manuscripts that have the same characteristics as the dated exemplars are given the same dates. Those having characteristics intermediate between those of the dated exemplars are dated between them. Those apparently more primitive or more developed in their characteristics than any dated exemplar are dated earlier or later. Sometimes the theory of constant rate of evolution is also followed. The datings so determined may be only very rough approximations. If they depend, for example, on the script, a range of several centuries may be possible, so little did the professional book hands change for some alphabets.

Occasionally there is clear evidence that conclusions based on the evolutionary theories would be incorrect: carbon-14 analysis of the wrappings of the Dead Sea Scrolls suggests that the script found in some scrolls is not archaic but archaized. Obviously, too, the conclusions are no truer than the theories. Theories of constant rates of change are tenable only in the physical sciences. Consistent evolution seems to obtain in many other fields, but historians cling to a pendulum, poets to a cyclical, theory of human behavior.

Still other methods of dating depend upon evidences of physical disturbance in one manuscript or book which will explain the condition of another, or normal practice in one which is abnormal when taken over unchanged in another. Such dating will be only relative—earlier, later—but may be all that is needed.

In *The Descent of Manuscripts*, A. C. Clark has developed at great length the bibliographical evidence of omissions and dittographies, whether or not they have been recognized and corrected by a scribe.[49] If these tend to run to standard lengths or multiples of the standard, they indicate the line lengths of the ancestors; if the ancestors are in existence, they may be thus identified. Errors running to more than one standard length in the same manuscript are evidence of the line lengths in a series of ancestors. Since individual lines will often vary from the standard, it will be more readily calculable from errors of several lines in length. Sometimes the omission or dittography will be exactly one line in the manuscript under observation; this indicates that it has been copied line for line from its ancestor, and gives further evidence for identification. Symptoms of page-for-page transcription from the ancestor are fragmentary last lines, run-overs from the last lines in the lower margin, and the expansion or contraction of the script. When spacing out or contraction comes at the end of quaternions only, and there are no breaks in the text at these points, the scribes have evidently been assigned each a certain part of a text to copy, the ancestor possibly having been broken up and distributed by quaternions among them. The evidence from spacing out and crowding together is equally useful with printed books.

Scribes copying line for line often saved themselves trouble when working from manuscripts in two columns by copying the first line of the second column in a page before copying the second line in the first column. A succession of copies might thus be made with exactly the same lineation, so that here the bibliographer cannot always be sure he has identified an immediate and not a more remote ancestor. And various possibilities may disturb the calculations. An ancestor written not in standard lines but in sense units will obviate any numerical relation among additions and omissions of lines or multiples of lines in its descendants. Only when there is evidence in the descendant of correction made in order to reproduce lineation is there a clue (for example, erasure of a word at the end of one line and appearance of the same word at the head of the next). Indentation for paragraphs in the ancestor will produce occasional short lines, which, if they fall within omissions or dittographies in the descendants, will upset the usual numerical correspondences. Since the scholar normally must estimate omissions and dittographies on the basis of the uncorrupted text, his calculations will be thrown off by passages in the ancestor that are already corrupt or corrected by insertion. A passage in the ancestor that is interrupted by flaws in the parchment will have the same effect. Sometimes the scribe of the ancestor will have expanded or contracted his script; sometimes several scribes with varying hands will have worked on the same manuscript; sometimes quaternions will have been formed from a different number of leaves; sometimes one of the columns on a page (normally the left one) will have been wider than the other or others.

In his *Introduction to Bibliography for Literary Students*, R. B. McKerrow gives a number of indications of the same general sort that are found in printed books.[50] Other things being equal, the handsomest edition, or the edition with the fewest errors in the mechanics of typography, is the first. In editions corresponding page for page, any abnormal crowding or spacing marks the later, just as with manuscripts. If the preliminaries have a separate or an interrupted run of signatures in one edition and not in another, the single series probably marks the later edition; certainly the indications are clear if there is a reference in the preliminaries to the printing of the text, or if in the edition with the single series of signatures the first page of the text falls in the same gathering with the end of the preliminaries. If one edition exactly fills a number of sheets whereas another is short or over a leaf or two, the first, representing an economy easy to obtain when one has printed copy, is doubtless the later. If paragraph breaks omitted in one edition correspond to those following a full line in the other, the omissions mark the later edition; there has not been enough white space in the earlier edition to attract the compositor's eye. If in two editions, corresponding page for page but not sheet for sheet, signatures correct in one appear also in the other but are there incorrect, the edition with the erroneous signatures is the later. If in one issue the watermarks are all the same, and in another they differ at just the places where the issues differ, the consistent series marks the earlier issue. A sharp eye will detect many another sign of priority of the same sort. In fact, with bibliographical evidence, rules cannot cover all the possibilities, and the bibliographer with no ability to make deductions for himself is lost.

A single example must serve for a host. In the 1730 edition of John Gay's *Wife of Bath* it is clear that the octavo impression preceded the quarto, which is printed from the same type as the octavo except for the signatures. Even one of these is the same in both. The abnormal appearance of the octavo type page on the quarto leaf shows that the type was set for the former. It would be a safe deduction that the octavo was printed first; it is a sure deduction, because the signature common to both is correct for the octavo only.

When bibliographers have recourse to the text to establish a family tree, they proceed in a different fashion from textual scholars. The more minute and unusual the correspondence between records, the more certain the close physical relationship. Since the unusual is likely to be wrong, the bibliographer is likely to lay stress on common errors as evidence. He is also likely to give weight to unusual spellings. On the other hand, mutilations in a manuscript that disturb the state of the text there recorded are not counted in bibliographical evidence unless there is evidence of a corresponding disturbance in another manuscript. Again, difference in method of transmission is accepted as causing variations and as requiring separate family trees. Hill says that a picture and a description of the picture are variants. Greg omits memorial transmission from his discussion as complicating it. Bibliographers are also likely to divide directional variations into grades according to the degree of probability that they represent real occurrences. A transposition is more certainly a mark of a later manuscript than is a more orthodox reading; a more orthodox reading is more certainly a mark of a later manuscript than is a reading more characteristic of the author. Faced with later readings in two different manuscripts, the bibliographer is not bound to decide that the manuscripts are collaterials. Instead he may weigh the directional variations and take as the ancestor the manuscript having the most more certainly earlier readings. He will proceed similarly when faced by conflation. When a manuscript seems to have more than one source for its text, he will determine by weighing the conflicting variations which manuscript is the principal ancestor. Sometimes he may be able to determine that a scribe copied from one manuscript for a time, then shifted to another.

Conflation may arise from chance coincidence in error by individual scribes or by the same scribe copying individual manuscripts; through editorial emendation by the scribe or by another; or through the consultation of another record, whether another manuscript or the memory. The different causes may sometimes be conjecturally identified; but if more than a single cause is operative, it may be difficult to distinguish their individual results. Chance coincidence should produce few and scattered conflicts. Editorial emendation should spring from obvious and easily correctible errors. Consultation of another record should produce a series of conflicts more or less consistent with one another in nature, or directional variations pointing from two or more states to another or to a group of others. Still another source for conflicting variations will be authorial revision, which will produce the same sort of conflicts as consultation of another record, except that their nature may not be uniform. It would seem that often the only way to decide between consultation of another record and authorial revision is on the basis of the likelihood that either can have occurred. The conflicts among the states of Dryden's *Mac Flecknoe*, for example, no doubt result from authorial revision, whereas those in the Greek New Testament must regularly arise from consultation of other records.

When the evidence indicates that extant manuscripts or their inferential ancestors descend from different revisions made by an author in his holograph or holographs, it may be possible to reconstruct these revisions and from them to form some conception of the author's procedure in producing them. A preliminary to the analysis proper is the determination by the usual bibliographical methods whether any of the extant manuscripts are holographs, whether any is descended from one of the others, whether any two or more are independently descended from a single revision, and whether any two or more have a common inferential ancestor not a holograph. (It may be impossible to determine whether there were one or more holographs; but since in bibliographical analysis each revision may be counted a descendant of the last, the exact number of holographs is immaterial.) Manuscripts of the third class should agree with reasonable consistency against the others in characteristics that are likely to have stood in the holograph; manuscripts of the fourth class should agree with reasonable consistency against the others in characteristics that are not likely to have been introduced by the author. Manuscripts of the second class are ignored. The common ancestors of the manuscripts in the third and fourth classes must be reconstructed; some of the ancestral readings may have to be represented as "x or y," "x or y or z," and so on. From the others and the inferential ancestors not holograph are reconstructed the revisions from which they descend.

Any reading found in two states independently descended from different revisions may be the result of coincidence or contamination, but it is equally possible that it represents multiple acceptance and rejection of the reading by the author himself. Therefore the revisions must be presumed to have these readings unless there is fairly clear evidence to the contrary. An author is quite as capable of changing from "laugh" to "smile," back to "laugh" again, and then back to "smile," as he is of proceeding from "form" to "frame" (Blake, "The Tiger," lines 19 and 24).[51] An author is also perfectly capable of making mistakes in first writing or in transcribing. In revising, he may make one change without at once noticing that he has thereby upset or confused the meaning of a neighboring context, and so on. Finally, the end product of his revision may not be the best state of the text in critical eyes. Therefore, in general, erroneous readings may not be excluded from the assessment of the process of revision. Errors found in two scribal states, if they are fairly clearly dependent for their form upon the correct reading, might be excluded as coincidences. Errors in an authorized edition, provided that it marked the end of the process of revision, might be excluded as not authoritative.

Variations resulting from defective manuscripts are obviously not to be considered, but decision is harder with readings found in a single scribal state. Almost certainly some of these are scribal changes, but there is, in general, no way of telling which ones; the recovery of another state may at any time, by producing a second example of the reading, show that even the errors were found in a holograph. These nonce readings, then, cannot be ignored, nor can they all be accepted as authoritative. Critical judgment may cull out those which are "impossible" in the context or in the author. A more conservative procedure would be to reject all those not markedly characteristic of the author. Still another procedure would be to divide the undecidables according to the proportion of the impossible to the probably authoritative nonce readings. It is an unhappy fact that the results of the analysis may be affected by the choices here.

When the revisions have been reconstructed, their variations can be written out and analyzed to determine the order in which they must have occurred if the author proceeded in the simplest and most systematic way to produce the variety of readings they present. I have elsewhere offered a method of performing this analysis.[52] It is sufficient to say here that two or more orderings of the revisions may be equally satisfactory in point of simplicity.

III

Mechanics of Calculation

What variants are significant to textual analysis? This is a different question from "What variants ought to be recorded in an apparatus criticus?" for the apparatus may contain a variety of information useful to others even when it is not used by the textual scholar. The bibliographer will have his demands, the linguist his. MacEdward Leach has said that editions of Middle English texts should include a record of every possible difference among the manuscripts, because we still have much to learn about such things as the orthography of the period.[1] But the only variations with which the textual analyst will concern himself are those in which the text (the pattern of ideas) is affected. Most spelling, punctuation, and so on is thus automatically eliminated. Capitalization, however, may mark personification, a comma may alter the sense of a word or a sentence ("Next to [Next, to] the sacred temple you are led"), a hyphen or an apostrophe may do the same ("His brows thick fogs, instead of glories, grace [Glories-Grace]," "As oils on water's [waters', waters] flow"), and so on.[2]

Where coöperative work is necessary in recording variants, the possibilities must be canvassed in advance and definite rules laid down, if the apparatus criticus is to be consistent and accurate. Doubtful types come upon after the work has begun will have to be excluded or the work begun again. A standard that seems to be widely accepted is that all variations in words, in grammatical forms, and in word order (*substantive variations*) are to be recorded; that most variations in spelling, punctuation, and so on (*accidental variations*) are to be ignored; and that those variations of the latter sort that markedly affect the sense are to be accounted *quasi-substantive* and recorded. Quasi-substantive variations are the presence or absence of the question mark and any alteration of the marks of separation and linkage, commas, quotation marks, hyphens, and so on that shifts the linkage of the words to one another—always provided that they are not obviously used or interchanged at random by the scribes. In any event the principles for determining the variations to be considered must be defined as rigidly as possible, and all the excluded variations that another scholar might conceivably wish to take into account must be listed in the apparatus.

Difficulties arise when one of the variants is wrong, but the larger context indicates clearly the correct reading. Is the meaning affected by the erroneous reading any more than by a misspelling that does not result in a new word? Something of the same problem arises with minor points of grammar. Is there any real difference in meaning between, say, "different from," "different than," and "different to"? Or between "to you ward" and "toward you"? In poetry the rules of meter may give a clue in such an instance, but often individuals may disagree as to whether the variations are significant. Names raise another difficulty: what is the boundary between variation in spelling and variation in name?

Dialectical variants and translations offer special problems. It would seem to be simpler to treat translations separately from the states in the original language and, if there is more than one version in any one language, to treat each by itself. Each will have its own earliest state, which may be connected to the state of the text in the original language that it most resembles. Of course the scholar must be alert for indications that some states in one translation have been influenced by another or by a fresh comparison with the text in the original language. Biblical collations, however, normally include the versions, the more unfamiliar languages sometimes cited in translation, and there seems to be no insuperable objection to analyzing all at once. This gives a hint concerning dialectical variants: if they are regular alternates for the original readings, they are the equivalents of the original readings and so may be ignored by the textual analyst.

The recording of variations seems best carried out on a series of cards, numbered, and, if they are numerous, tabbed, so as to permit easy arrangement and search. On each card should be entered—printed, if the project is a large one—the sigla of all the manuscripts to be examined, with as many special sigla as necessary for each manuscript having multiple readings caused by scribal correction. If the text is dealt with section by section, the manuscripts should be examined in the same order for each. It will be convenient to begin with the manuscript recording the fullest state of the text, unless some standard form of the text has become current. The first manuscript should be transcribed in full on the numbered cards, one line, verse, or other subdivision at the top of each card, the number of the card corresponding to the number of the subdivision of the text copied upon it. Only the variant readings of the subsequent manuscripts need be copied, in columns below those readings of the first manuscript with which they differ. When the manuscripts are examined, their sigla should be marked off in different fashions according as there are or are not variants or the manuscript is imperfect, but always marked in some fashion. It may be desirable to have a special place on the card for entering manuscripts lacking all the words on the card and for indicating how extensive the lacunae are. Thus there will be no doubt in any individual instance if all the manuscripts have been consulted. This is the method described by Manley and Rickert and used by them for *The Text of Chaucer's Canterbury Tales;*[3] it has proved to be just as useful for small projects as for large.

Simply because they are repeated so often, sigla should be as brief as possible. Perhaps ideally they ought also to indicate something of the manuscript or of the state of the text it records, though when there are very many this may not be practical. Thus the Greek minuscule manuscripts of the New Testament are usually identified simply by a serial arabic numeral; new discoveries may be communicated for numeration to those who prepare the supplements to Gregory's *Die Griechischen Handschriften des Neuen Testaments*. Von Soden, however, numbered the same manuscripts according to a system of classification he devised. Classification is a science in itself, and its complications daunt the average scholar, who is usually content to adopt sigla already established or to establish his own by some simpler method. The following examples of current practice are drawn partly from widely accepted systems and partly from those set up for the nonce by various scholars. Sigla may reflect the provenance of the manuscript:

A   Codex Alexandrinus of the Bible, whose earliest certainly traceable owner was the Patriarchal cell of Alexandria.

B   The Bannatyne Manuscript of Scottish poetry, copied out by George Bannatyne.

P   Codex Pithoeanus of the *Pervigilium Veneris*, once owned by Pierre Pithou, who first published the poem in modern times.

The present resting place of the manuscript:

W   Codex Washingtonianus of the Gospels, in the Freer Gallery of
Art, Washington, D.C.

L   The manuscript of Dryden's *Mac Flecknoe* now bound in Lambeth
Palace MS 711 Codex Cartaceus.

L   Laurentian MS 37.19 of Persius

The catalog number of the manuscript:

A   Chaucer's *Lak of Stedfastnesse* in British Museum Add. MS. 22139.

Co An eighteenth-century transcript of the copy of the *Lak of Stedfastnesse* in Cotton Otho A. XVIII, which was burnt in 1731.

The format of the book:

F1 The first folio of Shakespeare's *Comedies, Histories, & Tragedies.*

Q0 A fragment of an early quarto of his *1 Henry IV*, discovered after
the series Q1–Q8 was established.

The language:

Syr[Sin]   The Sinaitic Syriac manuscript of the Gospels, found in the
library of the Monastery of St. Catherine at the foot of Mount
Sinai.

D and *d*   Codex Bezae, the former the Greek, the latter the Latin
found in parallel columns in the manuscript.

The editor or edition:

ς   The Textus Receptus of the Greek New Testament, from Henri
Estienne (Stephanus), editor, printer, and publisher of the first
ↄeditions.

J   The edition of Cicero's *Letters to Atticus* printed by Jenson, Venice,
1470.

S.-S.   The Scott-Saintsbury edition of Dryden's *Works*, Sir Walter
Scott's notes revised by George Saintsbury.

The date of the edition:

1734   Pope's *Epistle to Dr. Arbuthnot*, first edition, 1734.

12   *The Examiners for the Year 1711*, first collected edition, 1712.

The order of printing:

1, 2, 3, 4, 5   The first five editions of Swift's *Tale of a Tub.*

1714a, 1714b, 1714c   The first three separate editions of Pope's *Rape
of the Lock.*

A, B, C   The first three editions of Nashe's *Pierce Penilesse.*

The script or material of the manuscript:

E and 1   Codex Basileensis in each case, but the former an uncial, the
latter a minuscule, manuscript of the Gospels.

p[45]   One of the Chester Beatty Biblical papyri.

The evaluation set on the state of the text:

ℵ Codex Sinaiticus of the Bible, an uncial manuscript that from the lateness of its discovery would normally have been assigned a Roman or Greek capital far down in the alphabet, and that its discoverer (Tischendorf) rated as at least equal in importance to those assigned the sigla A and B.

C and c Codex Gudianus and Codex Laurentianus 66.39 of Suetonius, the latter regarded as inferior to the former by the editor (Preud'homme) using these sigla.

It will be seen that the same manuscript may have different sigla assigned to different parts of its contents. Occasionally also two or more closely related manuscripts are assigned the same siglum (D of the Gospels and Acts is Codex Bezae, D of the Pauline Epistles is Codex Claromontanus). When the different manuscripts have to be cited in the same context, they are identified by added numerals or by superscript abbreviations in most cases, though one may not be so identified by common agreement Syr^{Cu}, Syr^{Sin}; D, D^{Paul}). Sigla indicative of editors may have added to them a number, usually in superscript arabic numerals, marking a specific edition referred to ($Rowe^1$, $Rowe^2$, or Rowe i, Rowe ii). Sigla indicative of format are regularly followed by a serial number, which will indicate the chronological order of the edition within the format if this is determinable.

Compounded sigla are often devised, as Ff for the four Shakespeare folios, Pope+ for Pope and a specified list of subsequent editors of Shakespeare, ♭ for a group of uncials recording the ecclesiastical text of Mark, fam^{13} for the so-called Ferrar group of manuscripts, usually found in agreement. One such siglum may include another, as ω is used for the whole group of inferior manuscripts of Juvenal, ψ for the seven of these cited by Housman in his edition. Exceptions to the usual agreements are then indicated in parenthesis, as ♭ ($-$K), or in some other convenient way.

Since sigla have normally been assigned to the manuscripts rather than to the states of the text recorded, editors have devised methods of indicating different states in the same manuscript. An asterisk following a siglum indicates the original reading of a manuscript. It will be used when the manuscript has been corrected by only one hand or by hands that cannot be distinguished, but it can always be used when it will make the context clearer. When several correcting hands are identifiable, it is customary to assign them superscript letters indicating their chronological order, as $ℵ^b$ for the second corrector of Codex Sinaiticus. The various correctors of Codex Pithoeanus (P) of Juvenal, however, have been lumped together as p. The original readings and the corrections in Codex Mediceus 49.18, Cicero's *Letters to Atticus*, have been identified as M^1 and M^2. Scholars working with texts in early printed books, where any one copy may have any combination of corrected and uncorrected forms, must also devise methods of identifying the various states of proof correction.

Charlton Hinman has designed and built optical devices for comparing books and microfilms of books and a few of these are available in the great libraries, but usually the scholar must proceed as with manuscripts.

In comparing the manuscripts, the scholar will naturally seek optimum conditions of light, air, comfort, quiet, and freedom from interruption. The work space should be capacious, and all necessary tools, as magnifying glass, ultraviolet lamp, and so on, within arm's reach. If variants are not recorded by the method described above, it is often helpful to hold a blank card under the line being read in each manuscript. The scholar should come fresh to the work and should not carry it on for long periods of time, for accuracy decreases with fatigue. He stops too late if he works until he notices a decrease of efficiency. Comparisons may be made visually by one person, or one can read aloud to another or even to several others. No doubt accuracy becomes increasingly hard to obtain as more persons are engaged in the process, though printers' proofreading is regularly done by two persons together because of the considerable saving of time. The results of the comparison should be checked at least once, preferably by someone else. According to the so-called laws of chance, a check performed with the same efficiency as the initial comparison should reduce its errors more or less by half; two additional checks will be required to halve the remaining errors, and correspondingly more to halve them again, so that three checks are usually all that are feasible. A better way to insure accuracy is to approach the work with the expectancy of attaining it, to proceed letter by letter and point by point without impatience, and to derive satisfaction from both the perfection and the value of the results. The "laws of chance" do not necessarily apply, as conscientious typists demonstrate every day.

Ideally, the manuscript itself should be examined. Reproductions are subject to all sorts of unexpected failures to perform their function. If a reproduction is used, it ought first to be checked with its original as minutely as if it were another manuscript.

When the collation of the manuscripts is complete, it must be transferred from the cards in condensed form for general use. For textual analysis, the lemma, or base reading from which the others are thought of as varying, may be the first reading recorded on the cards. If it is burdensome to write out all the sigla, the lemma may be the reading found in the largest number of manuscripts. Each lemma should be followed by a square bracket or some other mark to set it off from the rest of the entry, and then by the sigla of the states agreeing in the base reading, unless for reasons of space or time these are omitted (if the collation is printed, the mark following the lemma may be omitted if the lemma is set in a different type face from the rest of the entry). If the sigla are written out, they are separated from the variant or variants by a semicolon or other mark of division. The variant readings follow in turn, each with the sigla of the states in which it is found, and each separated from the next by a mark of division. The variations are identified by the number of the subdivision of the text in which they occur; strictly, the number need precede only the first variation in each subdivision, but it is usually more satisfactory to identify every variation in this fashion. In a very large apparatus, the variations in each subdivision may have a paragraph to themselves. When there is more than one variation within the subdivision of the text, they may be separated by a vertical rule if periods are not used to conclude all the variations. If the variations involve passages of more than a few words and there are variations within variations, it may be convenient when the collation comes to be printed to indicate the smaller differences in parentheses after the requisite sigla in the series that agree otherwise in the larger difference. Or it may be easier to indicate the smaller differences, together with the requisite sigla, in parentheses in the middle of the citation of the larger variant; the sigla within the parentheses will then appear again following the larger variant reading. Similarly it is often convenient to condense two or three variations into one statement for printing. If so, it may also be convenient to substitute marks of elision for the various parts of the second and subsequent readings that agree with the first. Summary statements of sigla, such as "al plus," are not sufficiently indicative for textual analysis.

In the inflected languages a lemma is not always strictly necessary, but its regular use much facilitates the computations attendant upon textual analysis. If the variation is an add-omission, it is well to include in lemma and variant readings a word at each extremity that does not vary, though here again it may be convenient simply to use the abbreviations "om." and "+." If the same word appears twice in a line, verse, or other subdivision by which the variations are identified, it is often convenient to label the occurrences 1^0, 2^0, and so on rather than to repeat the preceding word of the context in lemma and variant reading, but to give the preceding word will make the passages more easily identifiable in the manuscript or book having the variant reading. When the variation is in punctuation, the preceding word is always necessary in the lemma; in the variant readings it can be replaced by a wavy dash ($\sim$). Where the variant is omission of punctuation, it will be unmistakably indicated by a caret ($\sim_\wedge$).

When the critical apparatus is published separately, the lemma should be the reading of some more or less standard and easily available edition. When the critical apparatus is made part of an edition, of course the lemma must represent the reading of the edition text. In either event, the description of the variations may have to be rewritten. Quentin wisely cautions, however, against unnecessarily recopying textual notes, since errors tend to creep in just as they worked their way into the states of the text being analyzed. Imperfect and fragmentary states, especially, must be carefully checked when rewriting variations.

Greg has provided a convenient method of writing variations for most calculations. Where only simple variations are involved, Σ represents the sum of a number—usually the larger number—of states in agreement, and only those varying from them have their lemmas written out. In order to avoid misunderstandings, the sigla of states defective at a point of variation should be written as subscripts to the Σ; the sigla of fragmentary states, when they are present and agree with Σ at a point of variation, should be written as superscripts. If the Σ is used in complex variations, it can only represent the sum of the states having one of the variant readings; the sigla for the other two or more groups of states must be written out and separated by colons.

If the problem is complex, it is sometimes better to have the full set of sigla before the eyes. The sigla of states defective at any point of variation, set aside when compound variations are reduced to their components, or subtracted to solve a conflict, should be entered in brackets. It must be remembered that these sigla have in common nothing beyond being omitted from consideration in the analysis of the particular variation. A state that is wholly or nearly unpunctuated may be considered defective in this respect, and its siglum bracketed as necessary in recording variations in punctuation.

It will usually be helpful to tabulate the variations according to type, with a list of the examples of each type. If any of the examples are directional, it is well to mark them in some fashion. If as the analysis proceeds any of the types must be set aside to resolve a conflict, the analyst should return to the table and annotate it clearly. If the problem is a simple one, it will be easy enough to classify the types at once according to their indication of the form of the diagram, as in the first example below; but if there are complexities, it is usually simpler to arrange them in order as they occur.

In analyzing simple variations, it is probably best to work consistently with the smaller sides of the variations, and from the smaller of these to the larger—that is, to begin with the type–1 variations. The terminal states will thus be at once identified, and the terminal groups built up from them in an orderly way. Finally, the groups and any odd terminal states will only have to be joined by a single link, if there are two, or by individual links to a node, if there are three or more. In the following example, the method of calculation with Σ is also shown:

A:BCDEFGHIJKLM	Σ:A	A——[Σ]
B:ACDEFGHIJKLM	Σ:B	B——[Σ]
BC:ADEFGHIJKLM (no C:ABDEFGHIJKLM, or	Σ:BC Σ:C)	B——C——[Σ]
BCD:AEFGHIJKLM (no D:ABCEFGHIJKLM, or	Σ:BCD Σ:D)	B——C——D——[Σ]
E:ABCDFGHIJKLM	Σ:E	E——[Σ]
F:ABCDEGHIJKLM	Σ:F	F——[Σ]

EF:ABCDGHIJKLM $\quad\quad$ Σ:EF

$$\begin{matrix} E \\ \\ F \end{matrix} \!\!\!\Big\rangle\!\!-\![\Sigma]$$

G:ABCDEFHIJKLM	Σ:G	G——[Σ]
H:ABCDEFGIJKLM	Σ:H	H——[Σ]

GHI:ABCDEFJKLM $\quad\quad$ Σ:GHI
(no I:ABCDEFGHJKLM, or $\quad$ Σ:I)

$$\begin{matrix} G \\ \\ H \end{matrix} \!\!\!\Big\rangle\! I\!-\![\Sigma]$$

EFGHI:ABCDJKLM $\quad\quad$ Σ:EFGHI

$$\begin{matrix} E \\ F \\ \\ G \\ H \end{matrix} \!\!\!\Big\rangle\!\!\!\Big\rangle\!\!-\![\Sigma]$$

J:ABCDEFGHIKLM   Σ:J   J——[Σ]

K:ABCDEFGHIJLM   Σ:K   K——[Σ]

L:ABCDEFGHIJKM   Σ:L   L——[Σ]

JKLM:ABCDEFGHI   Σ:JKLM   K—M—[Σ]
(no M:ABCDEFGHIJKL, or Σ:M)

A single state, A, and three groups of states are excluded from being intermediary between the members of the others. The four must then radiate:

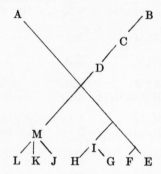

When the states fall into only two groups, such as A—B—[Σ] and C—D—[Σ], one of the links is omitted when the groups are connected, thus: A—B—D—C.

When complex variations are present, it is simpler to begin with one of the smaller groupings, and not to try to develop the relationships in a second group until those in the first have been defined. Assume the following series of variations:

1. ADGIJKLM:BC:EF:H
2. ABCDHIJKM:EF:G:L
3. ABCDJKLM:E:FGHI
4. A:B:CDEFGHIJKLM
5. ABCDEGHI:F:JKLM
6. AGHIJKLM:BCD:EF
7. A:BCDEFJLM:GHI:K
8. A:BC:D:EFGHIKLM:J

The analysis might proceed as follows:

A (4, 7, 8)   A—

BC (1, 8) + B:CD...(4) + BCD (6)
 (and no C:BD, BX:CD, or BCX:D)   B—C—D—

EF (1, 2) + E:FG... (3) + F:ABCDE... (5)
 (and no EX:FY)

GHI (7, cf. 3) + G:ABCDHI... (2) + H:ADGI... (1)
 (and no GX:HI, GI:HX, or I:GH)

E:FGHI:ABCDJKLM (3)

JKLM (5, cf. 1) + J:EFGHIKLM (8)
 + K:BCDEFJLM (7) + L:ABCDHIJKM (2)
 (and no JX:KLM, KX:JLM, LX:JKM, or M:JKL)

When conflation is present, or states are imperfect, the procedure is
little altered. Assume that we have the following set of variations
(bracketed sigla represent states imperfect at the point of variation):

1. A:BCDEFGHIJKLM
2. [B]:ACDEFGHIJKLM
3. BC:ADEFGHIJKLM
4. C:ADEFGHIJKLM[B]
5. BCD:AEFGHIJKLM
6. E:ABCDFGHIJKLM
7. BE:ACDFGHIJKLM
8. F:ABCDEGHIJKLM
9. EF:ABCDGHIJKLM
10. G:ABCDEFHIJKLM
11. H:ABCDEFGIJKLM
12. GHI:ABCDEFJKLM
13. EFGHI:ABCDJKLM
14. J:ABCDEFGHIKLM
15. K:ABCDEFGHIJLM
16. L:ABCDEFGHIJKM
17. JKLM:ABCDEFGHI

The type–1 variations show that A, B, E, F, G, H, J, K, and L are terminal, and that C may be, depending upon its relationship to B. The type–2 variations show that GHI is a terminal group and JKLM another, in which I and M respectively may be intermediaries. Variations 3 and 5 conflict with 7, and 7 conflicts with 9 and 13. The conflicting agreements, may be tabulated thus:

BC	EB
BCD	EF
BE	EFGHI

The tables show that the following partial diagrams are obtainable:

B:CDF(GHI)—2, 7
BC:DF(GHI)—3
C:DF(GHI)[B]—4
BCD:F(GHI)—5, 13
F:BCD(GHI)—8, 9
(GHI):BCDF—12

C:DEF(GHI)—3, 4
CD:EF(GHI)—5, 13
E:CDF(GHI)—6, 7
F:CDE(GHI)—8
EF:CD(GHI)—9
(GHI):CDEF—12

In the first diagram C may be an intermediary, because when B is present it either agrees with C or stands alone. The two diagrams will overlie as follows:

Variation 7 having been set aside by the overlay, variations 1, 5, 13, and 17 show that A, BCD as a group, EFGHI as a group, and JKLM as a group are all terminal. Since no further grouping is possible, the four radiate. The final diagram, with the states within the groups GHI and JKLM differentiated, will therefore be:

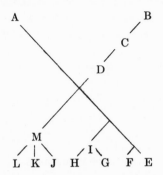

Variation 7 should then be marked in the table as a reminder that its readings are conflated.

When the number of states is large, it may be desirable to check the correctness of the solution by some other method than repeating it. In a table of the disagreements of each state with each of the others, any sigla that never disagree do not represent states but manuscrips recording the same state. In a table of the agreements of each state with each of the others in *one* example of each type of simple variation necessary to establish the scheme (substituting simple variations that would have given the same information for any complex variations from which the scheme was in fact derived), the diagram will be proved correctly drawn if the number of variations is one less than the total of extant states and hypothetical intermediaries and if the number of disagreements of each state with any other state is one, when they have no intermediary, and one more for each intermediary.

Greg's approach to complex variations suggests an additional check upon the analysis. A complex variation in which the second reading developed out of or replaced the first, the third, the second, and so on is tantamount to a series of simple variations: each new reading is potentially the last, and differs from all that have gone before. Thus $x{\rightarrow}y{\rightarrow}z$ may be represented by the series $x{:}yz$ and $xy{:}z$, $w{\rightarrow}x{\rightarrow}y{\rightarrow}z$ by $w{:}xyz$, $wx{:}yz$, and $wxy{:}z$, and so on. If the alternate readings independently developed out of or replaced the first, each new reading is actually the last

in its line of descent, and they never even potentially agree against the old reading. Thus $y \leftarrow x \rightarrow z$ may be represented by $y{:}xz$ and $xy{:}z$, and $x \leftarrow w \rightarrow y$ by $x{:}wyz$, $y{:}wxz$, and $z{:}wxy$, and so on. Combinations of suc-
$$x \leftarrow w \rightarrow y$$
$$\downarrow$$
$$z$$
cessive and independent alternation of readings may be represented in corresponding fashion. This process of expressing complex variations in terms of simple is called *resolution*, and it is convenient to call the simple variations arrived at in this way *resolutions* to distinguish them from the simple variations actually occurring.

Because the readings of a complex variation pass directly from one to another, not all the possible resolutions are compatible. Further simplification of the analysis is therefore possible because only those resolutions of a complex variation need be considered which are compatible with the simple variations actually occurring, with the resolutions of other complex variations, and with each other. By itself a type–3 variation may be represented by some combination of two of the following resolutions: $x{:}yz$, $y{:}xz$, $z{:}xy$; a type–4 variation by three of the following: $w{:}xyz$, $x{:}wyz$, $y{:}wxz$, $z{:}wxy$, $wx{:}zy$, $wy{:}xz$, $wz{:}xy$; a type–5 by four of the following $v{:}wxyz$, $w{:}vxyz$, $x{:}vwyz$, $y{:}vwxz$, $z{:}vwxy$, $vw{:}xyz$, $vx{:}wyz$, $vy{:}wxz$, $vz{:}wxy$, $wx{:}vyz$, $wy{:}vxz$, $wz{:}vxy$, $xy{:}vwz$, $xz{:}vwy$, $yz{:}vwx$; a type–6 by five of the following: $u{:}vwxyz$, $v{:}uwxyz$, $w{:}uvxyz$, $x{:}uvwyz$, $y{:}uvwxz$, $z{:}uvwxy$, $uv{:}wxyz$, $uw{:}vxyz$, $ux{:}vwyz$, $uy{:}vwxz$, $uz{:}vwxy$, $vw{:}uxyz$, $vx{:}uwyz$, $vy{:}uwxz$, $vz{:}uwxy$, $wx{:}uvyz$, $wy{:}uwxz$, $wz{:}uvxy$, $xy{:}uvwz$, $xz{:}uvwy$, $yz{:}uvwx$, $uvw{:}xyz$, $uvx{:}wyz$, $uvy{:}wxz$, $uvz{:}wxy$, $uwx{:}vyz$, $uwy{:}vxz$, $uwz{:}vxy$, $uxy{:}vwz$, $uxz{:}vwy$, $uyz{:}vwx$; and so on. That is, the combination will consist of one less than the number of readings in the variation, to be chosen from a list of $2n + 1$ resolutions, where n is the number of possible resolutions for the next less complex variation.

It follows that if the textual scheme has been completely defined by simple variations, the compatible resolutions of any additional complex variations should each repeat one of the simple variations. It also follows that if the scheme has not been completely defined by simple variations, it ought to conform to the evidence of compatible resolutions of the complex variations. Assume the following analysis:

AB:CDE

CD:ABE

E:ABCD

A:C:BDE

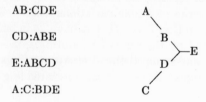

To check the work, the complex variation is resolved into its three possible resolutions: *x:yz* (*z* = BDE), *y:xz*, and *xy:z*. The third of these [= AC:BDE] is incompatible with the variation AB:CDE, but the other two [= A:CBDE, C:ABDE], taken with the simple variations, would give the diagram above. Therefore the diagram is correct.

If a great many states are to be analyzed, and especially if the collations are performed by different persons separately, the compilation of the apparatus criticus and the making of selections for the analysis of conflicts are an extremely tedious business and very likely to be inaccurate if done without any mechanical aids. One such aid is key sorting, that is, the separation of specially punched and notched cards by inserting a rod (the key) through the punches along the edges of the cards in a pack and lifting out those merely punched from those notched at the points of insertion. This means that the unwanted cards are lifted away from the rest. Cards can be bought ready-punched, and then individually notched as desired; can be punched by anyone with a drill press (the commercial standard is four ⅛-inch holes to the inch), and notched as desired; or can be individually punched and notched in one operation by a keyboard machine. Notching can be done with scissors, if necessary, but various kinds of specially designed notching punches are available, from the simple ticket-punch type through a whole range of more complicated devices. The punches may run around all four sides of the cards in a single or double row. One corner of the cards will be, or should be, cut off to allow immediate recognition of any that have been inserted upside down or back to front in the pack.

The methods now to be described are used by the McBee Company in its Keysort system. With a single row of holes, six holes are required to represent the numbers 0 to 9. One is "single figure" (SF), which in combination with the holes for 0, 1, 2, 4, and 7 represents these numbers; the holes for 1, 2, 4, and 7 in combination will represent the remaining digits. With a double row of holes, the column for "single figure" may be eliminated, and some space saved. The outer row will then represent 0, 1, 2, 4, and 7, when they are to stand alone; the inner row will represent the same numbers when they are to be combined with others. Letters may be represented by individual punches, or more compactly by a combination of numbers, representing the section of the alphabet in which they fall, and their place in the section. If the alphabet is divided into thirds, a group of only three holes will indicate the section (single figure, 1, and 2), and the standard group of six holes the place within the section (or, if two rows of holes are used, fronts of two and five holes are sufficient); A would be 1-1, J would be 2-1, R would be 2-9, and so on. Variations on these methods are possible.

If the cards are notched subsequent to punching and the identification of the holes is not printed or mimeographed on the face of each card, a master guide may be prepared by laying one of the punched cards over an unpunched card of the same dimensions and writing through the holes the number or letter represented by each. The cards may then be laid over this guide in turn, and the holes to be opened into notches may be quickly marked. When sorted, the cards should be held supported without excessive pressure, so that those to be lifted out will withdraw easily and not bring with them any that ought to remain. If the cards are small, they can be placed between two blocks of wood. If the cards show any tendency to stick to or catch on each other, the key should be vigorously shaken.

Exactly the same sorting process may be accomplished by machines which can sense punches in cards. For IBM machines, a standard card of eighty columns is used. The cards are punched on another IBM machine. On these cards, each column may represent any number from 0 to 9 or a letter, and information may thus be entered more compactly than on a Keysort card.

One card, whether for Keysorting or machine sorting, is used for each reading of each state in each variation. The earliest groups of holes or of columns may be used to identify the variation by the smallest standard unit of text—paragraph, section, sentence, Biblical verse or fraction of verse, poetical line—and by an additional arbitrary number for the specific variation within the unit (if there is only one, it should still be numbered, since the examination of additional states may turn up another). This information comprises a *field*.

Another field may be used to identify the reading by arbitrary number. If we have "wikked":"mede":"neid":"greid," we can number them 1, 2, 3, and 4. The field should be made large enough to cover all reasonable possibilities; two digits will allow up to 99 different readings (type–99 variation) to be noted, and ought to be sufficient under most conditions. On the other hand, if no more readings than 9 (type–9 variation) are likely to occur, allowing a second column will waste time and space. Decisions of this sort must be made carefully, for once the system of punching has been decided upon, it cannot be altered without discarding all the work previously done. States omitted from the record of a variation may be given zero in this field.

A third field may be used to identify the state of the text. Although it·

is not always absolutely necessary, it will usually simplify matters if numbers are substituted for sigla normally expressed in letters.

The remaining columns on an IBM card may be used for comment or for the variant reading itself, but neither may contain more letters and spaces than there are remaining on the card. The corresponding information would be entered by hand or typed on the face of a Keysort card. If it is desirable to read what is punched on the IBM cards, an interpreting machine will sense the punches and type the information at the top of the cards. This seems a useful precaution in any event, to facilitate checking the accuracy of the punching.

Different arrangements may suggest themselves for different projects, but the fields should always be arranged with that most used at the head, that least used at the end, so as to conserve time both in notching or punching and in sorting. In Keysort cards, fields having space for two or more digits must always be filled, that is, zero (and "single figure" if necessary) must be punched in any unused columns: 1 will be 01 or 001 and so on.

Obviously a base copy of the text will be required with which individual manuscripts or previously prepared collations of one or more manuscripts may be compared. In the base copy, the variations and variant readings will be numbered and written out just as they are to be on the cards: each variation will be identified by unit of text, and arbitrary number within the unit (this latter number may at first represent the variation's position within the unit, but examination of additional states may at any time make it truly arbitrary), and each variant reading in the variation will be written out and given a number. Sigla need not be entered in the base copy, only on the cards, for the apparatus criticus can be prepared from the cards at any time and quickly prepared again as new states are discovered and their variants recorded on cards with the others.

It is not necessary to describe the Keysorting operation in detail. Assume a poem of 125 lines, no line having more than nine variations and no variation more than nine readings. The operator sorts first for line 001, three operations: first, he sorts the cards with zero for the first digit; from these he sorts those with zero for the second digit; and from these he sorts the cards with 1 for the final digit. He sorts next for variation 1. Finally he sorts for reading 1. He copies the sigla from the cards for line 001, variation 1, reading 1. He then puts these cards in a permanent file, and sorts those having reading 2 from the other cards for variation 1 of line 001. When he has finished with the cards for line 001, he turns to the cards having zero for the first two digits and sorts the cards for line 002. When he has finished with the cards for line 009, he sorts the cards having 1 for the second digit. From these he sorts the cards having zero for the second digit (line 010). And so on. If there are many states of the text, it will be helpful also to sort the sigla by tens.

Keysort cards may also be used in analyzing conflicting variations. Each card will represent one conflict. Each of its fields will have space for entering all of the states, the first field for those that may be subtracted singly to resolve the conflict on that card, the others for those groups that must be subtracted in groups, one group being entered in each field.

If IBM cards are used, a collating machine will sort them in any desired fashion, and an accounting machine will print the critical apparatus, or any other information desired from them.

Finally, IBM cards may be fed into an electronic computer, or the information transferred to magnetic tape for use in such a computer. These computers can deal almost instantly with a very large number of items of information. In textual studies, the total of items for each problem is estimated by multiplying estimated number of states by estimated number of variations by estimated largest number of variant readings in any one variation. Not every computer may have a "memory" of the size necessary. These computers can be instructed not only to print the apparatus criticus but to solve conflicts among variations. In addition, the whole process will be performed in a matter of a few hours at most. But working out the instructions for the machine is a task often requiring weeks of effort by highly skilled specialists, and the costs of operating the computer, even if not borne by the analyst himself, may be prohibitive. One textual scholar who has used a computer in his work is the Reverend John William Ellison, working with selected passages from some hundreds of manuscripts of Luke, but his method of procedure results in a series of sheets each giving the agreements of one state with each of the others in various categories.[4] The analyses outlined in this book would be performed in a different way.

IV

Examples

A typical example of a simple problem is to be found in Dryden's epilogue to Etherege's *Man of Mode*.[1] Before Dryden's death the play went through three editions, each of which records the same state of the text of the epilogue. Three seventeenth-century manuscripts of the epilogue have been described by scholars who have been strongly attracted to some of their readings. The problem lies in the relationship of the states in the manuscripts to that in the editions.

The printed state may be called Q, since the editions of the play are all quartos; the states in the manuscripts may be numbered arbitrarily as M1 (British Museum MS Sloane 203, f. 95r), M2 (Sloane 1458, f. 23r–v), and M3 (Bodleian MS Don. b. 8, pp. 558–559). The text of Q (from the first edition) and such collation as is necessary in the solution of the problem follow:

The *EPILOGUE by Mr Dryden.*

Most Modern Wits, such monstrous Fools have shown,
They seem'd not of heav'ns making but their own.
Those Nauseous Harlequins in Farce may pass,
But there goes more to a substantial Ass!
Something of man must be expos'd to View,
That, Gallants, they may more resemble you:
Sir *Fopling* is a Fool so nicely writ,
The Ladies wou'd mistake him for a Wit.

69

And when he sings, talks lowd, and cocks; wou'd cry,
10   I vow methinks he's pretty Company,
So brisk, so gay, so travail'd, so refin'd!
As he took pains to graff upon his kind.
True Fops help Natures work, and go to school,
To file and finish god-a'mighty's fool.
Yet none Sir *Fopling* him, or him can call;
He's Knight o' th' Shire, and represents ye all.
From each he meets, he culls what e're·he can,
Legion's his name, a people in a Man.
His bulky folly gathers as it goes,
20   And, rolling o're you, like a Snow-ball growes.
His various modes from various Fathers follow,
One taught the Toss, and one the new *French* Wallow.
His Sword-knot, this; his Crevat, this design'd,
And this, the yard long Snake he twirls behind.
From one the sacred Perriwig he gain'd,
Which Wind ne're blew, nor touch of Hat prophan'd.
Anothers diving Bow he did adore,
Which with a shog casts all the hair before:
Till he with full Decorum brings it back,
30   And rises with a Water Spaniel shake.
As for his Songs (the Ladies dear delight)
Those sure he took from most of you who Write.
Yet every man is safe from what he fear'd,
For no one fool is hunted from the herd.

Title   The EPILOGUE by Mʳ Dryden.] The Epilogue written by Mʳ
Dryden and spoken by Smith or Sʳ ffopling. M2; Epilogue to Sʳ Fopling
Flutter, the play made by Mʳ Etheridge. M3; *wanting* M1.   1 shown,]
Q, M3; ∼ₐ M1; ∼. M2.   2 seem'd] Q, M2–3; seem M1.   3 Those] Q;
Such M2; These M1, M3.   6 they] Q, M1; hee M2; it M3.   8 Wit.]
Q, M2; ∼ₐ M1; ∼, M3.   10 I vow] Q, M1–2; I, now M3.   12 *After
this line M2 has two others:* Labouring to putt in more as Mʳ Bayes/
Thrums in Additions to his ten yeares playes.   14 file] Q, M1, M3;
fill M2.   14 god-a'mighty's] Q, M1, M3; God Almighty, M2.   14 fool]
Q, M1–2; Toole M3.   14 *After this line M3 has two others:* Labour, to
put in more, as Master Bayes/Thrumms in Additions to his ten-yeares
playes.   15–16 *In M2 these lines follow the line here numbered 20.*   22
taught the] Q, M2–3; taught a M1.   23–24 *In M2 these lines follow the
line here numbered 30.*   24 he] Q, M2–3; that M1.   25–26 *Omitted from
M2.*   26 nor touch of Hat] Q, M1; nor Hatt M3.   28 a shog] Q, M1;
the shog M2; one shogg M3.   30 a] Q, M1; his M2–3.   32 took ...
who] Q, M1; takes ... that M2–3.   33 man] Q, M1, M3; one M2.
34 For] Q, M1, M3; And M2.

The variations may be more simply analyzed if they are tabulated without the readings:

a.	Q M2 : M1 : M3	title, 8
b.	Q M3 : M1 : M2	1
c.	Q M2 M3 : M1	2, 22, 24
d.	Q : M1 M3 : M2	3
e.	Q M1 : M2 : M3	6, 28
f.	Q M1 M2 : M3	10, 14 (*bis*)
g.	Q M1 M3 : M2	12, 14 (*bis*), 15–16, 23–24, 25–26, 33, 34
h.	Q M1 : M2 M3	12 and 14 (couplet), 30, 32
i.	Q M1 : M3 [M2]	26

The three type–1 variations, *c, f,* and *g,* show that the three manuscripts record terminal states. The type–2 variation, *h,* indicates that Q and M1 form a terminal group, and that M2 and M3 form another. The exclusion in the complex variation *d* indicates that Q cannot be intermediary between M1 and M3 and so is terminal. The other variations do not conflict with these. The general diagram is therefore:

None of the variations are directional, for although some of the readings are certainly wrong, there is nothing to show that the "right" readings are not plausible emendations. George Thorn-Drury, who first described M3,[2] thought its readings in lines 6 and 10 "worthy of serious consideration," and H. F. B. Brett-Smith took them into his edition of Etherege's *Dramatic Works.*[3] Brett-Smith also accepted the additional couplet found in M2 and M3 as authoritative, but supposed Dryden had rejected it. Willard Thorp, who first described M2,[4] thought that in the order of its lines it was nearer than any other state "to what its author intended." The editors of the California Dryden, however, did not feel the force of these arguments. To them the order of lines in M2 did not seem superior to that in the other states, nor did the reading of M3 in line 6 seem more satisfactory than that of Q and M1 or than that of M2. Neither did they seem inferior. On the other hand, "I vow" in line 10 seemed a better reading than "I, now" (aye, now), and it seemed easier to suppose that the couplet peculiar to M2 and M3 was not authoritative. Dryden was lampooned in the character of Bayes in Buckingham's *Re-*

hearsal (1671). Therefore Brett-Smith's conclusion that the lines were a "hit at Buckingham" did not seem so satisfactory as Thorn-Drury's and Thorp's that they were a hit at Dryden. And there seemed no reason why Dryden should have seized this opportunity for humorous or sardonic self-reflection.

The dates of the records do not help us with the special diagram, for we know certainly only that of Q (first edition, 1676). The three manuscript versions are all found in commonplace books or miscellaneous collections of various dates and are not themselves dated (the volume containing M2 is dated 1677 on its first page, but what relationship this date has to the date of M2 itself we can not determine; it may mark the beginning or the end of the owner's work on his volume or any time between). The California editors felt that none of the manuscripts was a likely ancestor of the printed text. If it is fair to take the next step and conclude that the manuscripts are transcripts at one or more removes of the printed text, the final textual diagram will be:

A diagram of the bibliographical relationship of the manuscripts to the editions would differentiate the latter.

A fairly simple example in which conflicting variations occur is to be found in the manuscripts and first edition of Chaucer's *Complaint to his Purse*, as collated by George B. Pace.[5] The manuscripts are A, A2, CC1, CC2, F, Ff, H, H2, M, and P; the first edition is Cx. There are two textual states in H2; only the corrected state is here considered. Pace's apparatus contains certain nontextual evidence: spelling errors and variant spellings such as occur in lines 11 (*yelownesse:yowlenes*), 16 (*worde:worlde*), 19 (*shave:shae*), and 25 (*harmes:harmous*); eleven variant forms, *ye:yow, be(beo):been(bene, ben, bien):bethe, as:als, mote:must(e):moste, elles:ell, myn:my, syn:sith, wil:wol(l)e, of:o:off, by:be, mowen:mow:may*; and exact English-French correspondences. Pace's text (based on Ff) and the rest ⌐f his apparatus (adjusted also in formal details) follow:

The complaynt of Chaucer to his Purse

To yow my purse and to noon other wight
Complayn I for ye be my lady dere
I am so sory now that ye been lyght

ffor certes but yf ye make me hevy chere
5 Me were as leef be layde vpon my bere
ffor whiche vnto your mercy thus I crye
Beeth hevy ageyne or elles mote I dye

Now voucheth-sauf this day or hyt be nyght
That I of yow the blisful sovne may here
10 Or se your colour lyke the sonne bryght
That of yelownesse had neuer pere
Ye be my lyfe ye be myn hertys stere
Quene of comfort and of gode companye
Beth heuy ayeyne or elles mote I dye

15 Now purse that ben to me my lyves lyght
And saveour as doun in this worlde here
Oute of this tovne helpe me thurgh your myght
Syn that ye wil nat bene my tresorere
For I am shave as nye as any frere
20 But yet I pray vnto your curtesye
Bethe hevy ayen or elles mote I dye

Lenvoy de Chaucer

O conquerour of Brutes albyon
Whiche that by lyne and free eleccion
Ben verray kynge this songe to yow I sende
25 And ye that mowen all oure harmes amende
Haue mynde vpon my supplicacion

Title and 1–14 *wanting in CC1.*   *Title* The complaynt of Chaucer to his Purse] ... Chaucers ... M; ... vnto ... Cx, M; ... his empty ... Cx, P; A supplicacion to Kyng Richard by chaucier H2; Chaucer (*only*) A2; *wanting in* A, CC2, Ff, H.   1 to] *om.* CC2.   2 be] *om.* A2, H.   3 so] *om.* Cx.   3 now] *om.* A2, H.   4 ffor] That A; But P.   4 yf] *om.* A, CC2, Cx, P.   4 ye] + now Cx.   4 hevy] any A.   5 as] A CC2.   5 leef] + to A2, CC2, H, M.   5 vpon] on A2, H.   5 my] a Cx; *om.* A2, H, P.   6 your] you M.   7 mote I] y muste M.   8 hyt] yet Cx, P.   10 Or] To A2, H.   10 se] shew H2.   10 lyke] as A2, H; lyche to H2.   11 of] + yowre A2, H, M.   11 yelownesse (Ie-lownesse H)] eye low-nesse A2; the lewdnesse Ff.   11 had] hath A2, H, M.   11 neuer] no A2, H, M; neuer no CC2; neuer his H2.   12 lyfe] light A2, H.   12 stere] feere A2, H.   13 of] *om.* A.   13 gode] all CC2; *om.* A2, H, H2, M.   14 mote I] y muste M.   15–26 *wanting in CC2.*   15 Now] Yee H2.   15 to me] *om.* M.   15 lyves] lif my A2, H; hertis M.   16 saveour as] souerayn lady A2, H, M.   16 doun in this worlde] in this worlde

doun CC1, H2; *om*. doun M.   17 Oute of] Of lich CC1.   17 thurgh]
by Cx; þis M.   17 your myght] night M.   18 tresorere] tresour CC1.
19 as nye] *om*. Ff.   19 as] + ys F, Ff.   19 any] a F.   20 *instead of
this line A2, H, M repeat line 6.*   20 yet] *om*. Cx.   20 your curtesye]
you curtiously CC1.   21 mote I] I A; y must M.   *Heading* and
22–26 *wanting in A, A2, H, M. Heading* Lenvoy de Chaucer] *om*. de
Chaucer H2, P; + vnto the kynge Cx.   24 songe] *om*. CC1, Cx, P.
25 oure] my CC1, F; *om*. Cx, P.   25 harmes] harme F; mys CC1.
26 Haue] Haþe H2.

All the states except H are terminal: CC1, CC2, Cx, H2, and M stand
alone in type–1 variations; A stands alone only when CC1 is wanting,
but the apparently complex variation in line 21 is really a compound of
two type–1 variations; F and Ff stand alone only when CC2 is wanting,
but, to look ahead, CC2 is not immediately related to either; besides, Ff,
A2 and P stand alone in type–3 variations in which the states they agree
with elsewhere have new partners.

With one exception the variations in which at least two states agree
against at least two others are in conflict. The exception is Σ:A2 H, and
these two states therefore form a terminal group, in which A2 is terminal.
The apparent agreement in the title of Cx and M against F and P may
be ignored; P's title is in French, and the *a* therein corresponds equally
to *to* (F) and to *vnto*. The other variations are as follows:

A CC2 Ff H : A2 : Cx F M P : H2 [CC1] title
Cx P : F M [A A2 CC1 CC2 Ff H H2] title
A CC2 Cx F Ff H2 M P : A2 H [CC1] 2, 3, 5, 10 (*bis*), 12 (*bis*)
A CC2 Cx P : A2 F Ff H H2 M [CC1] 4
A Cx F Ff H2 P : A2 CC2 H M [CC1] 5, 11 (presence of *no*)
A CC2 F Ff H2 M : A2 H P : Cx [CC1] 5
A A2 CC2 F Ff H H2 M : Cx P [CC1] 8
A CC2 Cx F Ff H2 P : A2 H M [CC1] 11 (*tris*)
A Cx F Ff P : A2 H H2 M : CC2 [CC1] 13
A CC1 Cx F Ff H2 P : A2 H : M [CC2] 15
A CC1 Cx F Ff H2 P : A2 H M [CC2] 16, 20
A A2 Cx F Ff H P : CC1 H2 [M CC2] 16
A A2 CC1 Cx H H2 M P : F Ff [CC2] 19
A A2 H M : CC1 Cx F Ff H2 P [CC2] omission of heading and 22–26
CC1 Cx F Ff : H2 P [A A2 CC2 H M] heading
CC1 Cx P : F Ff H2 [A A2 CC2 H M] 24
CC1 F : Cx P : Ff H2 [A A2 CC2 H M] 25

These seventeen variations contain twenty-five conflicts, which may be diagrammed as follows:

A CC2——Ff H   CC2 H————M   P————————H   M————Cx F P

| 1-4 | | 1-5 | | 1-6 | | 1-8 |

Cx P——F M   A Ff——Cx F P   F M——A CC2 Ff   H——A CC2 Ff

A Ff——Cx F P   F——Cx M P   Ff——Cx F P   CC2————A2 H M

| 1-9 | | 1-13 | | 1-14 | | 4-5 |

H————M   Ff————A H   A H————M   A Cx P——F Ff H2

P————————A2 H   A————————Cx P   P————H2   P————————A2 H

| 4-6 | | 4-14 | | 4-15 | | 5-6 |

A CC2——F Ff H2 M   A2 H M——F Ff H2   Cx——F Ff   A F Ff H2——CC2 M

M————————A2 H   P————A2 H   P————A2 H   P————H2

| 6-8 | | 6-9 | | 6-14 | | 7-15 |

A CC2 F Ff H2——P   A F Ff——H2 M   F Ff H2——A M   Cx——F Ff

A————A2 H M   P————————H2   CC1——Cx P   F ———— Ff

| 9-14 | | 12-15 | | 12-16 | | 12-17 |

Cx F Ff P——H2   Cx F Ff——CC1   H2————F Ff   CC1—— -H2

M——Cx F P   M————A2 H   F————Ff   P— Cx CC1   H2————P

| 11-1 | | 11-6 | | 13-17 | | 15-16 | | 15-17 |

H————A Ff   A——A F Ff H2   CC1 ——H2   H2————F Ff   Ff— Cx

The largest number of states that can be analyzed together is six. Two of the possible groupings of six will overlie. The partial variations for both groupings are given at once:

H : A2 : Cx F M : H2 [CC1]

Cx : F M [A2 CC1 H H2]

Cx F H2 M : A2 H [CC1]

Cx : A2 F H H2 M [CC1]

$$-Cx$$

A2 ＼　　　　F
　　H ＼　／ H2
　　　M ／　＼ CC1

Cx F H2 : A2 H M [CC1]

F H2 M : A2 H : Cx [CC1]

A2 F H H2 M : Cx [CC1]

Cx F H2 : A2 H M [CC1]

Cx F : A2 H H2 M [CC1]

CC1 Cx F H2 : A2 H : M

CC1 Cx F H2 : A2 H M

A2 Cx F H : CC1 H2 [M]

A2 CC1 Cx H H2 M : F

A2 H M : CC1 Cx F H2

CC1 Cx F : H2 [A2 H M]

CC1 Cx : F H2 [A2 H M]

CC1 F : Cx : H2 [A2 H M]

−CC1

A2   F
   H   Cx
   M   H2

A2   Overlay   F
   H   Cx
   M   CC1
       H2

The overlay can be enlarged further by dropping A2, CC1, and H and adding Ff. The calculations and results follow:

Ff : Cx F M : H2   Cx F Ff H2 : M

Cx : F M [Ff H2]   Cx F Ff H2 : M

Cx F Ff H2 M   Cx F Ff : H2 [M]

Cx : F Ff H2 M   Cx H2 M : F Ff

Cx F Ff H2 : M   M : Cx F Ff H2

F Ff H2 M : Cx   Cx F Ff : H2 [M]

F Ff H2 M : Cx   Cx : F Ff H2 [M]

Cx F Ff H2 : M   F : Cx : Ff H2 [M]

Cx F Ff : H2 M

M   F
H2   Ff
      Cx

A2   Overlay   F
  H   Ff
  M   Cx
      CC1
      H2

Two more groupings of five states give diagrams that can be overlaid, and this overlay can then be overlaid on the previous one to give the final diagram. The partial variations for both sets of five states are given at once:

A CC2 Ff : Cx P : H2

Cx P [A CC2 Ff H2]

A CC2 Cx Ff H2 P

A CC2 Cx P : Ff H2

A Cx Ff H2 P : CC2

A CC2 Ff H2 : P : Cx

A CC2 Ff H2 : Cx P

A CC2 Cx Ff H2 P

A Cx Ff P : H2 : CC2

A Cx Ff H2 P [CC2]

A Cx Ff H2 P [CC2]

A Cx Ff P : H2 [CC2]

A Cx H2 P : Ff [CC2]

A : Cx Ff H2 P [CC2]

Cx Ff : H2 P [A CC2]

Cx P : Ff H2 [A CC2]

Cx P : Ff H2 [A CC2]

−H2

−P

Overlay of the above

Final overlay

The two earliest manuscripts are those recording A and F, which belong to the first half of the fifteenth century. All the other states date from the last half of the century. There are three variations that are more or less certainly directional, *hevy:any* in line 4, *yelownesse (Ie-lownesse):the lewdnesse:eye lownesse* in line 11, and *saveour as:souerayn lady* in line 16. It is certainly more likely that *hevy* is Chaucer's reading than that it is the inspired witticism of a scribe, and A, which reads *any*, may therefore be accepted as a descendant. Conceivably, *yelownesse* might result in *the lewdnesse* (Ff), through **yelowdnesse*, **ye lewdnesse*, but the wrong reading by no means suggests the right; the same is true of the pair *Ie-lownesse*

(H) and *eye lownesse* (A2). Therefore Ff and A2 may be accepted as descendants. Finally, it seems safe enough to class *souerayn lady* as a pious alteration of *saveour*, and to accept A2, H, and M, which have the former reading, as descendants. Under the circumstances F may be accepted as the ancestor of the other states. The simplest conceptual scheme of their relationship is therefore:

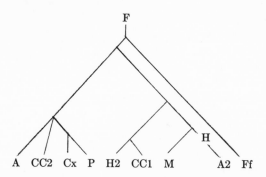

The nontextual evidence cited by Pace does not suggest any alternate bibliographical relationship for the manuscripts and Cx; so the textual scheme may be accepted as a bibliographical scheme also. Pace's tree, redrawn to correspond as closely as possible to the above, is as follows:

The differences, which lie in the placing of CC1 and CC2, and in the choice of ancestor, spring from a variety of causes. In the first place, Pace did not count the title or the heading of the envoy as part of the text. In the second place, he set aside the agreements of A, CC2, Cx, and P in line 4, and of CC1 and H2 in line 16, as accidental coincidence (he also passed over the agreements of A2, H, and P in line 5, and of CC1 and F in line 25). Finally, as he developed his terminal groups, he supposed that the intermediaries between the individual manuscripts and between the groups of manuscripts were necessarily their ancestors.

Next, an instance of authorial revision, using collations of nine states of Dryden's *Mac Flecknoe*, abstracted from a fuller apparatus published by G. Blakemore Evans.[6] That this is authorial revision, and not scribal conflation, is indicated by the extreme complexity of the conflicts: it is impossible, given the nature of the poem, that so many copyists should have compared so many exemplars. The manuscripts are designated by Evans B, C, F, H, I, L, and M, the editions 82 and 84. The unauthorized edition of 1682 is found in two states; only the corrected state is here considered. Similarly, in the manuscripts only the corrected readings are listed. Three of the latter, B, C, and I, are imperfect in varying degree, and two more, H and M, which are almost without punctuation, are to be considered imperfect in this respect. The lemmas are from 84, which, since it is everywhere available in reprints and the poem is a long one, is not reproduced here.

Title Mac Flecknoe] + A satyre LB; + or A Satyr upon the *True-Blew-Protestant Poet*, T.S. 82; *C wants title and lines 1–46; I wants title and lines 1–152.*   6 Through] In F.   6 Realms] Realm L.   10 the State] his State L.   11 which of all] well which of H.   11 was] were 82 L B M.   12 War] Wars 82 L B F M.   14 who] y^t L H F.   19 make] have B.   21 on] an H.   23 *Sh*—'s] *Shad*— 82.   23 genuine] Gloomy H.   27 the] that H.   29 of] to L B.   31 dunce] Prince F.   31 than] *om.* B.   33 And] I 82.   33 clad] Cloath'd 82 M L B; drest H.   33 *Norwich* Drugget] Drugget Russet 82 M; rusty drugget L; Russell drugget H; rustick drugget B F.   36 of] att H.   37 the] a 82 B M.   39 well tim'd] well tun'd L H F.   41 Hymn] him B.   41 Commander] Commanders 82.   42 was ne'er in *Epsom* Blankets tost] in Epsom Blankett nere was tost L.   42 Blankets] Blankett L M.   43 new] now H.   44 still] she L.   44 trembling] Trembles 82 B F M L.   44 thy] his M.   45 At] As M.   46 squeaks for fear,] squeaks, for feare H B F; squeakes for feare L M.   47 *C begins.*   47 Echoes] Eccho 82.   48 from] to H.   50 As at the Morning Toast, that Floats] And gently waft the over all 82.   50 Toast] Tide C.   50 Floats] wafts F M.   51 *B wants lines 51–150.*   51 thy] y^e H.   52 Papers] Paper 82.   53 *Andre's*] *Andrew's* 82 H F M.   54 Not] Nor L C F.   54 of] in F.   54 rhime:] $\sim$; 82; $\sim$, L; $\sim_\wedge$ H F M; $\sim$. C.   55 Though . . . excell;] $\sim$, 82 C; $\sim_\wedge$ L H M; ($\sim$) F.   55 sense] verse L C.   56 fell,] $\sim$; 82 F; $\sim_\wedge$ H M; $\sim$. C.   58 bore] wore 82M.   59 he ne'er would] he'd never M.   59 *Villerius*] Valerius L C F H.   . 61 of] for F.   64 to] by 82 L H C F M.   64 Walls] wall H.   65 fears] fear C F.   67 of] on H.   67 it] is L; was C.   69 Of all the Pile an

empty name] An Empty name of all the Pile 82.   71 loves] Love 82 F.
72 Where] Here F.   72 Mother-Strumpets] mother waters H.   73
silence] silent C.   75 form'd] nurst M.   77 Where] And H.   79
Buskins] Buskin L C.   82 this Monument] these Monuments 82.
82 vanisht] Varnisht 82 M.   83 Pure] Their H.   84 war] warrs F.
86 *Sh—'s*] *Shad—* 82.   88 Pile] Isle 82 H M; place L C.   89 a] yᵉ F.
90 *Psyches*] psyche C.   92 *Humorists*] Hum'rist L.   92 it] his Pen
82; he L C F M.   96 of] o' th C.   96 Fame] Pomp 82 L F M C.   97
and] to 82 M.   98 Carpets] Carpet 82 L H F M.   99 scatter'd] letter'd H.   100 come] came H.   103 Sh—] Shadwells L.   104 Bilk't]
Bill'd C.   104 Yeomen] Women H.   105 *H—*] *Herringman* 82 L M
C F; *Herringham* H.   107 Throne] State 82 L F M.   108 *Ascanius*]
Ascaines H.   109 and] the H.   110 Brows] brow C.   110 glories,
grace] Glories-Grace 82.   111 arround] about 82 C.   112 to] from C.
112 Altars] Altar H.   114 swore] *Sworn* 82.   114 should] could F.
115 till] to 82 C.   117 Ne'er to have peace with Wit, nor truce with]
Wou'd bid defiance unto Wit and 82.   117 nor] or L C.   121 He] Was
82.   121 mighty] lusty C.   124 Lore] Love 82 H C.   124 young]
long M.   125 Loyns] Lungs H.   126 Poppies] Poppey 82 L C F M;
Popery H.   128 at] as H.   128 that] the C.   132 admiring] ad-
vancing 82.   134 *Syre*] Brether'n H.   134 of] on 82.   135 shed] ∼:
82; ∼; L; ∼, C F.   136 Full on the filial dullness] Dulnesse L.   136
on] of 82 H C.   136 dullness:] ∼ₐ 82 L H C F M.   138 At] And L.
138 burst] broke L H C F.   138 prophetick] poetick F.   139 Heavens]
Heaven 82 L H C F M.   140 farr] fair 82 L H C M.   141 Dominion]
dominions L C.   142 And] But F.   143 Kingdom] Kingdoms 82 L C.
143 let him] may he 82.   144 paus'd] said C.   144 and] *om.* H.   144
cry'd] said L C.   145 thus,] ∼ₐ 82 L H C F M.   146 new Ignorance]
& arrogance F.   147 thou] then H.   148 and] a 82; *om.* M.   150
Yet] And H.   150 thy] the H.   150 toyl] Soul 82; soil L C M H.
151 *B is again present.*   151 in] with 82 M.   152 Make] Lett H.   152
Loveit] love it's L.   153 *I begins.*   153 Let] And H.   153 charm] fill
L.   154 in] by C.   155 still] let C.   155 shall] yᵗ L; still C.   157
by] of 82 M.   157 thy] thine H F.   159 future] after 82 L H B C F
M.   160 Issue] Issues 82 L H C F M.   160 thy] thine 82.   161 men]
man F.   162 All] As H.   162 full of] like to 82 B M.   163 *S-dl-y*]
Sydney 82.   164 wit thy hungry] hungry wit thy C.   165 cull] smell
H; pull F.   167 and top] on th' top 82.   167 and in each] in every
H B.   168 *Formal's*] formal L.   168 will] Wit 82 H B M.   169 un-
sought] untaught H.   169 quill] will C.   170 does] doth 82; do L.

170 *Dedications*] Dedication M.   175 *Johnson*] Johnsons M.   175
has] hath 82 L.   175 part;] ∼, 82 B; ∼‸ L H C F M.   176 What share]
For w^t L C.   177 Where] What I.   177 on] or 82 L H C F M I.   178
And] Or 82 L H B C M; To F.   178 Arts] art L C.   179 he] in H.
179 *Nicander's*] Alcanders F M.   180 dust] Durst 82 M.   181 Whip-
stitch] Whip-stick F.   181 my] *mine* 82 L B C M.   182 dwindled]
windled H.   183 When] Where 82 H B F M.   183 Muse] scenes M.
183 *Fletcher*] *Fletchers* 82 H C M.   184 thou] then H.   184 dost] does
F.   185 transfus'd] transfuse L H B C F.   185 Oyl] Oyls 82 L H B C
F M.   185 on] and H.   185 Waters] Water 82.   187 Province]
Promise 82 B.   187 wondrous] Boasted H.   188 New Humours to in-
vent] T'invent new humours still C.   188 for] to B.   189 thy] the 82
L H B C M.   190 one] each L C.   191 makes] make L.   191 writ-
ings] writing M.   191 lean] lame 82.   192 changes] Charges 82.   192
bends] bend L.   193 thy] my F.   196 But] Yet M.   196 sure
thou'rt but] sure thou art 82 L H B C; thou art but F M.   197 gentle]
feeble M.   197 feebly] gently M.   198 smiles] smile C.   198 sleep]
Witt H.   199 sett'st] sets 82; sitt'st M.   202 does] doth 82.   203
thee] the 82 H.   204 mild] wild 82; kind L C.   207 Altars] trophys
L C.   208 Ten] a H M.   209 diff'rent] differing F.   209 talents]
Talent 82 L C M.   210 own] one 82.   213 sent] let M.   213 de-
claiming] declining 82 H B F.   214 his] the 82.   214 robe] Robes 82.
217 double] doubled 82 B.

The pattern of the variations will be more readily comprehended from
the following table:

1. B L 82 : F H M 84	[C I]	title (A satyr)
2. B F H L M 84 : 82	[C I]	title, 23, 33, 41
3. B F H L M 82 84: C	[I]	title–46 (omission)
4. B F H L M 82 84: I	[C]	title–152 (omission)
5. B H L M 82 84: F	[C I]	6, 31
6. B F H M 82 84: L	[C I]	6, 10, 42, 44
7. B F L M 82 84: H	[C I]	11, 21, 23, 27, 36, 43
8. B L M 82: F H 84	[C I]	11
9. B F L M 82: H 84	[C I]	12, 44
10. B M 82 84: F H L	[CI]	14, 39
11. B: F H L M 82 84	[C I]	19, 31, 41
12. B L: F H M 82 84	[C I]	29
13. B L M 82: F 84: H	[C I]	33
14. B F: H: L: M 82: 84	[C I]	33

15.	B M 82: F H L 84	[C I]	37
16.	B F H 82 84: L M	[C I]	42
17.	B F H L 82 84: M	[C I]	44, 45
18.	B F H: 82 84	[C I L M]	46 (position of comma)
19.	B F H 82 84: L	[C I M]	46 (some punct: no punct.)
20.	B C F H L M 84: 82	[I]	47, 50
21.	B C F L M 82 84: H	[I]	48, 152
22.	B F H L M 84: C	[I 82]	50
23.	B C H L 84: F M	[I 82]	50
24.	B: C F H L M 82 84	[I]	51
25.	C F L M 82 84: H	[B I]	51, 64, 67, 72, 77, 83, 99, 100, 104, 108, 109, 112, 125, 128, 134, 144, 147, 150¹, 150²
26.	C F H L M 84: 82	[B I]	52, 69, 82, 86, 110, 114, 117, 121, 132, 134, 143
27.	C L 84: F H M 82	[B I]	53
25.	C F L : H M 82 84	[B I]	54
29.	C H L M 82 84: F	[B I]	54, 61, 72, 84, 89, 114, 138, 142, 146
30.	C: F: L: 82: 84	[B H I M]	54 (punct.)
31.	C L: F H M 82 84	[B I]	55, 79, 141, 144
32.	C 82: F: L: 84	[B H I M]	55 (punct.)
33.	C: F 82: L 84	[B H I M]	56 (punct.)
34.	C F H L 84: M 82	[B I]	58, 82, 97
35.	C F H L 82 84: M	[B I]	59, 75, 124
36.	C F H L: M 82 84	[B I]	59, 138
37.	C F H L M 82: 84	[B I]	64, 139
38.	C F: H L M 82 84	[B I]	65
39.	C: F H M 82 84: L	[B I]	67
40.	C H L M 84: F 82	[B I]	71
41.	C: F H L M 82 84	[B I]	73, 90, 96, 104, 110, 112, 121, 128, 144
42.	C L: F 84: H M 82	[B I]	88
43.	C F H M 82 84: L	[B I]	92, 103, 136, 138
44.	C F L M: H 84: 82	[B I]	92
45.	C F L M 82: H 84	[B I]	96
46.	C 84: F H L M 82	[B I]	98
47.	C F L M 82: H: 84	[B I]	105, 126
48.	C H 84: F L M 82	[B I]	107
49.	C 82: F H L M 84	[B I]	111, 115
50.	C L: F H M 84	[B I 82]	117
51.	C H 82: F L M 84	[B I]	124
52.	C H 82: F M 84	[B I L]	136
53.	C F: L: 82: 84	[B H I M]	135 (punct.)

54.	C F L 82: 84	[B H I M] 136 (punct.), 145 (punct.)
55.	C H L M 82: F 84	[B I] 140
56.	C L 82: F H M 84	[B I] 143
57.	C F H L 84: M: 82	[B I] 148
58.	C H L M: F 84: 82	[B I] 150
59.	B C F H L 84: M 82	[I] 151
60.	B C F H M 82 84: L	[I] 152
61.	B C F I L M 82 84: H	153, 162, 169, 179, 182, 184, 185, 187, 198
62.	B C F H I M 82 84: L	153, 168, 191, 192
63.	B F H I L M 82 84: C	154, 155, 164, 169, 188, 198
64.	B F H I M 82 84: C: L	155
65.	B C F H I L 84: M 82	157, 180
66.	B C I L M 82 84: F H	157
67.	B C F H L M 82: I 84	159, 185
68.	B I 84: C F H L M 82	160
69.	B C F H I L M 84: 82	160, 163, 167, 185, 191, 192, 202, 210, 214^1, 214^2
70.	B C H I L M 82 84: F	161, 181, 184, 193, 209
71.	B M 82: C F H I L 84	162
72.	B C I L M 82 84: F: H	165
73.	B H: C F I L M 82 84	167
74.	B H M 82: C F I L 84	168
75.	B C F H I M 84: L: 82	170
76.	B C F H I L 82 84: M	170, 175, 183, 191, 196, 197^1, 197^2, 213
77.	B C F H I M 84: L 82	175
78.	B 82: C F L: I 84	[H M] 175 (punct.)
79.	B F H I M 82 84: C L	176, 178, 190, 207
80.	B C F H L M 82 84: I	177
81.	B 84: C F H I L M 82	177
82.	B C H L M 82: F: I 84	178
83.	B C H I L 82 84: F M	179
84.	B C L M 82: F H I 84	182
85.	B F H M 82: C I L 84	183
86.	B F I L 84: C H M 82	183
87.	B C F H L: I M 82 84	185
88.	B 82: C F H I L M 84	187, 217
89.	B: C F H I L M 82 84	188
90.	B C H L M 82: F I 84	189
91.	B C H L 82: F M: I 84	196
92.	B C F H I L 84: M: 82	199

93. B C F I L M 84: H 82	203
94. B F H I M 84: C L: 82	204
95. B C F I L 82 84: H M	208
96. B F H I 84: C L M 82	209
97. B F H 82: C I L M 84	213

With one exception, Evans could find no clear evidence that any state was descended from any other or that any two or more had a common ancestor short of Dryden's holograph. He took I to be a descendant of 84. Even I shows one conflated reading (line 177) in its 65 lines (it is the most imperfect of the states); so for the purposes of illustration it may be counted as possibly reflecting authorial revision.

The type–1 variations show B, C, F, H, I, L, M, and 82 to be terminal. Since 84 does not stand alone when B or I is present, it may be intermediary between either or both of these states and the rest, but conflation obscures the evidence (cf. variations 67, 68, 81, etc.).

Every variation in which at least two states agree against at least two others is in conflict with some other; such too is the complexity of the conflicts that no more than four states can be analyzed together, and of the sets of four the only overlay is specious:

$$
\begin{matrix} C & & I \\ & \diagup\!\diagdown & \\ L & & F \end{matrix}
\;+\;
\begin{matrix} C & \\ & \diagdown\!\!\!-84\!\!-\!\!I \\ F & \end{matrix}
\;\neq\;
C \diagup\!\diagdown \begin{matrix} & I \\ & \diagup \\ 84 \\ \diagup\!\diagdown \\ L \quad F \end{matrix}
$$

It is necessary, then, to turn instead to the relative incidence of the conflicting variations, and to determine which of them occur the most often alone and supported by compatible variations. It is well to review the conditions for compatibility in the present instance, because of the complexity of some of the variations and the imperfect nature of some of the states. The rule is that Σ:AB is compatible not only with Σ:ABX, but also with Σ:A:BX or, if A is wanting, with Σ_A:BX, and with Σ:AX:B or, if B is wanting, with Σ_B:AX. Thus, although Σ:CL occurs most often alone and in compatible variations of the pattern Σ:CLX, nevertheless Σ:B 82 and its compatible variations occur more often.

The totals are as follows: Σ:B 82, 73 occurrences of this and compatible variations; Σ:CL, 58 occurrences of this and compatible variations; Σ:I 84, 54 occurrences of this and compatible variations; Σ:FH, 45 occurrences of this and compatible variations; Σ:BM 82, 45 occurrences of this and compatible variations; Σ:FHI 84, 28 occurrences of this and compatible variations. It seems from these and the type–1 variations that the general diagram will be as follows:

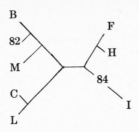

Except for 82 and 84, the states cannot be dated relative to each other. It is more or less certain that the fragmentary states, B, C, and I, are not the ancestors of any of the others. Probably H and 82 are not, because they have readings that can never have come from Dryden's pen (*Herringham* in line 105, etc., in H; line 50, etc., in 82). No doubt 84 is not the ancestor of any except possibly I, because it was reproduced with only insignificant changes in subsequent apparently authorized editions during Dryden's lifetime; it must have descended from his final holograph revision. This leaves F, L, and M as possible ancestors. But all these states stand alone in type–1 variations so often that some of their peculiar readings must, it would seem, be scribal, and the states therefore descendants. There are two readings, both found only in C and L, that are not too obviously wrong and yet are the sort a careful author might change, "verse" in line 55 (which is tautological), and "trophys" in line 207 (which is not so accurate as "altars"). If these are genuine early authoritative readings, then the final diagram will take the form:

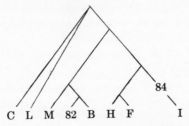

The order of the states at the foot of the diagram is partly arbitrary: possibly C and L should be interchanged, perhaps B should be to the left of M and 82, and so on. This diagram, since it purports to indicate the course of Dryden's revisions, is not textual but bibliographical.

The final examples illustrate the analysis of Biblical texts, the end for which this volume was initially designed. The first to be considered is the Greek text of Philemon in fourteen states recorded in ten uncial manuscripts. The text and collation given below are taken from Tischendorf's eighth edition.[7] Tischendorf's notices of the minuscules are often given in summary, and so are of no use to the textual analyst. As before, alternate spellings, alternate forms, and other information not germane to purely textual analysis have been passed over; in other respects, Tischendorf's apparatus has been adjusted only slightly, so that his on the whole admirable system may be illustrated.

The states to be analyzed are as follows: א*, Sinaiticus, fourth century; אᶜ, Sinaiticus as corrected, seventh century; A, Alexandrinus, fifth century; C*, Ephraemi rescriptus, fifth century; C² Ephraemi rescriptus as corrected, sixth century; D*, Claromontanus, sixth century; Dᶜ, Claromontanus as corrected, ninth century; E*, Petropolitanus, ninth century; E** Petropolitanus as corrected; F, Augiensis, ninth century; G, Boernerianus, ninth century; K, Moscuensis, ninth century (so C. R. Gregory; Silva Lake argues for the eleventh century[8]); L, Angelicus, ninth century; P, Porfirianus, ninth century. In the collations, it must be remembered that א alone stands for both א* and אᶜ, C alone for both C* and C², and so on. It must also be remembered that whatever these sigla represented to Tischendorf they here represent states of the text.

ΠΡΟΣ ΦΙΛΗΜΟΝΑ

1 Παῦλοσ δέσμιοσ Χριστοῦ 'Ιησοῦ καὶ Τιμόθεοσ ὁ ἀδελφόσ Φιλήμονι τῷ ἀγαπητῷ καὶ συνεργῷ ἡμῶν 2 καὶ 'Απφίᾳ τῇ ἀδελφῇ καὶ 'Αρχίππῳ τῷ συνστρατιώτῃ ἡμῶν καὶ τῇ κατ' οἶκόν σου ἐκκλησίᾳ. 3 χάρισ ὑμῖν καὶ εἰρήνη ἀπὸ θεοῦ πατρὸσ ἡμῶν καὶ κυρίου 'Ιησοῦ Χριστοῦ.

4 Εὐχαριστῶ τῷ θεῷ μου πάντοτε μνείαν σου ποιούμενοσ ἐπὶ τῶν προσευχῶν

---

*　προσ φιλημονα ut אA. Item DEFG αρχεται προσ φιλημονα . . . KLP παυλου (L του αγιου αποστολου παυλου) επιστολη προσ φιλημονα [C wants the title and the text through vs. 2]

1.　δεσμιοσ : D*E* αποστολοσ | χριστου ιησου cum אADᶜE**FGKP . . . D*E*L ιησου χριστου | ο αδελφοσ : DEF om o | αγαπητω : addunt vero D*E αδελφω

2.　απφια : D* αφφια, FG αμφια | αδελφη cum אAD*E*FGP . . . DᶜE**KL αγαπητη | τω ante συνστρατ. : F om | τη et εκκλησια : D* την et εκκλησιαν

3.　πατροσ ημων (F υμων) et[iam] אᶜ . . . א* om ημων

μου, 5 ἀκούων σου τὴν ἀγάπην καὶ τὴν πίστιν ἣν ἔχεισ πρὸσ τὸν κύριον Ἰησοῦν καὶ εἰσ πάντασ τοὺσ ἁγίουσ, 6 ὅπωσ ἡ κοινωνία τῆσ πίστεώσ σου ἐνεργὴσ γένηται ἐν ἐπιγνώσει παντὸσ ἀγαθοῦ τοῦ ἐν ὑμῖν εἰσ Χριστόν. 7 χαρὰν γὰρ πολλὴν ἔσχον καὶ παράκλησιν ἐπὶ τῇ ἀγάπῃ σου, ὅτι τὰ σπλάγχνα τῶν ἁγίων ἀναπέπαυται διὰ σοῦ, ἀδελφέ. 8 Διὸ πολλὴν ἐν Χριστῷ παρρησίαν ἔχων ἐπιτάσσειν σοι τὸ ἀνῆκον, 9 διὰ τὴν ἀγάπην μᾶλλον παρακαλῶ· τοιοῦτοσ ὢν ὡσ Παῦλοσ πρεσβύτησ, νυνὶ δὲ καὶ δέσμιοσ Χριστοῦ Ἰησοῦ, 10 παρακαλῶ σε περὶ τοῦ ἐμοῦ τέκνου, ὃν ἐγέννησα ἐν τοῖσ δεσμοῖσ, Ὀνήσιμον, 11 τόν ποτέ σοι ἄχρηστον, νυνὶ δὲ καὶ σοὶ καὶ ἐμοὶ εὔχρηστον, ὃν ἀνέπεμψά σοι, 12 αὐτόν, τοῦτ' ἔστιν τὰ ἐμὰ σπλάγχνα. 13 ὃν ἐγὼ ἐβουλόμην πρὸσ ἐμαυτὸν κατέχειν, ἵνα ὑπὲρ σοῦ μοι διακονῇ ἐν τοῖσ δεσμοῖσ τοῦ εὐαγγελίου, 14 χωρὶσ δὲ τῆσ σῆσ γνώμησ οὐδὲν ἠθέλησα ποιῆσαι, ἵνα μὴ ὡσ κατὰ ἀνάγκην τὸ ἀγαθόν σου ᾖ ἀλλὰ κατὰ ἑκούσιον· 15 τάχα γὰρ διὰ τοῦτο ἐχωρίσθη πρὸσ ὥραν, ἵνα αἰώνιον αὐτὸν ἀπέχῃσ, 16 οὐκ ἔτι ὡσ δοῦλον ἀλλὰ ὑπὲρ δοῦλον, ἀδελφὸν ἀγαπητόν, μάλιστα ἐμοί, πόσῳ δὲ μᾶλλον σοὶ καὶ ἐν σαρκὶ καὶ ἐν κυρίῳ· 17 εἰ οὖν με ἔχεισ κοινωνόν, προσλαβοῦ αὐτὸν ὡσ ἐμέ. 18 εἰ δέ τι ἠδίκησέν σε ἢ ὀφείλει, τοῦτο ἐμοὶ ἐλλόγα. 19 ἐγὼ Παῦλοσ ἔγραψα τῇ ἐμῇ χειρί, ἐγὼ ἀποτίσω· ἵνα μὴ λέγω σοι

---

5. την αγαπ. κ. τ. πιστιν cum ℵACFGKLP . . . DE τ. πιστ. κ. τ. αγαπ. | προσ τον cum ℵDᶜFGKLP al[teris] fere omn[ibus] [presumably including E] . . . ACD* εισ τον | ιησουν : D*E add χριστον

6. οπωσ : FG ινα πωσ | η κοινωνια et. ℵᶜ . . . ℵ* η διακονια | αγαθου : FG praem[ittunt] εργου | του εν cum ℵDEFGKL . . . AC om του | εν υμιν cum ℵFGP . . . ACDEKL εν ημιν | εισ χριστον sine additam cum ℵ*AC . . . ℵᶜDEFGKLP add ιησουν

7. χαραν cum ℵACDEFG . . . KLP χαριν | πολλην εσχον cum ℵACFGP; item D*E πολλην εσχομεν . . . Dᶜ (sed πολλ. εχομ.) KL (sed εχωμεν) εχομεν πολλην | και παρακλησιν : ℵ om | επι τη : D*L εν τη

8. εν χριστω παρρησ. εχων : L παρρησ. εν χρι. εχων . . . D* παρρ. εχω εν χρι. ιησου, DᶜE παρρη. εχων εν χρι. (E add ιησου)

9. αγαπην : Α αναγκην | νυνι cum ℵCDEFGKLP . . . A νυν | χριστου ιησου cum ℵACP . . . DᶜEFGKL ιησου χριστου . . . D* om utrumque

10. ον cum ℵCDEFGKLP . . . A add εγω | δεσμοισ sine μου cum ℵ*AD*FG . . . ℵᶜDᶜEKLP add μου

11. και σοι cum ℵ*FG . . . ℵᶜACDEKLP om και | ανεπεμψα : D*E* επεμψα | σοι sec[utus] c[um] ℵACD*E* . . . DᶜE**FGKLP om

12. αυτον cum ℵ*AC* . . . ℵᶜC²DEFGKLP praem συ δε | σπλαγχνα sine additam cum ℵ*AFG . . . ℵᶜCDEKLP add προσλαβου

13. μοι διακονη (P -νει) cum ℵACDEFGP . . . KL (-νει) διακονη μοι

14. σησ (post τησ) : F om | κατα εκουσιον : D* εκουσιον

15. εχωρισθη : P add σου | απεχησ : L -χεισ

16. FG om αλλα υπ. δουλ. | αδελφον et. ℵᶜ : ℵ* om | ποσω δε : P om δε

17. με cum ℵACDEFGLP . . . K εμε

18. σε : K om | οφειλει (L ωφειλει) : FG add τει

19. αποτισω : D* αποδωσω | προσοφειλεισ (L προσωφ-) : D*E* add εν κυριω

ὅτι καὶ σεαυτόν μοι προσοφείλεισ. 20 ναί, ἀδελφέ, ἐγώ σου ὀναίμην ἐν κυρίῳ· ἀνάπαυσόν μου τὰ σπλάγχνα ἐν Χριστῷ.

21 Πεποιθὼσ τῇ ὑπακοῇ σου ἔγραψά σοι, εἰδὼσ ὅτι καὶ ὑπὲρ ἃ λέγω ποιήσεισ. 22 ἅμα δὲ καὶ ἑτοίμαζέ μοι ξενίαν· ἐλπίζω γὰρ ὅτι διὰ τῶν προσευχῶν ὑμῶν χαρισθήσομαι ὑμῖν.

23 Ἀσπάζεταί σε Ἐπαφρᾶσ ὁ συναιχμάλωτόσ μου ἐν Χριστῷ Ἰησοῦ, 24 Μάρκοσ, Ἀρίσταρχοσ, Δημᾶσ, Λουκᾶσ, οἱ συνεργοί μου.

25 Ἡ χάρισ τοῦ κυρίου Ἰησοῦ Χριστοῦ μετὰ τοῦ πνεύματοσ ὑμῶν.

20. χριστω cum ℵACD*FGLP . . . DᶜEK κυριω. Ceterum desunt reliqua in FG
21. υπερ a cum ℵACP . . . DEKL υπ. ο | ποιησεισ : L -σησ
22. προσευχ. υμων : L om υμ.
23. ασπαζεται cum ℵACD*EP . . . DᶜKL ασπαζονται
25. του κυριου absque ημων ℵP . . . ACDEKL add ημων | πνευματ. υμων sine αμην cum AD* . . . ℵCDᶜEKLP add αμην

Subscriptio: ℵC προσ φιλημονα (in A periit), DE προσ φιλημ. επληρωθη . . . P προσ φιλημ. εγραφει απο ρωμησ, K προσ φιλημονα εγραφη απο ρωμησ δια ονησιμου οικετου, L του αγιου αποστολου παυλου επιστολη προσ φιλημ. και απφιαν δεσποτασ του ονησιμου και προσ αρχιππον τον διακονον τησ εν κολοσσαισ εκκλησιασ· εγραφη απο ρωμησ δια ονησιμου οικετου.

Seven of the states are excluded from being intermediaries by type–1 variations: ℵ*, A, D*, F, K, L, and P. All the other variations except Σ:ℵ*:F (verse 3) are in conflict. They are as follows:

a.　Σ: ℵ* ℵᶜ 7
b.　Σ: ℵ* ℵᶜ AC* C² D* E* 11 (reciprocal of ee below)
c.　Σ: ℵ* ℵᶜ AC* C² P [FG] 21 (reciprocal of v below)
d.　Σ: ℵ* ℵᶜ AC* C² P: D* 9
e.　Σ: ℵ* ℵᶜ F G P 6
f.　Σ: ℵ* ℵᶜ P [FG] 25
g.　Σ: ℵ* AC* 12
h.　Σ: ℵ* AC* C² 6
i.　Σ: ℵ* AD* FG 10
j.　Σ: ℵ* AFG 12
k.　Σ: ℵ* FG 11
l.　Σ: AC* C² 6
m.　Σ: AC* C² D* 5
n.　Σ: AD* [FG] 25
o.　Σ: C*C² title etc. (omission)
p.　Σ: D*:FG [C*C²] 2 (name)
q.　Σ: D*Dᶜ E* E** 5
r.　Σ: D* Dᶜ E*E** [AFG] subscription (επληρωθη)
s.　Σ: D* Dᶜ E*E**: L 8 (transposition)
t.　Σ: D* Dᶜ E*E** F [C*C²] 1
u.　Σ: D* Dᶜ E*E** FG [C* C²] title (αρχεται)
v.　Σ: D*Dᶜ E*E** KL [FG] 21 (reciprocal of c above)
w.　Σ: D*E* 11, 19

x.   Σ: D*E* [C*C²] 1
y.   Σ: D*E*E** 5, 8 (add ιησου)
z.   Σ: D*E*E** [C*C²] 1
aa.   Σ: D*E*E**:DᶜK:L 7 (tense, person, and mood of εχω)
bb.   Σ: D*E*L[C*C²] 1
cc.   Σ: D*L 7
dd.   Σ: DᶜE*E**K 20
ee.   Σ: DᶜE**FGKLP 11 (reciprocal of *b* above)
ff.   Σ: DᶜE**KL [C*C²] 2
gg.   Σ: DᶜKL [FG] 23
hh.   Σ: FG 6(bis), 16, 18, 21 to end (omission)
ii.   Σ: KL 7 (transposition), 13 (transposition)
jj.   Σ: KL [AFG] subscriptio (δια ονησιμου οικετου)
kk.   Σ: KLP 7
ll.   Σ: KLP [AFG] subscriptio (εγραφη απο ρωμησ)
mm.   Σ: KLP[C*C²] title (παυλου επιστολη)
nn.   Σ: LP 13 (mood)

The necessary tables appear below:

ℵ*ℵᶜ	ℵᶜℵ*	Aℵ*ℵᶜC*C²D*E*	C*ℵ*ℵᶜAC²D*E*
ℵ*ℵᶜAC*C²D*E*	ℵᶜℵ*AC*C²D*E*	Aℵ*ℵᶜC*C²P[FG]	C*ℵ*ℵᶜAC²P[FG]
ℵ*ℵᶜAC*C²P[FG]	ℵᶜℵ*AC*C²P[FG]	Aℵ*ℵᶜC*C²P:D*	C*ℵ*ℵᶜAC²P:D*
ℵ*ℵᶜAC*C²P:D*	ℵᶜℵ*AC*C²P:D*	Aℵ* C*	C*ℵ*A
ℵ*ℵᶜFGP	ℵᶜℵ*FGP	Aℵ*C*C²	C*ℵ*AC²
ℵ*ℵᶜP[FG]	ℵᶜℵ*P[FG]	Aℵ*D*FG	C*AC²
ℵ*AC*		Aℵ*FG	C*AC²D*
ℵ*AC*C²		AC*C²	C*C²
ℵ*AD*FG		AC*C²D*	
ℵ*AFG		AD*[FG]	
ℵ*FG			

C²ℵ*ℵᶜAC*D*E*	D*ℵ*ℵᶜAC*C²E*	DᶜD*E*E**	E*ℵ*ℵᶜAC*C²D*
C²ℵ*ℵᶜAC*P[FG]	D*ℵ*AFG	DᶜD*E*E**[AFG]	E*D*DᶜE**
C²ℵ*ℵᶜAC*P:D*	D*AC*C²	DᶜD*E*E**:L	E*D*DᶜE**[AFG]
C²ℵ*AC*	D*A[FG]	DᶜD*E*E**F[C*C²]	E*D*DᶜE**:L
C²AC*	D*DᶜE*E**	DᶜD*E*E**FG[C*C²]	E*D*DᶜE**F[C*C²]
C²AC*D*	D*DᶜE*E**[AFG]	DᶜD*E*E**KL[FG]	E*D*DᶜE**FG[C*C²]
C²C*	D*DᶜE*E**:L	DᶜK:L:D*E*E**	E*D*DᶜE**KL[FG]
	D*DᶜE*E**F[C*C²]	DᶜE*E**K	E*D*
	D*DᶜE*E**FG[C*C²]	DᶜE**FGKLP	E*D*[C*C²]
	D*DᶜE*E**KL[FG]	DᶜE**KL[C*C²]	E*D*E**
	D*E*	DᶜKL[FG]	E*D*E**[C*C²]
	D*E*[C*C²]		E*D*E**:L:DᶜK
	D*E*E**		E*D*L[C*C²]
	D*E*E**[C*C²]		E*DᶜE**K
	D*E*E**:L:DᶜK		
	D*E*L[C*C²]		
	D*L		

E**D*D∘E*
E**D*D∘E*[AFG]
E**D*D∘E*:L
E**D*D∘E*F[C*C²]
E**D*D∘E*FG[C*C²]
E**D*D∘E*KL[FG]
E**D*E*
E**D*E*[C*C²]
E**D*E*:L:D∘K
E**D∘E*K
E**D∘FGKLP
E**D∘KL[C*C²]

Fℵ*ℵ∘GP
Fℵ*AD*G
Fℵ*AG
Fℵ*G
FG:D*[C*C²]
FD*D∘E*E**[C*C²]
FD*D∘E*E**G[C*C²]
FD∘E**GKLP
FG

Gℵ*ℵ∘FP
Gℵ*AD*F
Gℵ*AF
Gℵ*F
GF:D*[C*C²]
GD*D∘E*E**F[C*C²]
GD∘E**FKLP
GF

KD*D∘E*E**L[FG]
KD∘:L:D*E*E**
KD∘E*E**
KD∘E**FGLP
KD∘E**L[C*C²]
KD∘L[FG]
KL
KL[AFG]
KLP
KLP[AFG]
KLP[C*C²]

LD*D∘E*E**K[FG]
LD*E*[C*C²]
LD*
LD∘E**FGKP
LD∘E**K[C*C²]
LD∘K[FG]
LK
LK[AFG]
LKP
LKP[AFG]
LKP[C*C²]
LP

Pℵ*ℵ∘AC*C²[FG]
Pℵ*ℵ∘AC*C²:D*
Pℵ*ℵ∘FG
Pℵ*ℵ∘[FG]
PD∘E**FGKL
PKL
PKL[AFG]
PKL[C*C²]
PL

The analysis may begin with a group of six states, C*, C², D∘, E**, F, and G:

C* C² : D∘ E** F G	title, etc. (omission), 5, 6 (bis), 9, 11
D∘ E** F : G [C* C²]	1
D∘ F G : E** [C* C²]	1
D∘ E** : F G [C* C²]	2 (bis)
D∘ E** G : F [C* C²]	2
C* C² D∘ E** G : F	3, 14
C* C² F G : D∘ E**	5, 8 (transposition), 20
C* C² D∘ F G : E**	5, 8 (add ιησου)
C* C² D∘ E** : F G	6 (tris), 10, 11, 12, 16, 18, 21 to end (omission)
C* C² F G : D∘ : E**	7 (tense and person of εχω)
C* : C² D∘ E** F G	12
C* C² : D∘ E** [F G]	21, subscriptio (επληρωθη)
C* C² E** : D∘ [F G]	23

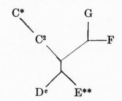

The diagram may now be extended by working with various groups of four states, as follows:

(1) $\aleph^*$ A C* C²

$\aleph^*$ A : C* C²	title, etc. (omission), 10, 12	
$\aleph^*$: A C* C²	3, 5, 6 (tris), 7, 11, 16, 25	
$\aleph^*$ C* C² : A	9 (bis), 10, 25, subscriptio	
$\aleph^*$ A C* : C²	12	

$$\aleph^* \diagdown\mathllap{}\ \text{C*—C²} \qquad \text{A}\diagup$$

(2) D*Dᶜ E* E**

D* E* : Dᶜ E**	1 (bis), 2, 11 (bis), 19
D* E* E** : Dᶜ	1, 5, 7, 8, 23
D* : E* E** Dᶜ	2 (bis), 5, 7, 9, 10, 14, 20, 25

D*—E*—E**—Dᶜ

(3) $\aleph^\circ$ P D* E*

$\aleph^\circ$: D* E* : P	title
$\aleph^\circ$ P : D*E*	1 (quater), 5 (bis), 6, 7, 8 (bis), 11, 19, 21, 25, subscriptio
$\aleph^\circ$ E* P : D*	2 (bis), 5, 7, 8, 10, 14, 19, 25
$\aleph^\circ$ D* E* : P	7, 11, 13
$\aleph^\circ$: D* E* P	7
$\aleph^\circ$ P : D* : E*	9
$\aleph^\circ$ D* P : E*	20

$$\aleph^\circ\diagdown\ \diagup\text{D*} \qquad \text{P}\diagup\ \diagdown\text{E*}$$

(4) F G K L

F G : K L	title (bis), 2 (bis), 6 (tris), 7 (bis), 10, 11, 12, 13, 16, 18, 21 to end (omission)
F G K : L	title, 1, 7, 8, 13, 15, 18, 19
F : G K L	1, 2, 3, 14
F G : K : L	7
F G L : K	17, 18, 20
K : L [FG]	22, subscriptio

$$\text{F—G}\diagup^{\text{K}}_{\text{L}}$$

The five partial diagrams overlie as follows:

A number of readings seem to have resulted from homoeoteleuton:

2 αρχιππω τω : αρχιππω F
6 αγαθου του : αγαθου A C
11 ον ανεπεμψα : ον επεμψα D* E*
14 τησ σησ : τησ F
16 δουλον αλλα υπερ δουλον : δουλον F G
16 δουλον αδελφον : δουλον ℵ*
18 ηδικησεν σε : ηδικησεν K
22 προσευχων υμων : προσευχων L

Certain other readings seem to have resulted from a scribe's desire for symmetry of expression:

1, 2 φιλημονι τω αγαπητω . . . και απφια τη αδελφη : φιλημονι τω αγαπητω αδελφω . . . και απφια τη αδελφη D* E* ; φιλημονι τω αγαπητω αδελφω . . . και απφια τη αγαπητη E** ; φιλημονι τω αγαπητω . . . και απφια τη αγαπητη Dᶜ K L
3, 5 και κυριου ιησου χριστου . . . τον κυριον ιησουν : και κυριου ιησου χριστου . . . τον κυριον ιησουν χριστον D* E
20 εν κυριω . . . εν χριστω : εν κυριω . . . εν κυριω Dᶜ E K

One reading apparently results from harmonization to Paul's usual salutation:

1 δεσμιοσ : αποστολοσ D* E*

One reading may have occurred through dittography:

5 εχεισ προσ : εχεισ εισ A C D*

One reading appears to be a gloss:

19 σεαυτον μοι προσοφειλεισ : + εν κυριω D* E*

One reading may be a grammatical correction by a scribe:

23, 24 ασπαζεται σε επαφρασ . . . μαρκοσ, κτλ. : ασπαζονται σε επαφρασ . . . μαρκοσ, κτλ. Dᶜ K L

Finally, the omissions in C*, C², F, and G are certainly not original.

These readings show that ℵ*, A, C*, C², D*, Dᶜ, E*, E**, F, G, K, and L are descendants. The dates of the manuscripts show that ℵᶜ and P cannot be the ancestors of the others. Since ℵᶜ and P always have the better readings, and D* and E* consistently agree against them in directional readings, the final diagram will conform to the pattern:

ℵᶜ　P　Σ

The relative dates of the manuscripts will then require that C*, C², E*, and E** be removed from being intermediary between the ancestor and ℵ*. The tree will therefore be:

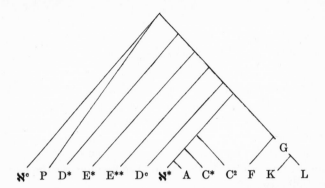

This is a textual, not a bibliographical, scheme.

Too many extant states of the text have been omitted from the analysis for the diagram to be called definitive, but it will serve as an illustration of the method. The text of the ancestor here could be established when D* or E* or both agree with ℵᶜ or P and when ℵᶜ and P agree together. The other readings would remain in doubt, though no one would quarrel with Tischendorf's choice of the earliest attested readings in these instances. Under the circumstances, Tischendorf's text is what the ancestor here could be accepted as reading, except that in verse 6 it would read Χριστὸν Ἰησοῦν, in verse 10 δεσμοῖσ μου, in verse 11 σοί (without καί), in verse 12 σὺ δὲ αὐτόν and σπλάγχνα, προσλαβοῦ, and in verse 25 ἀμήν.

In time the full collations necessary for a more final analysis will be available, and the necessary mechanical aids to calculation will have been provided. That happy day, it is to be hoped, is not far in the future.

Finally, a problem where the texts are different enough to be accepted as independent works, and yet are clearly interdependent in some fashion—even in many considerable passages to the point of agreeing in the sequence of words. This is the problem posed by the Gospels, which in the past has been divided into the "Synoptic problem" and the "Johannine problem." A solution to the Synoptic problem that has been widely accepted, though with individual reservations and modifications of detail, is the so-called "four document hypothesis" put forward by Canon B. H. Streeter in *The Four Gospels*. Streeter's diagram (p. 150) is essentially as follows:

Matthaean source   Mark   Q   Lucan source

"Proto-Luke"

Matthew   Luke

More tentatively Streeter assigns an "Antiochene tradition" as an additional separate source for Matthew, and a separate source for the first two chapters of Luke, which he conceives not to have stood in "Proto-Luke." The letter Q represents a body of Jesus' sayings, some of them set in historical contexts. The diagram ought also to have shown lines of descent to Mark and Q from a common ancestor, since Streeter maintains that some of the information in Mark was also found in Q. There should then also be lines of descent from a special Markan source to Mark and from a special Q source to Q to account for the material that is not common to both.

Those who have followed the reasoning in the present volume will recognize that Streeter's is a diagram expressive of literary history, and will wish to know, perhaps, what textual and bibliographical trees would require such a complicated synthesis. There is no bibliographical evidence, for the original manuscripts have vanished, and the details upon which a bibliographical analysis would be based have either vanished from their descendants or are the subject of considerable dispute. There is evidence, for example, that the original ending of Mark was early lost, but where Streeter argues that Matthew did not know the perfect text (p. 343), Goodspeed is confident that he did know it.[9] The textual tree, according to Streeter and many others before and since is:

The tree is not intended to indicate that Matthew was written before Luke (as a matter of fact, Streeter, p. 150, puts it five years later).

It is at once clear that such a textual tree does not support the larger diagram. The evidence for it as given by Streeter (pp. 151–152, 157–169) is as follows:

1. Of the material in Mark, about 90 per cent appears in Matthew, about 50 per cent in Luke, and in both often in the same words.

2. In the passages where the wording is largely identical in all three, Matthew and Mark sometimes agree against Luke, Mark and Luke

welcoming crowd shouted, in the words of Psalm 118, εὐλογημένος ὁ
ἐρχόμενος ἐν ὀνόματι κυρίου, "blessed is he who comes in the name of the
Lord" (Matthew 21:9; Mark 11:9; Luke 19:38; John 12:13), but Luke
and John add ὁ βασιλεὺς, "the king," in apposition to ὁ ἐρχόμενος. (d, e) All
four Gospels have accounts of Jesus' being anointed with costly ointment
by a woman while he was at a banquet (Matthew 26:6–13; Mark 14:3–9;
Luke 7:36–50; John 12:1–8); if these are all variant accounts of the same
event, as some scholars would have it, then Matthew and Mark agree
that the woman anointed Jesus' head, while Luke and John agree that
she anointed his feet, and Luke and John add that she wiped his feet
with her hair. (f) At Jesus' arrest, the Gospels all tell how one of his
followers cut off the ear of one of those arresting him (Matthew 26:51;
Mark 14:47; Luke 22:50; John 18:10); Luke and John add that it was
the left ear, τὸ δεξιόν. (g) All four Gospels tell of Peter's triple denial that
he knew Jesus (Matthew 26:69–74; Mark 14:66–72; Luke 22:56–60; John
18:17, 25–27); Matthew and Mark add that at his third denial he cursed.
(h) All four Gospels agree that Pilate asked Jesus, σὺ εἶ ὁ βασιλεὺς τῶν
Ἰουδαίων, "are you the king of the Jews," and that Jesus replied, σὺ
λέγεις, "you say . . ." (Matthew 27:11; Mark 15:2; Luke 23:3; John
18:33–37—John has some intervening dialogue); but Matthew and Mark
continue, using much the same phrasing, with an account of how Jesus
caused Pilate to wonder at his refusal to answer his accusers, whereas
Luke and John continue instead with Pilate's finding, again using nearly
the same words, that Jesus had committed no crime. (i) Luke and John
agree that Pilate repeated this finding for the third time after the mob
demanded Jesus' crucifixion (Matthew 27:23; Mark 15:14; Luke 23:22;
John 19:6). (j) All four Gospels say that the mob cried out twice for
Jesus' crucifixion, but only Matthew and Mark add the detail that the
second time they shouted louder, περισσῶς (Matthew 27:23; Mark 15:14;
compare Luke 23:23; John 19:15). (k) Just before Jesus was crucified,
he was offered wine to drink, according to Matthew 27:34 and Mark
15:23; Luke and John omit this detail, which would follow Luke 23:33a
and John 19:17. (l) In the sentence telling of the women who followed
Jesus to the place of crucifixion, Matthew 27:55 and Mark 15:40 begin
ἦσαν, "there were," and Luke 23:49 and John 19:25 begin εἱστήκεισαν,
"there stood." (m) In describing the tomb where Jesus was laid (Matthew 27:60; Mark 15:46; Luke 23:53; John 19:41), only Luke and John
conclude by saying that no one had been buried there before (this is not
quite the same thing as saying that it was new). (n) And in describing
Jesus' burial (as before, and John 19:42), only Matthew and Mark close

their accounts with Joseph's closing the door of the tomb with a stone; Matthew has καὶ προσκυλίσας λίθον μέγαν τῇ θύρᾳ τοῦ μνημείου ἀπῆλθεν, Mark has καὶ προσεκύλισεν λίθον ἐπὶ τὴν θύραν τοῦ μνημείου.

(2) Mt Lk:Mk Jn.   (a) In recording John's saying that he baptized only in (or with) water, Matthew 3:11 and Luke 3:16 begin ἐγὼ μὲν βαπτίζω, "I indeed baptize," while Mark 1:8 and John 1:26 begin simply ἐγώ . . . , "I . . ."   (b) All the Gospels give an account of the feeding of the five thousand (Matthew 14:15–21; Mark 6:35–44; Luke 9:12–17; John 6:5–13), but only Mark and John record a protest from among the disciples, when faced with the task of feeding the multitude, that two hundred denarii would not buy bread enough (this detail would come in Matthew 14:16 and Luke 9:13*b*). (c) In the four accounts of the woman's anointing Jesus, Matthew and Luke simply say she used ointment, employing different forms of μύρον, where Mark and John specify that she used oil of nard or spikenard, agreeing in the words μύρου νάρδου πιστικῆς. (d, e) All the Gospels say that Peter followed Jesus into the high priest's house or palace, where he sat among the servants and was questioned by them (compare Matthew 26:58, 69; Mark 14:54, 67; Luke 22:55, 56; John 18:18, 25), but only Mark and John say he warmed himself at a fire there, both using ὁ Πέτρος . . . θερμαινόμενος in the first passage, Mark using τὸν Πέτρον θερμαινόμενον and John using Σίμων Πέτρος . . . θερμαινόμενος in the second. (f) In recording the second of the mob's outcries for Jesus' crucifixion Matthew 27:23 and Luke 23:23 have passive constructions, but Mark 15:14 and John 19:15 have the active construction σταύρωσον αὐτόν, "crucify him!"

(3) Mt Jn:Mk Lk.   (a) In citing Isaiah 40:3, Matthew 3:3 and John 1:23 read that Isaiah said these words (Matthew has λέγοντος, John εἶπεν), where Mark 1:2 and Luke 3:4 read "it is written," γέγραπται, in Isaiah. (b, c) In recounting John's explanation of his baptizing and his prophecy of the one who was to come after him (Matthew 3:11, Mark 1:7, 8; Luke 3:16; John 1:26, 27), Matthew and John have ἐν ὕδατι, "in water," and ὁ . . . ἐρχόμενος, "the one who is coming," where Mark and Luke have ὕδατι, "with water," and ἔρχεται, "comes." (d) Describing how Jesus came to ride into Jerusalem in his triumphal entry (Matthew 21:1–7, Mark 11:1–7; Luke 19:28–35; John 12:14–15), only Matthew and John say that this was a fulfilment of the prophecy in Zechariah 9:9. (e) In Jesus' dialogue with Pilate, only Mark and Luke introduce his words σὺ λέγεις with a participial phrase, ἀποκριθεὶς αὐτῷ, "answering him," as well as with a verb. (f) In describing Jesus' death on the cross, Matthew 27:50 and John 19:30 read respectively ἀφῆκεν τὸ πνεῦμα and

παρέδωκεν τὸ πνεῦμα, "he gave up the ghost"; Mark 15:37 and Luke 23:46 say it in one word, ἐξέπνευσεν. (g) Finally, in saying that Jesus was laid in a tomb, Matthew 27:60 and John 19:41 have different forms of one word for "tomb," μνημεῖον and Mark 15:46 and Luke 23:53 have another word, μνήματι, though only Sinaiticus and Vaticanus among the manuscripts cited by Nestle have μνήματι instead of μνημείῳ here in Mark.

This combination of type–2 variations requires the following general diagram, but without requiring that any one Gospel be understood by any one letter:

Two of the type–2 variations seem directional. The addition of ὁ βασιλεὺς listed under (1) (c) looks like a gloss on the quotation from the Psalm. The omission of reference to Peter's cursing listed under (1) (g) looks like a pious alteration. If these are directional variations, they are of the type

Mt Mk → Lk Jn

Taken out of context, the shorter version of Jesus' saying listed under (1) (a) would generally be accepted as the more original, but each version is appropriate to its context; the longer versions would be less appropriate in Luke and John, and it may be then that Luke and John simply abbreviated Jesus' original saying for their own purposes.

Although the Gospel of John is traditionally the last to have been written—written, too, according to tradition, to supplement the others—and though modern scholars often, perhaps customarily, regard it as a derivative work, still there are passages where its narratives seem earlier in form than the corresponding narratives of the Synoptics. Thus, if John's account of how Jesus pointed out his betrayer (John 13:21–30) seems elaborated over those of the Synoptics (Matthew 26:21–25; Mark 14:18–21; Luke 22:21–23), on the other hand his simple statement that the disciples were afraid when they saw Jesus walking on the water (John 6:19) seems elaborated in Mark 6:49, 50, and further elaborated in Matthew 14:26–31. Or again, if his account of the cleansing of the temple seems elaborated over those of the Synoptics—supposing that all the Gospels describe the same event (Matthew 21:12, 13; Mark 11:15–17;

Luke 19:45, 46; John 2:13–17)—on the other hand his simple statement that Jesus found a young ass to ride in his triumphal entry into Jerusalem (John 12:14) seems to be elaborated in the Synoptic accounts of how the ass was found (Matthew 21:1–3, 6, 7; Mark 11:1–7; Luke 19:28–35).

Taking all the evidence into account, it appears that the simplest final diagram for the four Gospels is this:

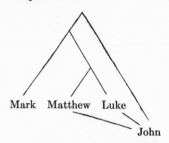

This is a textual diagram, but as there is no bibliographical evidence to the contrary it may serve also as a bibliographical diagram. How it might be interpreted by the literary historian has already been suggested in the discussion of the Synoptic problem.

I cannot close without alluding to the discovery in the vicinity of Khirbet Qumran of manuscripts that record states of the Hebrew text sufficiently diverse from those lumped together as Massoretic to have revitalized the problem of the text of the Old Testament. The method of analysis set forth in the preceding pages is adequate to the solution of this most important question also.

Notes

NOTES TO CHAPTER I

Preliminary Distinctions
(Pages 1–8)

[1] Silva Lake, *Family* II *and the Codex Alexandrinus* (London, 1936), p. 17, n. 1.

NOTES TO CHAPTER II

Rules of Analysis
(Pages 9–50)

[1] Silva Lake, *Family* II *and the Codex Alexandrinus* (London, 1936), pp. 17–18; Mark 3:2.

[2] Lake, *op. cit.*, p. 26, n. 10; Mark 9:6.

[3] F. W. Hall, *A Companion to Classical Texts* (Oxford, 1913), p. 162; Virgil, *Aeneid*, vi. 139.

[4] Donald F. Bond, "The Text of the *Spectator*," *Studies in Bibliography*, V (1952–1953), 110, n. 2; *Spectator* 262.

[5] Collation in G. Blakemore Evans, "The Text of Dryden's *Mac Flecknoe*," *Harvard Library Bulletin*, VII (1953–1954), 38.

[6] Kirsopp and Silva Lake, *Family 13 (The Ferrar Group)* (London, 1941), p. 93; Mark 10:18.

[7] Aulus Gellius, *Noctivm Atticarvm*, ed. Carolus Hosius (Lipsiae, 1903), I, x.

[8] *Major British Writers* (New York, [°1954]), I, 215.

[9] Hall, *op. cit.*, p. 169; Livy, iii.35.9.

[10] Bond, *op. cit.*, pp. 123, 112; *Spectator* 267, 376.

[11] Hall, *op. cit.*, p. 182; Cicero, *Verrine Orations*, 2. *Act.* iv. 49.

[12] On the whole subject of numbers see Hall, *op. cit.*, pp. 180–181.

[13] *Biblia Hebraica*, ed. Rud. Kittel, ed. alt. amend. stereo. l, ed. alt. amend. stereo. (Lipsiae, 1909), p. 370; I Samuel 2:16.

[14] Hall, *op. cit.*, p. 173.

[15] Bond, *op. cit.*, p. 125; *Spectator* 113.

[16] Dryden, *Annus Mirabilis*, 39.

[17] Ronald B. McKerrow, *An Introduction to Bibliography for Literary Students* [2d imp.] (Oxford, [1928]), p. 257.

[18] Hall, *op. cit.*, p. 176; Aristophanes, *Acharnians*, 91.

[19] Hall, *op. cit.*, p. 176; Euripides, *Iphigenia in Aulis*, 396.

[20] Bond, *op. cit.*, p. 125; *Spectator* 224.

[21] Aulus Gellius, *ed. cit.*, I, 94.

[22] Gall, *op. cit.*, p. 179; Iamblichus, *Exhortation to Philosophy*, ch. 9.

[23] A. C. Clark, *The Descent of Manuscripts* (Oxford, 1918), p. 35; Nonnius, 107.27 and 114.25.

[24] McKerrow, *op. cit.*, p. 196; Nashe, *Pierce Penilesse*.

[25] Hall, *op. cit.*, p. 188; Xenophon, *Cyropaedia*, v. 5. 23.

[26] Hall, *op. cit.*, p. 188; Pliny, *Epistles*, i. 20. 14.

[27] McKerrow, *op. cit.*, p. 198; Nashe, *Pierce Penilesse*.

[28] Archibald Hill, "Some Postulates for Distributional Study of Texts," *Studies in Bibliography*, III (1950-1951), 82.

[29] John 1:52; collation in Kirsopp and Silva Lake, *op. cit.*, p. 148.

[30] Clark, *op. cit.*, p. 1; Thucydides, iv.391.

[31] Clark, *op. cit.*, p. 1; Cicero, *In Behalf of Caelius*, §27.

[32] Clark, *op. cit.*, p. 3; *Hamlet*, V, i, 38–42.

[33] Clark, *op. cit.*, p. 3; *Hamlet*, V, i, 114–116.

[34] Clark, *op. cit.*, p. 8; Cicero, *De Natura Deorum*, i. 12.

[35] Clark, *op. cit.*, p. 8; Cicero, *De Natura Deorum*, ii. 81.

[36] Clark, *op. cit.*, pp. 1–31.

[37] Mark 3:28; collation in *Nouum Testamentum Graece Secundum Textum Westcotto-Hortianum: Euangelium Secundum Marcum*, ed. S. C. E. Legg (Oxonii, 1935).

[38] Hall, *op. cit.*, p. 192; Livy, xlii.17.8.

[39] Bond, *op. cit.*, p. 125; *Spectator* 210.

[40] Emily Bronte, "Through the Hours of Yesternight," from Hall, *op. cit.*, p. 193.

[41] Hall, *op. cit.*, p. 194; Propertius, iv. 8. 3.

[42] Hall, *op. cit.*, p. 196; Demosthenes, *Conon*, §26.

[43] Chaucer, *Parlement of Fowles*, 353, from Hall, *op. cit.*, pp. 196–197.

[44] Silva Lake, *op. cit.*, p. 135; Mark 13:25.

[45] Dryden, *Mac Flecknoe*, 72; collation in Evans, *op. cit.*, p. 39.

[46] Conveniently summarized in Henri Quentin, *Essais de Critique Textuelle (Ecdotique)* (Paris, 1926), p. 31.

[47] Burnett Hillman Streeter, *The Four Gospels*, 4th imp. rev. (London, 1930), pp. 115–116, 163–164.

[48] W. W. Greg, *The Calculus of Variants* (Oxford, 1927), pp. 36–42.

[49] Clark, *op. cit.*, pp. 1–48.

[50] McKerrow, *op. cit.*, pp. 184–199.

[51] *Poetical Works*, ed. John Sampson (London, 1914), pp. 85–88.

[52] "Dryden's *Mac Flecknoe*: The Case for Authorial Revision," *Studies in Bibliography*, VII (1955), 87–92. The method of analysis outlined in this paper is limited in

application: unmentioned assumptions, unrecognized at the time, are that none of the manuscripts dealt with is a holograph, and that each can be shown to descend from a different state of revision in the holograph or holographs. If any manuscripts have a common ancestor, it will be necessary to reconstruct it and work with it rather than with its descendants. The possibility that some manuscripts may be holographs indicates that the first axiom for the analysis must be modified unless it is agreed that nonce readings in holographs are to be ignored on the grounds that they are scribal errors, that is, errors committed by the author in his capacity as scribe and rejected as soon as recognized by him in his capacity as proofreader. If the axiom is modified, some method of identifying authoritative nonce readings must be devised, as well as some method of including in the analysis the changes of mind they require us to posit of the author.

In the earlier part of the discussion, it is assumed that there is only one holograph, from which the extant manuscripts radiate. The evidence will not support such a conclusion, for Hill is wrong and Greg is right as to the evidence for radiation. Instead, the situation described in the second paragraph on page 91 ought to be visualized from the beginning. The first mention of factoring the variants (p. 89) misleadingly suggests that it is the same as Greg's factoring of complex variants; and the factoring shown on pages 92–93 is not fully carried out. This factoring simply shows agreements between pairs of manuscripts. It is risky to ignore any hidden pairs or any that do not happen to stand alone in the simple variants. Therefore Σ:82BM should have been factored $(\Sigma_{82}:BM).(\Sigma_B:82M).(\Sigma_M82B)$; Σ:82HBM should have had six factors instead of only two; and so on. The conclusions as to Dryden's procedure in revision seem sound, nevertheless. The recovery of additional states of the text might force some changes, but so much uncertainty is inherent in the method.

NOTES TO CHAPTER III

Mechanics of Calculation
(Pages 51–68)

[1] MacEdward Leach, "Some Problems in Editing Middle English Manuscripts," *English Institute Annual, 1939* (New York, 1940), pp. 145–157.

[2] Dryden, *To His Sacred Majesty*, line 145 (the first edition and the reprint in the 1688 edition of *Annus Mirabilis*); and *Mac Flecknoe*, lines 110 and 185, for which see G. Blakemore Evans, "The Text of Dryden's *Mac Flecknoe*," *Harvard Library Bulletin*, VII (1953–1954), 39, 41.

[3] John M. Manley and Edith Rickert, *The Text of Chaucer's Canterbury Tales* (Chicago, [1940]), II, 3–12.

[4] I visited Mr. Ellison at the end of 1954. In 1957 he completed his Harvard Ph.D. dissertation, "The Use of Electric Computers in the Study of the Greek Text of the New Testament," which I have not seen. He has also, of course, engineered the compilation of the Concordance to the Revised Standard Version of the Bible (Nelson, 1957), though here, I should think, his problem was only one of sorting, not of true calculation.

NOTES TO CHAPTER IV

Examples

(Pages 69–102)

N.B. The variant titles in the first and second examples are analyzed as motifs, without regard for their word-for-word correspondences. In the third and fourth examples, the shortest titles (and the shortest subscriptio in the fourth example) are counted as bases that certain states agree in augmenting in ways in which the other states agree in not augmenting; and overlapping imperfections in the manuscripts are not counted as causing variations of the type *xyz:yz:z*. These procedures are not consistent with the treatment of the remaining variations.

[1] The following material was collected in preparing the text found in the first volume of *The Works of John Dryden*, ed. E. N. Hooker and H. T. Swedenberg (Berkeley and Los Angeles, 1956); see pp. 396–398 therein.

[2] G. Thorn-Drury, "Some Notes on Dryden," *Review of English Studies*, I (1925), 325–326.

[3] George Etheredge, *Dramatic Works*, ed. H. F. B. Brett-Smith (Oxford, 1927), II, 288, 294.

[4] Willard Thorp, "A New Manuscript Version of Dryden's Epilogue to *Sir Fopling Flutter*," *Review of English Studies*, IX (1933), 198–199.

[5] George B. Pace, "The Text of Chaucer's *Purse*," *Studies in Bibliography*, I (1948–1949), 103–121; Pace's tree is given on p. 107, his text on pp. 117–118, and his apparatus on pp. 120–121. I am indebted to the author and to the editor of *Studies in Bibliography* for permission to quote.

[6] G. Blakemore Evans, "The Text of Dryden's *Mac Flecknoe*," *Harvard Library Bulletin*, VII (1953–1954), 33–41. I am indebted to the author and to the President and Fellows of Harvard College for permission to quote.

[7] *Novum Testamentum Graece*, ed. Constantinus Tischendorf, ed. oct. critica maior (Lipsiae, 1869–1894), II, 895–901; for descriptions of the manuscripts, see III, 418–435.

[8] Silva Lake, *Family* II *and the Codex Alexandrinus* (London, 1936), pp. 10–11.

[9] Edgar J. Goodspeed, *A Life of Jesus* (New York, [°1950], pp. 224–225.

[10] *Novum Testamentum Graece*, ed. D. Eberhard Nestle and D. Erwin Nestle, ed. vicesima prima (New York, Stuttgart, [1952]).

[11] This list was compiled from Albert Huck, *Synopsis of the First Three Gospels*, 9th ed. rev. by Hans Lietzmann, English ed. by F. L. Cross (Oxford, 1954), checked against and once supplemented by the parallels noted by Streeter (see Streeter, *op. cit.*, p. 397; and (2) (d) in the list). The Greek quotations, however, are from Nestle rather than from Huck. Streeter's list of parallels between John and the other Gospels is mostly not of type-2 variations.

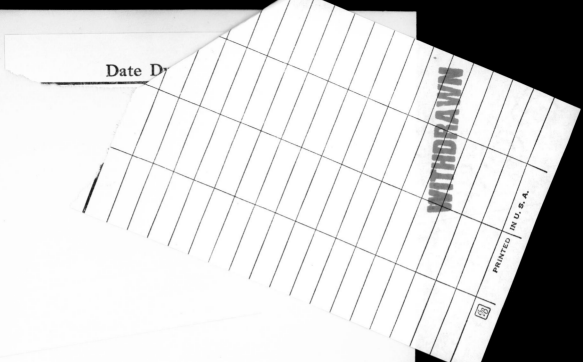